MW00899522

HOW TO START A
PROJECT MANAGEMENT
BUSINESS

And

Enjoy Life, Live Well, and Retire Rich

HOW TO START A PROJECT MANAGEMENT BUSINESS

And
Enjoy Life, Live Well, and Retire Rich

John Tuman Jr., P.E., PMP

Copyright © 2010 by John Tuman, Jr.

Published by Management Technologies Group, Inc.

ALL RIGHTS RESERVED.

No part of this publication may be reproduced, stored in a retrieval system, or transmitted in any form or by any means, electronic, mechanical, photocopying, recording, or otherwise without the written permission of the author.

ISBN 978-0-557-88506-0

Dedication

This book is dedicated to my friends and colleagues who were victims of the terrorist attack on the World Trade Center, September 11, 2001.

Acknowledgments

The foundation for a rich and enjoyable career is the people one works with and meets along the way. I have been especially fortunate to work, learn, and develop friendships with some of the most extraordinary and productive people in the field of project management. At the top of my list is Dr. David I. Cleland, who I consider the father of project management. Dave is the internationally recognized authority on project management and has published more books and technical papers on project management than any person I know. I have had the honor and privilege of contributing to several of Dave's books and working with him on a number of seminars and training sessions that we conducted in the United States and overseas. My fondest memories of working with Dave are the times we spent on the sidewalk cafés in Paris, drinking a few beers and sharing war stories.

Some of the other project management professionals who helped shape my professional career include Russell Archibald, David Frame, Lewis Ireland, Linn Stuckenbruck, Robert Youker, and Robert Yourzak. These individuals were the pioneer developers and providers of project management to universities, corporations, and governments around the world.

I also have to give credit to the many independent contractors (ICs) who worked for my company, especially Ron Anzalone, Tricia Cox, Pat McMackin, John Lee, Fred Williams, and Jeffery Wood, who provided skills, expertise, and professionalism to solve problems, set priorities, and accomplish critical tasks that made our clients' projects successful.

Finally, I have to acknowledge the dedication, support, and hard work of my business partner, my friend, my rock, my wife, Helen.

John Tuman, Jr.
Poinciana, Florida
September 11, 2010

The Author

John Tuman, Jr., P.E., PMP, was the president of Management Technologies Group, Inc. (MTGI), a United States consulting firm specializing in project management, organizational development and information technology. Mr. Tuman provided project management consulting, training and support services to major corporations in the United States and overseas.

Mr. Tuman also provided project management consulting services to the World Bank to support their development initiatives with China, Russia, and Ukraine as well as other Eastern European nations.

Prior to establishing MTGI, Mr. Tuman was a Project Manager and Program Manager on a number of major Aerospace R&D and production programs for the General Electric Company and AVCO Corporation. Later he became the Director of Special Projects for the A&E firm Gilbert/Commonwealth where he developed computer based project management systems for Nuclear Power Plant projects.

Mr. Tuman has given numerous presentations and seminars on management issues and problems in the United States, England, Europe, Africa, Asia and Russia. He is a contributing author to several textbooks on project management. He has published more than fifty technical papers and articles on management methods, systems and trends.

He is also the founding president of the Keystone Chapter of PMI and he has served on the publications board of the PMI's PM-Network magazine. In addition, he has been a member and a regular contributor to the International Project Management Association (IPMA). Mr. Tuman has developed and presented project management courses for Penn State University and the Project Management Institute (PMI).

John Tuman, Jr., has a M.S. degree in Computer Science and a B.S. degree in Mechanical Engineering. He is a registered professional engineer, a certified project management professional (PMP) and a certified change management consultant.

Mr. Tuman is retired and lives in Florida with his wife and their big Akita, Cato.

Introduction

Whenever I read the newspaper or watch TV, there is another story about corporate restructuring, downsizing, outsourcing, or reducing employee benefits. What happened to the good old days when you got a job, made a decent wage, married, bought a house, raised your family, sent the kids to college, worked until you retired, and moved to Florida with a decent pension?

When I graduated from Lafayette College in 1959 with a BS degree in Mechanical Engineering, everyone in my graduating class had a minimum of three job offers. The job offers were for good jobs with great starting salaries, generous benefits, and the opportunity for advancement. I started my career at the General Electric Company with the expectation that I would work on challenging assignments, advance up the corporate ladder, and stay there until I retired.

It was a wonderful time for the United States; the world desired our technological and management know-how and there was good reason for this. At the end of World War II, the United States was the most powerful nation in the world. By 1950, the United States gross national product (GNP) was about 45 percent of global product. It was great to be an American; we secured freedom for the world, and were now showing the world how to be creative and productive so that everyone could build a better life. After the United States dollar, the most sought-after thing was American know-how. We were the technologists, innovators, entrepreneurial leaders of the world; we shared freely of what we had and what we knew.

America gave generously of its resources, management expertise, and technical know-how. United States corporations had extensive technology-transfer programs; in every field, from agriculture to nuclear power, American consultants, engineers, and scientists traveled the globe to impart our expertise to other nations. Over time, countries like Japan, Germany, and Italy regained and even exceeded their prewar economic capabilities. More significantly, the so-called third world nations such as Singapore, Taiwan, and South Korea emerged to become international economic powerhouses.

Now fast forward to 1987 when my son graduated from college with a degree in Electrical Engineering. Upward of half of his class did not have a single job offer, and this was the situation at most colleges and universities across the nation.

Now jump to the present. As I write this book, we are in the midst of the most severe economic crash since the great depression. Job loss is the worst it has been since 1945; employment prospects for new graduates are grim, and those who do find jobs will live with lower wages for a good part of their careers. Individuals who have jobs live with the fear that their positions will be eliminated or sent overseas. The scars of this recession will last a long time.

It is obvious the good old days are gone forever. Today we live in a global economy, and every person who has a job is at risk of losing that job. As I see it, most working professionals have only two choices: live with the volatility, insecurity, and stress of today's job environment, or get out of that environment, start a business, and be the master of your own future.

Some thirty years ago I decided to get out of the corporate environment and to control my own destiny. This was not an easy decision; I had a mortgage, children in college, and bills to pay. Yet the stress of an unstable business environment plus the realization that my future was entirely controlled by someone else caused enough pain to motivate me to do something radical. I decided to give up a good-paying job and go on my own. Now this was not a sudden, rash move; I spent several years dreaming, planning, and getting ready. Every day I would ask myself, "if this were my company, what would I do in this situation?" At every opportunity I would think about how I would organize my business: the processes and procedures I would use, the products and services I would offer, and the clients I would assist. By the time I made the decision to go on my own, I had developed a comprehensive model of my business, and I had most of the tools in place to start operating. Most importantly, I had established business contacts and associations that enabled me to generate revenue from day one.

Like everyone else, I have made mistakes along the way, but I have learned from my mistakes and successes. I have prospered well beyond my wildest expectations. Today I am retired, live well, and pursue activities that enrich my life. I tell you this because what I am going to do in this book is to provide you the benefits of my experience. Specifically, I will give you a comprehensive guide to establishing a business that is well suited to the global marketplace. This business centers on project management and represents a new way of creating a company and earning a good livelihood in today's volatile economy.

Book Objectives

My objective is to show you how to set up and operate a unique business that is based on project management. This is not a get-rich scheme like buying and selling real estate with no money down, or day trading from your home office. A project management business is a serious, innovative, and timely business for knowledge workers. I will tell you how to start your business with minimum investment and minimum risk. I will explain how to run your business to generate a sizable income without working yourself to death, how to thrive during poor economic times, how to grow your business consistently to build wealth, and finally, how to manage your business and yourself so you will enjoy life, live well, and retire rich. This may sound like an unattainable objective, but believe me it is not. Everything presented in this book is based on actual experience, most of it mine; however, I have included experiences of several of my associates in order to give you a wide-ranging, practical guidebook.

What This Book Covers

This book focuses on the essentials of what it takes to build a successful project management business. I will not waste time discussing alternative approaches or options. I know from experience what works and what does not, and I have the battle scars to prove it. If my advice sounds opinionated, it is! Therefore, in this book I will:

- Explain what a project management business is and why it is ideal for today's global economy
- Show you how to start your project management business with little capital and minimum risk
- Define the skills, tools, processes, and procedures you will need to run a successful project management business
- Tell you how to make substantial and consistent profit from your business

- Present a model for managing your business and your life in a way that is balanced, enjoyable, and rewarding both emotionally and financially

This book will enable you to establish a unique business so you and your loved ones will enjoy life, live well, and retire rich.

Who Should Read This Book

Anyone who has the desire to be an entrepreneur, start a business, and be his or her own boss should read this book. In this book I will address several specific startup situations including:

- The working professional who is fed up, tired, or jaded by the corporate environment
- The employee who is facing job loss because of outsourcing, reorganization, or economic downturn
- The out of work professional
- The college graduate who cannot find a job
- The college student who is thinking about becoming an entrepreneur

The above list reflects a variety of needs and interests; however, it also reflects the circumstances of people I have mentored and worked with over the years to show them how to create their own project management business.

Value and Benefits

This book will save you time and money by showing you how to start your business without lawyers, accountants, and employees. Also, I will show you how to bootstrap yourself into business; thus, you will not have to borrow money to start your business, you will not have to write business plans, nor will you have to rent a fancy office.

A project management business is not for everyone. This book will help you determine if you have the appropriate temperament, the prerequisite skills, and ensure you are on the right path so you have the best possible chance for success from the outset.

Finally, this book will position you to control your destiny and to create both a value-based work life and a personal life which are the foundation for sustained happiness.

Contents

Chapter 1

Enjoy Life, Live Well, Retire Rich

The Quest for Happiness

The quest for happiness is universal. Are you happy with your life? Does your job enable you to be happy? Many of us work to earn money to buy things that will make us happy—the boat, the car, the wide-screen TV, the big house—the list goes on forever. However, once we have these things, we find that our joy is brief. What we experience is not happiness, but pleasure. By definition, pleasure is short lived. For many people, pleasure keeps us plodding along at our jobs like the proverbial donkey pursuing the carrot on a stick. Pleasure is not happiness; research shows that truly happy people are those who *control their destiny* and *pursue value-based goals.*

Controlling one's destiny means that your boss or your company does not determine your life and your livelihood; instead, you alone control your destiny through the decisions you make and the actions and effort you take. For me this means running my own business; making all the decisions that determine success or failure, and living a life driven by my creativity, energy, and values.

Value-based goals are those that give meaning, purpose, and deep satisfaction to life, and can include family, children, home, religion, community, profession, as well as social, political, intellectual, or creative accomplishments. My value-based goals encompass my family, my profession, and my physical and mental well-being.

To be happy, you need to earn a living in a way that enables you to control your destiny and to pursue your value-based goals; however, during your working years you also want to enjoy life, live well, and position yourself to retire rich. What does it take to make this possible?

Enjoy Life

First, to enjoy your life you must *love your work* and *control your destiny*. You will love your work if you are challenged and inspired without being crushed or ground down by the effort. In addition, you will love your work if you have the opportunity to develop and to apply your interests, talents, and skills to produce something of value.

Unfortunately, as an employee you cannot fully develop your abilities because to succeed, you need to conform to the norms and standards of the corporation. As you work at your job, the culture, processes, and procedures of the organization reshape your individuality to fit the desired corporate model. Hence, your ability to fully develop and apply your talents is constrained by your job. Furthermore, as an employee you learn to take orders. The needs and wishes of your superiors are spelled out for you, and you respond by accomplishing tasks within the standards of the organization.

Like it or not, almost every aspect of your life is structured by your job. When you sleep, eat, commute, shop, and spend your free time is dictated by your job. Some people can be quite happy in this environment; one corporate executive says that some people are company people in their bones. For many people, the company environment provides a sense of predictability and security. However, we know that in today's global economy there is no security.

When you work in a corporate environment, you cannot control your destiny. Your boss controls your destiny and your future; there is little you can do about it. Recent polls show that an overwhelming number of workers feel they have less job security and experience more job stress than twenty to thirty years ago. Worker anxiety centers on the corporate tendency to send jobs overseas or to eliminate jobs, especially during economic downturns. This in large measure explains the frustration and dissatisfaction that many people have with their jobs. Yet many people believe they have no choice but to keep working at their jobs; as a result, they do not fully enjoy life. This is a tragedy since the largest part of our lives is spent working.

If you look at the typical life cycle of the working professional, (see Exhibit 1-1) you know that during the first twenty years or so we are cared for by our parents who provide not only food, clothing, and shelter but also in most cases, our education. After that, we go on our own and spend the next forty to fifty years working at our jobs to earn a living to support the lives we build for ourselves. To a large extent, our jobs determine how well we will live during most of our adult lives.

Life Cycle of the Working Professional

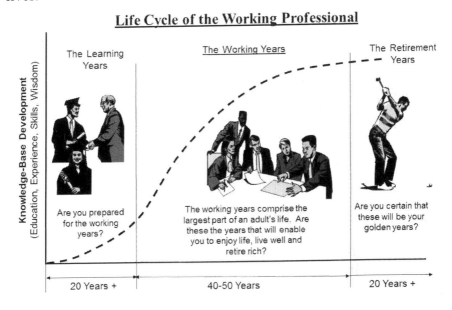

Exhibit 1-1

Live Well

In order to live well, you need enough *money* and *time* to support your desired lifestyle. We want a job that will give us satisfaction, but we also want to earn enough money so that we can live well. For the average professional man or woman, the net take-home pay is not sufficient to buy the house, the car, the college education for the kids, and everything else we would like to have in order to live well. As a result, a vast number of people go into debt and spend most of their lives paying their creditors. Certainly, if you are in debt, you can't save money for retirement. In today's economy, why can't the average professional person live a decent life and accumulate sufficient wealth for a comfortable retirement? There are three contributing factors at work: *wage stagnation, unstable job environment*, and *taxes*.

The Sunday, December 16, 1990, edition of the New York Times featured a major article titled, "Not Getting Ahead? Better Get Used to It." The gist of the article was that wages and family income did not rise fast enough to keep pace with inflation; hence, most Americans in 1990 are worse off than they were in the early 1970s. Now fast forward to 2006; a Bureau of Labor Statistics report shows that the average worker is no better off today than he was seven years ago. Among experts there is much debate about the cause of wage stagnation; however, the simple truth is that except for those at the very top of the corporate ladder, wages for most Americans have not increased enough to keep pace with inflation. Wage stagnation is one cause for limiting our standard of living; another is today's unstable job environment.

Virtually every type of job in America is at risk of being outsourced or eliminated. Moving jobs to low-wage countries like China or India enables American corporations to be competitive around the world; in addition, by establishing a foothold in these countries, United States corporations position themselves for long term growth as the target countries develop and prosper. Unfortunately, as these jobs are moved out of America, they are not replaced by new jobs. Coupled with job loss is the fact that, at every economic downturn, corporations resort to layoffs. Some employees who are laid off never return to their old jobs; some may find new jobs; others find jobs at lower salaries; still others, especially older workers, never find meaningful employment for the rest of their lives. At best, it takes years to recover from the financial loss of an extensive layoff, to say nothing of the great stress and anxiety placed on the breadwinner's family. Clearly, an employee cannot live well in today's volatile economic environment.

Wage stagnation and job loss are two major factors that work to limit our standard of living; however, the third and perhaps most insidious factor is taxes. Our tax laws make it impossible for the average working person to keep most of the money they earn. Actually, there are two distinct sets of tax laws in this country: one set for employees and one set for business owners. As we will see later, the tax laws for business owners offer tremendous advantages to build wealth, while the tax laws for employees do the opposite.

As an employee, you have to work more than five months out of the year just to pay taxes. In addition, if you are thrifty and save your money, you will be taxed on the interest you earn. Also, if you are smart and wisely invest your money, you will be taxed on your gains. To add insult to injury, you will be taxed again when you die. As an employee, you have very few options to shield your earnings from taxes. Yet in order to retire comfortably, you must accumulate wealth during your working life. For most wage earners this is difficult because there is not much left after all the bills and taxes are paid. The result is that a large majority of Americans are working harder and longer than ever before.

To truly enjoy life you need money, but you also need time; time for yourself, your family, friends, and community. Unfortunately, for most working professionals the job is all consuming. According to the International Labor Organization, Americans now work more hours than workers in any other industrialized nation. The adage: "Europeans work to live and Americans live to work," is painfully true when you consider that the French work a thirty-five hour week and the Germans a bit more. One expert reported that American working hours are longer now than they were forty years ago; furthermore, if the trend continues, Americans will soon be spending as much time at their jobs as they did in the 1920s. The impact of this situation on our daily life is staggering. Sleep deprivation is now a common problem, time spent with children is minimal, and stress is wide spread. Couple extended working hours with wage stagnation and taxes, and it becomes clear why most working Americans are pessimistic about their future. What kind of life will we have when we retire?

Retire Rich

To have a comfortable retirement you must build a nest egg that will sustain you for the rest of your life. This nest egg must be large enough to give you a decent and secure place to live, opportunities to travel and to socialize with family and friends, and an environment where you can maintain good mental and physical health. When you retire, your expenses will be reduced; nevertheless, you will still need about 80 to 90 percent of normal income. Some people can live on less; however, to enjoy life and live well in your retirement years you don't want to drastically down-size your lifestyle.

Unfortunately, because of corporate reductions in retirement benefits, wage stagnation, unemployment, taxes, and credit card debt, far too many Americans will have to reduce their lifestyle when they retire. Except for the fortunate few who rise to the very top of the corporate ladder, most employees will never retire rich. This is sad, because intelligent and ambitious men and women all across this country are building businesses that give them a fulfilling professional life as well as providing an income that enables them to enjoy life, live well, and retire rich. They are living the great American dream of owning and operating their own businesses.

For the working professional with a well-developed knowledge-base, there has never been a better time to start a business. Believe it or not, the right kind of business can thrive even during turbulent economic times. Globalization, information technology, and our *business tax laws* are the key factors that make it easier than ever before for an individual to build a business and accumulate wealth. The question is why more people don't make an attempt to venture on their own and pursue the great American dream?

The Great American Dream and Why Most People Will Never Realize It

If owning your own business offers so many opportunities to control your future and acquire wealth, why don't more people go into business? Many professional people I know talk about starting their own business, but few actually do it. Why? I am convinced that the root of the problem is that most of us are actually programmed to be employees.

Think about it; when you were growing up how many times did you hear your parents say, "study hard, and get a good education so you can get a good job." I heard this advice many times when I was growing up; frankly, it was the same advice I gave my children. We were all programmed to be employees. Why? Well, when you get a good job you will have an interesting career, wonderful benefits, a good income, live well, and someday retire with a nice pension. Perhaps at one time in our history, back in the 1950s and 60s, when America was the world's industrial leader, this was possible. But today we live in a global marketplace, and every job in America is in competition with jobs in every industrialized nation. As we well know, in our global marketplace, knowledge and information travel almost at the speed of light, allowing other industrialized nations to access and duplicate the know-how of another nation. The result is that the model of security for our parents, "the good job," does not exist today. Everyone who earns a living must have a new model, a model that they can construct, control, and implement for their own security and welfare. This is what this book is all about. I am convinced that if you have the right temperament, knowledge-base, and motivation you can become an entrepreneur, build a business, create wealth, and accomplish your value-based goals.

Build a Business and a Fulfilling Life

This book will show you how to build a business so you can control your future, enjoy life, live well, and even retire rich. Does this sound too good to be true? Believe me, it is true because I have done it for more than twenty years. Through good times and bad I have run my own company, Management Technologies Group, Inc. (MTGI), and I have earned a handsome living, worked on challenging projects, traveled the world, met interesting people, and never once looked back at the job I left in the corporate world. This was all possible because I created a new business model; the foundation for this business model is project management.

In the next chapters I will tell you what a project management business is all about, why it is an ideal business for the global economy, and how you can create and expand your own business. I will also spell out the personal attributes that will give you the highest probability for success. If you feel that you have what it takes to engage in a project management business, I will show you how to get started with minimum investment and minimum risk. In addition, I will lay out a twenty-five year plan, from business startup to retirement. In the course of showing you how to make your business a financial success, I will also show you how to avoid the pitfalls and problems that can prevent your business from being an enjoyable experience.

This book is based on my 40 plus years of experience as a business owner and a knowledge worker in the corporate world. In addition to my experience, I have included lessons learned from my colleagues and associates as well as study and research I have done over the years. This information will position you to create a unique and profitable business; however, this book is designed to be more than a business startup book. This book will take you from business startup, implementation, operation, and expansion, right down to business termination and your retirement. My goal is to give you a master plan for a successful business and a fulfilling life.

I am glad that I waited until I retired to write this book because my experience gives me a solid understanding of what it takes to be successful and happy. I strongly recommend to those readers who are in the early stages of their professional careers to pay attention to the advice and recommendations given in this book. The principles for success and happiness in your personal and professional life are deceptively simple. However, these simple truths are often shrouded by the pressures, pitfalls, and temptations of our modern world.

Summary

The main points of this chapter are:

- To be happy you must control your destiny and pursue value-based goals
- As an employee you cannot reach your full potential because you must mold yourself to a corporate model and culture
- Because of wage stagnation, job loss, and taxes most employees will not generate enough money or have enough time to enjoy life, live well, or retire rich
- You can overcome the limitations of a wage earner's life by becoming an entrepreneur
- Globalization, information technology, and our business tax laws make it easier than ever before for an individual to build a business and accumulate wealth
- The focus of this book is on how to set up, operate, and expand a project management business, and in the process enjoy life, live well, and retire rich

Chapter 2

Project Management
A New Business Model

A Business for Knowledge Workers

A project management business is a knowledge-based business that provides products and services to clients' projects. Furthermore, the business itself is organized and operated like a project. The business does not have a rigid organizational structure or a permanent staff of employees. The business does not need fancy offices, lawyers, accountants, and the trappings of most traditional businesses. The project management business presents the entrepreneur with an opportunity to earn a handsome living while doing value-added work that is interesting, exciting, and rewarding. In a project management business, you have the opportunity to see first-hand how your contributions positively influence a client's organizational efficiency, productivity and morale. However, to be successful you must understand the differences between a project and an ongoing or traditional business. Moreover, you must be certain that you have the right credentials and temperament to build and operate a project management business in today's highly competitive global marketplace.

Attributes of a Traditional Business

An entrepreneur starts a business to make money by providing a product or service at a competitive price. To be successful, the entrepreneur must consistently make a profit, enjoy what he or she is doing, and feel a sense of satisfaction about his or her accomplishments. This is a tall order for most businesses since the failure rate for a new business is high. Something like two out of three businesses will not make it to the fourth year.

When you think about the time, effort, and money that goes into starting a business you can understand the fear that many people have about taking the plunge. Let's face it; starting a new business in today's world is complex and risky. You need equipment, facilities, offices, supplies, and employees. There are a myriad of legal and financial issues to worry about; hence, you have to deal with lawyers, accountants and tax experts. In today's business environment, even a small venture requires substantial startup capital. To survive beyond the startup period, the business owner must not only provide a desired product or service at a competitive price, but must also operate effectively and efficiently. Typically this is accomplished through subdivision of work and specialization. Employees work on specific tasks in accordance with well-developed processes. The employees perform these tasks many times and get very good at what they do. Hence, the organization becomes more efficient over time and the business becomes more profitable. However, the problem in today's global economy is that things change quickly. The hot product or service you had last year may not be viable this year. In addition, the processes and procedures that were implemented to make the business operate effectively and efficiently may no longer be viable. This explains in part why many corporations and businesses have projects.

Characteristics of a Project

In the simplest of terms, a project is a unique undertaking to accomplish a specific objective on time and within budget. For most organizations, projects are a special endeavor or enterprise. For example, consider a typical corporate payroll department. The payroll department is responsible for getting the paychecks out to the employees at the prescribed time without fail. This task continues as long as the corporation stays in business. The payroll department staff does the same job week after week; thus, because of the repetition, the staff is very good at what they do. However, if the payroll department needs a new computer system, the system must be installed and operational without upsetting the department's ability to get the paychecks out on schedule. Typically, payroll personnel do not have the expertise required to install a new computer system. Therefore, a project team of computer specialists is brought in to install the system, get it running, and train department personnel. Once the new system is operational, the project is completed and the project team leaves. Installing a new computer system is a one-time effort, whereas the payroll department's functions are ongoing for the life of the business.

Today, modern corporations invest heavily in projects to create new products and services, to enhance efficiency and productivity, to comply with new laws and regulations, and to be more competitive. In fact, projects have become so important that some corporations are rewarding their CEOs based on project success. The October 18, 2006 issue of the Wall Street Journal reported that "Verizon Ties CEO Pay to Project Success Instead of Company Stock Performance." Clearly, major projects are important in assuring the future viability of a corporation. Moreover, we know that unless corporations invest in projects, they usually will not last long in today's highly competitive global economy. We also know that project success is related directly to an organization's project management capabilities.

Defining Project Management

Project Management's mission is to plan, schedule, organize, and direct project teams to accomplish the project objectives on time and within budget. Another way of looking at project management is to say that the goal of project management is to use corporate resources (see Exhibit 2-1) effectively and efficiently to accomplish project objectives on time and within budget. This is a significant responsibility when you realize that, in effect, project management is taking today's profits to build capabilities that will enable the corporation to generate revenue in the future. Clearly, if project management is not successful, the corporation will suffer.

The Mission of Project Management

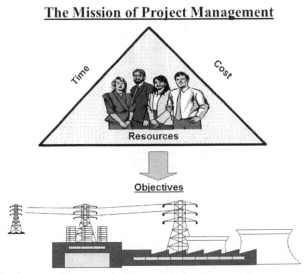

The mission of project management is to use company resources effectively and efficiently to accomplish project objectives on time, within budget.

Exhibit 2-1

Project managers, like functional managers (section managers, department managers, and division managers), get work done through people with specific skills. However, unlike a functional manager, the project manager's job is life limited. Thus, project teams are decommissioned, and personnel are reassigned to other responsibilities when a project is completed or terminated. Additionally, in most corporations, project management's role is to accomplish undertakings that are unique to the core business of the corporation. For example, an electric utility makes money by selling electricity; hence, its core business is the production of electrical energy. To generate electrical energy, the utility company builds power plants. Typically, the electric utility employs an A&E firm to design the plant and a construction company to build the plant. If the electric utility has a project management capability, it can manage the total project. If the electric utility has a limited project management capability, it can augment its staff with outside project management expertise. As projects become increasingly complex and more vital to corporations, we see a significant trend for corporations to rely more and more on outside project management support. Hence, there is an extraordinary opportunity for a project management business.

Uniqueness of a Project Management Business

A project management business provides products and services to corporations and government organizations that are engaged in projects. Moreover, as we stated before, in today's volatile economic environment, virtually every organization worldwide is engaged in some type of project in order to be competitive and remain viable. Thus, the forces of global competition that fuel the need for change, innovation, and improvement create the ideal setting for a project management business.

At this point, you might ask how a project management business is different from any other business, like consulting for example. Well, a project management business is unique because it has no employees, no formal office, minimal overhead, a simple infrastructure, and rarely, if ever, uses lawyers, accountants, or sales people. In simplest terms, a project management business is organized and run like a project. It builds a team for a specific undertaking, accomplishes the project's objectives, decommissions the team, and moves on to the next project. Hence, it is easy and simple to set up a project management business and it can be done with a small investment and limited risk. Based on my experience, I can definitely say that a project management business is ideal for men and women who have the temperament, skills, and drive to control their own destiny.

How to Make Money in a Project Management Business

As stated before, a project management business provides products and services to corporations that are engaged in projects. To be of value, these products and services must enhance the corporation's capability to manage their projects effectively and efficiently. The specific products and services that a corporation may need depend on the project's technology, industry, and competitive environment. In our project management business model, we define six business units (see Exhibit 2-2) that can address the needs of today's corporate projects.

These business units include: specialized products, specialized services, training, consulting, on-site support, and contracted project management. Each one of these business units can be an independent business or can be combined to offer clients a wide range of project management services. Let us look at how each business unit generates revenue.

Project Management Business Units

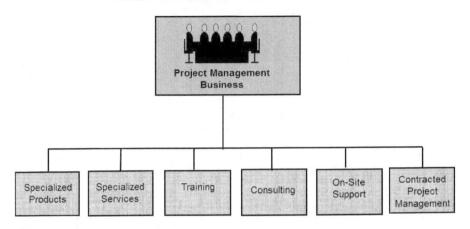

Exhibit 2-2

SPECIALIZED PRODUCTS

Organizations engaged in projects are constantly looking for tools to enhance their efficiency and effectiveness. Projects are important, they are expensive, and they are risky. If the project does not fully realize its objectives, or if the project fails, the corporation not only loses money, but also does not gain the competitive advantage needed to remain viable in the marketplace. Management literature is filled with horror stories of corporations that squander vast resources on projects that went down the tubes and virtually destroyed the corporation. So anyone who can provide a tool or a product to ensure project success has the potential to make money. I'll give you some examples.

Project planning is the foundation for project success, yet many corporations, especially those with limited project experience, have difficulty developing effective project plans. One project management entrepreneur has developed a handsome business by creating project-planning templates for clients. These templates aid the client's project teams to focus on the key tasks that must be performed to accomplish a particular project. The templates are unique because they are customized to the level of experience and capabilities of the client's project team. The templates not only force the project team to address all the requirements of a good project plan, but also provide management with a checklist and report card to assess their project team's performance.

In another example, a project management entrepreneur has developed a series of risk-assessment tools. These tools enable client project teams to assess risk issues inherent in their projects and to develop strategies for dealing with these risks. Another benefit of these tools is that they provide the project team with a powerful communication instrument to inform senior management of the challenges and difficulties the team faces. It enables the project team to raise issues and concerns based on risk data thereby avoiding the appearance of complaining or whining.

Specialized tools do not have to be sophisticated or complex. What is important is that they be practical and useful. In many cases, these tools come out of the daily work environment of those who were perceptive enough to see their value. Far too often, I hear people say what I do is so mundane no one would be interested in my ideas. Many of us do not realize how powerful our experience or ideas can be to others if we take the time to package them properly. If you want to move from the ranks of employee to that of entrepreneur, you must start by thinking that everything you do or know is important and can be useful to someone else. Constantly ask yourself how you can package your knowledge into a product or service that can be value-added to someone or some organization.

SPECIALIZED SERVICES

If you have worked in a certain field for a long time, you have built up a knowledge-base that can be translated into a project management service. For example, I have an associate who worked for a number of years as an estimator for a large construction company. Estimating is an art as well as a science, and good estimators can be a valuable resource to any organization that has to generate competitive bids to win jobs. If you bid too high, you do not win the job; bid too low, and you lose your shirt. My associate set up shop offering estimating services to organizations engaged in engineering and construction projects. Because of his extensive experience and expertise, he is able to command a premium fee for his services. He has expanded his business to include training and design to help clients develop or enhance their in-house estimating capabilities. This is an example of how an individual can package his experience and expertise to become an entrepreneur in his own field.

TRAINING

Training should be included in your project management business. No matter what you offer by way of a product or service, there is always an opportunity to sell training related to your product or service. Training can be a stand-alone business. I know a number of people who have made a handsome living by doing just project management training. Training is an ideal way to promote other project management offerings like consulting, support, or some specialized product or service. As you shall see in the next section, training can be a powerful marketing tool.

Training programs can deal with a wide range of project management process, procedures, tools and techniques. However, most clients are interested in learning how to make project management work more effectively in their organization. Thus, customized training programs that address specific client needs or problems are more in demand than off-the-shelf programs that are readily available from most training and consulting firms.

Our company got started by doing project management training. We found that in every one of our training sessions we were getting first-hand insight into specific client problems and needs. It did not take much business acumen to recognize that we could also offer products or services to help our clients.

In addition to getting first-hand information about the client's project needs and problems, training also enables you to keep abreast of trends in the business environment. As we all know, the corporate environment periodically embraces hot management topics or fads such as, TQM, Reengineering, Management by Walking Around, just to name a few. If you can get a sense of these emerging, hot topics early enough, you can pick your niche, develop your product or service, and carve out a piece of the market to beat the competition. Training is also the perfect vehicle to promote your expertise as a consultant.

CONSULTING

By definition, consulting seeks to offer the client a value-added benefit. Thus, the client should be able to do something better, faster, smarter, more efficiently, and more effectively because of the consulting service you offer. Consulting in general covers a world of topics, but in our business model we concentrate on consulting as it relates to projects.

Typically a client hires a project management consultant when the client's project is in trouble. The consultant will review the projects plans, schedules, budgets, and organization to identify problems and make recommendations for corrective action.

Clients also engage consultants at the front end of a project to provide support or make independent assessments of how things are going. Clients also hire consultants to build or enhance their project management capability.

To provide consulting services, you need substantial project management experience and expertise. Furthermore, you should be a certified Project Management Professional (PMP). Go to *www.pmi.org* for information on the Project Management Institute (PMI) certification program. If you have the appropriate experience and credentials, project management consulting can be interesting, exciting, and highly rewarding financially.

ON-SITE SUPPORT

Up to this point, we have been talking about the project management business units in which one individual does all the work. However, if you want to grow your business and generate revenue in the seven-figure range, you have to leverage your capabilities by engaging additional personnel. As we said in the previous chapter, in a project management business we do not hire employees; our business is too dynamic for that. Rather, we engage independent contractors to work on our project for the life of that project only. Later, we will talk about the hiring and managing of independent contractors as well as some of the IRS regulations to be considered. However, at this stage, we simply want to point out that there are opportunities to assist clients by providing staff to augment their project teams. In many cases, it is highly advantageous for the client to bring in outside project staff for a particular undertaking. Otherwise, the client must take personnel from their typically lean, functional departments or hire permanent personnel.

You will be able to generate revenue on every project management personnel that you assign to the client's project. The amount of markup you can realize by providing on-site staff to the client will depend to some extent on whether your support people work under the client's direction or operate independently, relying on your processes, procedures, tools and techniques.

CONTRACTED PROJECT MANAGEMENT

Contracted Project Management is a value-added service that will enable you to generate a premier revenue stream. In a contracted project management arrangement, you are hired to run the client's project. Our company has had engagements where we provided one individual to act as the project manager who was responsible for directing the client's project personnel. We also had assignments where we provided the project manager, all the project personnel, as well as the processes, procedures, tools, and techniques.

Contracted project management provides the most demanding, exciting, and rewarding aspect of a project management business. And as corporations downsize in response to negative business cycles, there are increasing opportunities for entrepreneurs who offer a complete portfolio of project management services. As I look back at the years I was in business, I find that many financially rewarding periods came during some of the worst business downturns.

Building Your Project Management Business

Using my business model, you can structure your company to offer the specific products and services you feel you are qualified to provide. If you operate several business units, you can smooth out the peaks and valleys of any business cycle and substantially increase your revenue. However, a number of factors will determine how large an operation you want to build, such as your capability as a business manager, your income requirements, and the style and quality of life you want to live. We will consider those factors later in this book.

A Twenty-five Year Plan

My goal is to show you how to start and operate a project management business so you can enjoy life, live well, and retire rich. A project management business is not a quick-rich scheme; it is a knowledge-based business that offers products and services to manage corporate projects.

With this plan, you can start your business on a shoestring, and if you work diligently, live sensibly, save, and invest wisely, you should, within twenty-five years, be able to retire rich. Along the way you can carve out an exciting career, get involved in challenging projects, meet interesting people, travel, and have sufficient time and money to enjoy life and live well.

The plan outlines the life cycle of a project management business from concept, start-up, operation, expansion, optimization, and wind down (see Exhibit 2-3).

The basic activities in each phase of this twenty-five year plan are as follows:

Phase 1—Concept

In Phase 1, dream your business before you start your business. Take your time to think about the kind of company you want to own; be certain that you really want a business and not a job. If you have a job, keep working at your job until you are certain that you really want to start a business. Be certain to assess your skills to determine if you have the abilities and the temperament to succeed in a project management business (see Chapter 3).

If you are comfortable with your capabilities and you have what it takes to be successful, then start thinking seriously about how you want to design and construct your company. Consider the advantages and disadvantage of various approaches, research existing companies, and identify the attributes that make them successful. Develop a conceptual design and specification of how you want to run your company and the products and services you want to offer. Also, think about the type of life you want to live as an entrepreneur and the amount of money you want to earn to support your desired lifestyle.

Be certain to identify potential clients for your company. Determine the types of products and services that potential clients obtain from outside providers and develop a list of the top, three companies that procure products and services that are in line with what you hope to offer. Develop various startup plans and schedules; keep dreaming and planning until you are ready to actually start building your company.

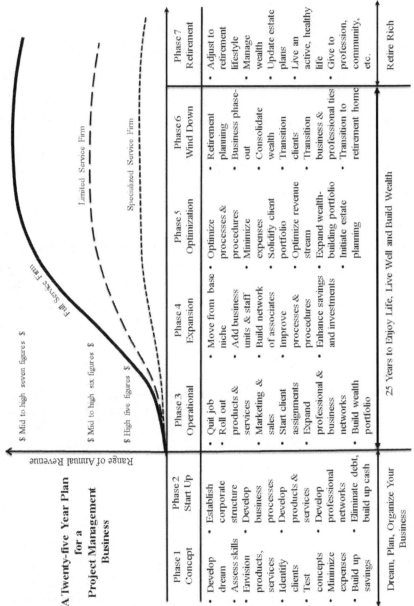

A Twenty-five Year Plan for a Project Management Business

Range of Annual Revenue

$ Mid to high seven figures $
$ Mid to high six figures $
$ High five figures $

Full Service Firm
Limited Service Firm
Specialized Service Firm

Phase 1 Concept	Phase 2 Start Up	Phase 3 Operational	Phase 4 Expansion	Phase 5 Optimization	Phase 6 Wind Down	Phase 7 Retirement
• Develop dream • Assess skills • Envision products, services • Identify clients • Test concepts • Minimize expenses • Build up savings	• Establish corporate structure • Develop business processes • Develop products & services • Develop professional networks • Eliminate debt, build up cash	• Quit job • Roll out products & services • Marketing & sales • Start client assignments • Expand professional & business networks • Build wealth portfolio	• Move from base niche • Add business units & staff • Build network of associates • Improve processes & procedures • Enhance savings and investments	• Optimize processes & procedures • Minimize expenses • Solidify client portfolio • Optimize revenue stream • Expand wealth-building portfolio • Initiate estate planning	• Retirement planning • Business phase-out • Consolidate wealth • Transition clients • Transition business & professional ties • Transition to retirement home	• Adjust to retirement lifestyle • Manage wealth • Update estate plans • Live an active, healthy life • Give to profession, community, etc.

Dream, Plan, Organize Your Business

25 Years to Enjoy Life, Live Well and Build Wealth

Retire Rich

Exhibit 2-3

Phase 2—Start-up

In Phase 2, get serious about actually starting your business. Formalize your ideas and concepts, and start building your company. Create a formal corporate structure, and design the processes, procedures, and systems you will need to run your business. In addition, develop the products and/or services you plan to offer clients, and work on building your professional and business networks. Furthermore, work at gaining recognition and building market contacts. At the end of this phase, you should have everything in place to start doing business the first day you leave your job and go on your own (see Chapters 4 and 5).

Note that I have not specified a time span for Phase 1 or Phase 2. I believe that it is important to take enough time to develop your dream and then build your business infrastructure before you go on your own. However, if you are out of work you have to decide if you want a job or you truly want to start a business. If you are out of work and want to start a business, you don't have time to do much dreaming—you have to implement a crash program and get up to speed as quickly as possible.

Phase 3—Operation

In Phase 3, make your company operational and roll out the products and/or services you will offer clients. Implement your marketing and sales program, and actively cultivate your top three potential clients to promote your portfolio of products and services. In this phase, concentrate on building your experience base and gaining recognition as a premier project management provider. Start building your wealth portfolio by implementing a consistent and balanced savings and investment program.

It will take three to five years to establish a firm client base and satisfy yourself that you have made the right decisions and are on the right career path. When you have a solid client base, a well-developed portfolio of products and services, and feel comfortable with what you are doing in your personal and professional life, then it is time to get serious about growing your company. See Chapters 6 and 7.

Phase 4—Expansion

In Phase 4, move your business from your base niche and expand into new profit centers. In addition, build a network of associates and independent contractors and take on assignments that are more diverse. In this phase, determine how big you want to grow your company to support your desired lifestyle; furthermore, enlarge your savings and investments programs in concert with the growth of your business revenue.

Your entrepreneurial acumen will be tested in Phase 4, you will establish the type of lifestyle you want to live, and the level of wealth you want to create.

By the end of this phase, you will have taken your business to a level that meets your personal goals and lifestyle; furthermore, you should have a solid, successful business you can be proud of. You will have refined your processes and procedures for maximum business efficiency and effectiveness; you will also have established a solid portfolio of clients that you can count on for a steady stream of revenue. In addition, you should have built up a substantial savings and investment portfolio.

Phase 4 may run five years or more depending on how long it takes you to reach your comfort level. See Chapters 8, 9, 10, and 11.

Phase 5—Optimization

In Phase 5, consolidate functions, eliminate any marginal business activities, and make refinements and modifications to ensure continued, stable operations. In Phase 5, you reach a level of business that meets your professional and lifestyle objectives and you should maintain this level of business until you are ready for retirement.

Throughout Phase 5 you expand your savings and investment program to maximize your wealth portfolio to position yourself for a comfortable retirement. Phase 5 may run ten years, more or less, depending on your particular situation and personal goals. See Chapters 12, 13, 14, 15.

Phase 6—Wind Down

In Phase 6, you are on the glide path to retirement. Plan how to wind down your business—turn it over to your children, sell it, or just put it into hibernation. Plan now how you will transition to retirement and how you will live and fill your days in retirement. In Phase 6, consolidate your wealth portfolio and update your estate plans. The wind down phase can take five to seven years. See Chapters 16, 17, 18 and 19.

Phase 7—Retirement

In Phase 7, terminate or significantly reduce your full-time business involvement and devote your energies to your retirement goals and life. In addition, you actively manage your wealth portfolio, finalize your estate plans, and develop and document your final-wishes. Hopefully, your retirement will run thirty years or more. See Chapter 20.

The above twenty-five year plan lays out a nominal schedule for a project management business. The duration of the plan is really up to the individual entrepreneur. Some individuals may reach their goals quickly and move into retirement at an early age. Others who love their work may never retire, but simply adjust their workload to suit their maturing lifestyle. Regardless of the route you choose, I know you will find your life fulfilling and rewarding.

Clearly, a project management business offers many opportunities to carve out an exciting career, provide a superior income, and build wealth. Nevertheless, before you go any further, you must determine if this is the right business for you. Are you qualified to run a project management business and will you love what you are doing? If you are not qualified, you will fail, and if you are not suited for this business, you will be miserable. Therefore, I strongly recommend that you study the next chapter carefully to help you determine if you are pursuing the right course of action and not spending time and money on an effort that will not pay off.

Summary

The key points of this chapter are:

- A project management business is a knowledge-based business
- A project management business provides products and services to client projects

- A project management business has no permanent employees, no formal office, minimum overhead, and a simple infrastructure

- A project management business consists of six business units: specialized products, specialized services, training, consulting, on-site support, and contracted project management

- Each one of these business centers can be an independent business or be integrated to offer clients a wide range of project management services

Chapter 3

Is This the Right Business for You?

An Important Consideration

A Project Management business offers unparalleled opportunities to generate substantial income while engaging in interesting and challenging work. However, this is not a business for everyone. To ensure maximum probability of success, I recommend that you carefully read the "Criteria for Success" given below and take the "Self-Assessment" to determine if you have the potential to thrive in a project management business. You do not need to meet every facet of the "Criteria for Success." If you are weak in any particular area, you must determine how this may impact your chances to build and operate a profitable business and what you must do to overcome your limitations. Furthermore, be certain that you have the right temperament for this type of business. You do not want to create an environment that conflicts with your psychological makeup.

This chapter is important because I have seen too many would-be entrepreneurs spend time and money pursuing business ventures they were not suited for. There is nothing worse than throwing yourself into a business that you wind up hating and ultimately fail in. Hence, if you read the following and find that Project Management is not a business for you, then the cost of this book has saved you a lot of time, money, and grief.

Criteria for Success

To succeed in a project management business you must have three things: Vision, Knowledge-Base, and Entrepreneurial Spirit (see Exhibit 3-1). The degree to which you can meet all facets of these three elements will determine largely your ability to attract clients, successfully accomplish projects, generate significant revenue, and enjoy what you are doing.

Criteria for Success

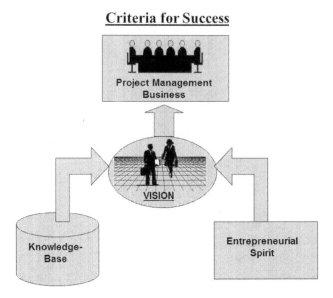

Exhibit 3-1

VISION

Your vision is the picture, the mental image, the dream, of what you want your business and your life to be. Your vision must be clear and focused for as long as you run your business. It is important to take the time to fully develop your dream; you must know exactly what you want to do and how you are going to do it. In addition to pointing your business in the right direction, your vision will help to define and shape all of the components that make up your knowledge-base and entrepreneurial spirit. More importantly, your vision will not only shape your business but will also shape your life.

KNOWLEDGE-BASE

Project management is a knowledge-based business. In order to provide the expertise that clients need, you must have a knowledge-base suited to the business or industry you plan to work in. A knowledge-base consists of your education, experience, skills and professional credentials (see Exhibit 3-2). Most importantly the core, the integrating and binding force of your knowledge-base, is wisdom.

Knowledge-Base

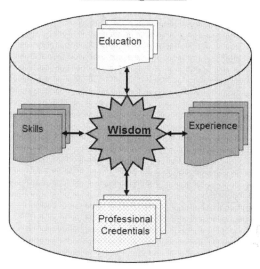

Exhibit 3-2

Education—The first component of a knowledge-base is education. In today's competitive global environment, education is critical to business success. At a minimum, the project management practitioner needs a college education, preferably with an advanced degree. Since the range of modern projects is so diverse, it is difficult to define which area of education is most appropriate. However, I find that in most cases your degrees should be compatible with the business or industry you plan to work in. Since most of my work focused on engineering, construction, and information technology my BS in Engineering and MS in Computer Science were very appropriate. Nevertheless, I always made it a point to expand my academic portfolio by taking specialized courses. Hence, I augmented my engineering and information technology background with courses in business, finance, economics, law, history and art. I am a strong advocate of life-long learning. Continually upgrading your academic credentials not only helps to ensure business success but also contributes to a more meaningful and richer life.

Experience—The second component of a knowledge-base is experience. When I went out on my own I had almost twenty years of industrial experience under my belt, most of it related to managing high tech projects. Hence, I could talk to a client with confidence and could address a wide range of project situations and problems. Project-related experience and project management training are paramount to running a project management business. However, if you are just starting your working career you may not have an extensive experience base to draw upon. In this case, you need to focus on a specialized skill, product, or service that addresses a particular client need or problem.

Skills—The third component of a knowledge-base is skills. This means that you know how to apply your education and experience to different situations and problems. You demonstrate your skills by how quickly you assess client needs and problems and implement solutions that are realistic and cost effective. I can recall one engagement where I made a study of the client's project management organization and gave management a presentation on how the organization should function and why it was having problems. After I made my presentation the executive in charge responded by saying, "I have people who have worked for me for five or more years and they still don't understand how and what I am trying to do here, yet you come in and in a matter of days present a clear and concise picture." The comment was flattering; however, it was no great feat on my part because I had been in similar situations with other clients in other industries. The ability to use your education and experience and apply it to a new situation is what skill is all about.

Professional Credentials—The fourth component, professional credentials, represents the badges you earn because of your education, experience, and skills. Professional credentials are important because they signify to the world that your education, experience, and skills have been investigated, proven, and certified by a government or professional organization. For example, to get my Professional Engineering License (PE), I had to meet proscribed educational and experience requirements and I had to pass the PE test. Once I met all the requirements, I was awarded a PE license. The license enables me to perform certain types of engineering work and obligates me to ethical and legal standards. Having my PE license provides a recognized measure of credibility to my clients and gives them a comfort level when we are dealing with engineering problems and technical issues. A professional license not only indicates competency in a particular area but also demonstrates your initiative and willingness to work hard to establish your professional credentials.

A very important credential for anyone working in Project Management is the Project Management Institute (PMI) Professional Certification. When you meet PMI's educational and experience requirement and pass their comprehensive test, you will be certified as a Project Management Professional or PMP. You do not need to be a PMP to work in the field of project management or to run your project management business; however, it does provide a measure of competitive advantage over those who are not certified. I have noticed in recent years that many firms, in their solicitations for project management services, specifically require PMP certification. I know from experience that having my PMP certification gave me a definite business advantage over my competitors who were not certified Project Management Professionals. Virtually all professional organizations have some type of certification program, so I would strongly recommend that you seek certification in your professional arena.

Wisdom—Education, experience, skills, and professional certifications are all important to building a solid knowledge-base for your project management business. However, the single most important element for ensuring long-term, lasting success for your business is wisdom. Wisdom cannot be taught. Wisdom is a wise way of thinking, the ability to use common sense, insight, and good judgment to deal with all matters in both your business and personal life. Wisdom is the sum of everything you have ever learned or experienced. A person with wisdom has the ability to determine the right thing to do, at the right time, in the right way. Wisdom is the integrating force of your knowledge-base.

One final word about knowledge-base; to ensure maximum opportunity for business success and to give your company competitive advantage, you want to have a rich and comprehensive knowledge-base. However, this does not mean you need to have everything in place before you start your business; as an entrepreneur, you will expand your knowledge-base over time.

If you compare the knowledge-base of the entrepreneur with that of the employee (see Exhibit 3-3), you will note that the entrepreneur continues to build a rich knowledge-base over the life of their professional career. The diversity of assignments and the challenges that the entrepreneur undertakes contribute to their knowledge-base. On the other hand, an employee becomes proficient at his or her job and eventually slips into a comfortable, well-worn groove. I have found that entrepreneurs who develop an extensive and in-depth knowledge-base tend to generate the highest income. Therefore, I stress the importance of continually challenging yourself by engaging in lifelong learning.

Knowledge-Base Development and Earning Power

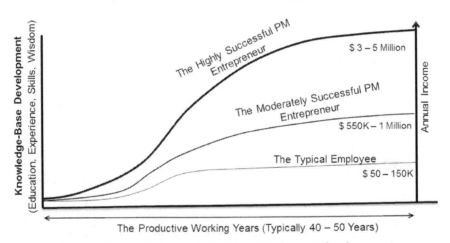

There is a strong correlation between knowledge-base development and earning power. The typical employee's knowledge-base will peak in 10 to 15 years. The successful entrepreneur will continue to develop his or her knowledge-base over the life of his or her working career, thereby increasing earning power.

Exhibit 3-3

ENTREPRENEURIAL SPIRIT

Several times in this book I emphasize the importance of ensuring that in your heart you want to have a business, not a job, and you truly want to be your own boss and in complete control of your destiny. To make this happen you must have an entrepreneurial spirit. In my view, this spirit consists of five critical components (see Exhibit 3-4): temperament, motivation, discipline, energy, and ethics.

Entrepreneurial Spirit

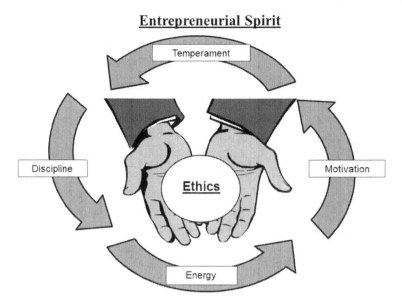

Exhibit 3-4

Temperament—Temperament determines if you have the personality or make up to be an entrepreneur. Largely, temperament defines your comfort level in a particular environment. If you are comfortable with the structure, routine, and regimentation of your job, you are probably well suited to be an employee. On the other hand, if you can live in an environment where you do not get a paycheck at regular intervals, or you have to work on your own for long periods of time, you may have the makings of an entrepreneur. I believe that entrepreneurial temperament really boils down to not being afraid of the unknown. If you are reasonably comfortable with ambiguity and confident that you can control your destiny, then you have the temperament of an entrepreneur. Temperament is important because it separates the employee from the entrepreneur. However, temperament is not enough to ensure success—you also need motivation.

Motivation—Motivation is the drive to make it happen. Many business books say that you must have a passion to start your own business. I think that passion is a good metaphor for describing the kind of intense drive needed to achieve your business aspirations. To succeed you must be motivated; however, thinking about starting a business because you just lost your job may not be the right kind of motivation. Virtually everyone I have ever known who decided to start a business because they lost their job has failed. As far as I am concerned, if you have not thought about it and dreamed it for a long time, you are probably not sufficiently motivated. For my readers who are considering going on their own for the first time, I recommend that you read this book through at least once, and then sleep on it for a while. Then go back and read key chapters to help you visualize what your business could look like. If you find yourself getting excited, constantly thinking about how you could run your own show, then you are probably generating the level of passion needed to start your own business. But keep in mind that no matter how strong your motivation, you will never succeed unless you have the discipline to move forward.

Discipline—Discipline is the self-control, the self-management that is vital to organizing and directing your business and your personal life. Self-discipline is particularly vital to a project management business because you are in charge of and responsible for every facet of your business. We all have likes and dislikes about the things we do. I like interacting with clients, I enjoy problem solving, and I feel energized directing my project teams. However, I do not like writing reports, I do not like paying bills, or doing quarterly tax reports and the myriad of other administrative details required to run my show. But I know that if I do not discipline myself to take care of these requirements, the little things have a habit of becoming big problems. Over the years I have seen many of my fellow entrepreneurs who did not have a strong, disciplined approach to their business eventually fail because of neglect or sloppiness. Discipline is the self-regulation necessary to keep your business on a stable platform. However, to meet the competition and grow your business you need energy.

Energy—Energy is composed of two components: the *psychological drive* and the *physical capacity* to do the work. The psychological drive is the enthusiasm and the spirit that sustains you through the inevitable ups and downs of any business. On the other hand, your physical energy determines that you can get the work done over the long haul. There will be periods of intense work effort, perhaps a lot of travel, not to mention conflicts and problems that may require immediate attention. In many respects, your ability to sustain yourself through the best of times and the worst of times will depend on how much energy you can muster. And of course, the energy you can bring to bear will relate directly to your health. I cannot overemphasize the importance of keeping in good physical condition and maintaining good health. Set up a regular exercise program, maintain a proper diet, and avoid the well-known health assassins—drugs, alcohol, and smoking. Your health is the single most important asset for your business and your life.

As important as energy, discipline, motivation, and temperament are to your success, the one component that overarches all of these regarding entrepreneurial spirit is ethics.

Ethics—Ethics is the guiding light that determines how you carry out your business and your life. Ethics represents principles that ensure that you will make the right decisions and exercise the right behavior in any situation. Over the course of my career in business and industry, I have witnessed many situations where an individual was tempted to behave unethically for business or personal gain. Often these individuals gave in to the dark side, only to find out later that their actions came back to haunt them and harm them in some way.

In business as well as in your personal life, many temptations can lead you down the wrong track. If you do not have a strong ethical standard, you can falter and make a serious mistake. As far as I am concerned, ethics is the single most important force that integrates temperament, motivation, discipline, and energy to produce that critical mass I call entrepreneurial spirit.

If after reading this chapter you feel that you are comfortable with the criteria for success, be sure to take the self-assessment given in the next section. Be honest with yourself and make the assessment as objectively as possible. You must determine if you can go it alone or if you are really a company person at heart.

Self-Assessment

The self-assessment utilizes the criteria discussed above to help you evaluate your strengths and weaknesses to determine if you are suited to undertake a project management business. Keep in mind that you may not have all the specified attributes, but the more you have, the greater are your chances for success and happiness in your business and your life.

Knowledge-Base

Education—List your educational credentials. Do you have the educational credentials appropriate to the field, business, or industry that you plan to work in? Talk to vendors, suppliers, associates and clients to determine the educational credentials you need to compete in your chosen arena. List your educational strengths and weaknesses. Identify specific areas where you must make improvements *before* you start your project management business.

Experience—Summarize your experience. Is your experience relevant to the arena you plan to work in? Do you have sufficient depth of experience to be considered an authority or expert in a specific area or niche? Identify strengths and weaknesses. If your experience base is very limited, determine how you may compensate for this limitation by emphasizing other attributes.

Skills—List your skills. Are you comfortable applying your skills to new situations? Do you consider yourself to be an investigator, problem solver, innovator, trainer, or mentor? List your primary strengths and weakness. Identify the specific work tasks that give you the most satisfaction.

Certifications—List all of your certifications. Are you licensed in any specific profession, certified in project management, or any other discipline? In what areas of project management are your certifications most relevant?

Wisdom—Do you make decisions quickly based on your gut feelings, or do you take time to collect data, make an analysis, and then formulate a decision. Would you classify your decision making as bold and courageous, or conservative and safe? How successful has your decision making been in the handling of your personal finances, professional career, and family life? Identify the three worst decisions you ever made and why you made them. Identify the three smartest decisions you ever made and why you made them. Determine if you are pragmatic and shrewd, or idealistic and evenhanded. Are you wise, and do others think you are wise? Do you feel confident that you will be able to wisely navigate all the circuitous demands of the business world?

Summarize all your findings and determine your knowledge-base strengths and weaknesses; furthermore, determine what you think is your primary area of expertise. Keep in mind that this initial appraisal is to get you started in the area that offers you the most likelihood of success. Over time your knowledge-base will grow and expand in tune with the assignments and challenges you undertake and the degree of learning and study you engage in over your lifetime.

Entrepreneurial Spirit

Temperament—What kind of work do you love? What gives you the most challenge, satisfaction, and feeling of accomplishment? What kind of work do you find tedious, boring, unfulfilling? What kind of work environment do you prefer—working as an individual contributor or working as part of a team?

Do you enjoy traveling to distant places to work with clients, or would you rather spend most of your time working out of your home office? Are you energized by working with project teams or one-on-one with a specific individual? Are you comfortable making presentations to a large group? Can you think on your feet and display confidence, self-reliance, and objectivity? Are you good at building interpersonal relationships and establishing trust and respect with associates and client personnel? Do you do well in an unstructured environment, or do you prefer well established routines? How well do you handle criticism, conflicts, and setbacks? Do you believe that you alone control your destiny, or does your future depend more on luck and the environment you live and work in?

Motivation—Why do you want to start your own business? Are you committed to making it happen? Do you honestly have the passion to start you own business, or is this something that just caught your fancy? Would you rather have a good job than deal with the risk of starting a business?

Discipline—What has been your history for completing projects that you start? Do you start out with a lot of excitement and energy only to have second thoughts as you work toward your objective? Or, are you the type that never gives up no matter what? Do you have a systematic approach to getting things done? Do you make daily to-do lists, weekly schedules, and long range plans? Do you feel compelled to work on tasks on your to-do list, or do you respond to situations as they occur? Be honest; are you highly self-disciplined or do you tend to go with the flow?

Ethics—Do you have a well-established standard of ethics based on your religion, morals, or personal values and principles? Do you believe you do what is right all the time, or are your actions based on the circumstances at that time?

Personal Attributes

Take a hard look at yourself. How good is your health, your physical fitness, and your mental attitude? Are you battling any addictions, facing family problems, or dealing with personal issues that create distractions and stress?

Financial Status

Do you have sufficient savings to support yourself and your family during business start-up? Have you eliminated all credit card debt or other personal debt? If not, how long will it take you to be free and clear of all personal debt? What other financial obligations do you have—alimony, child support, student loans, etc. Can you manage these obligations while you start up a new business? How do you classify your spending habits—disciplined, average, or subject to periods of impulse buying? Do you have a budget and do you stick to it? Based on your financial status, when can you afford to leave your job?

Family Situation

Take a hard look at your family situation. Do you have a stable family environment? What are your family obligations; are you a caregiver or have kids in college? What do you have by way of backup resources: working spouse, grandparents to watch the kids, etc., or other outside support network?

The self-assessment is not designed to discourage you from becoming an entrepreneur. Far from it, the self-assessment's primary objective is to help you develop a clear picture of your strengths and weaknesses. Then you have to decide if you are well positioned to succeed. Otherwise, you need to establish a program to address your limitations or look for a different type of business venture.

Summary

Some of the more important points of this chapter are as follows:

- The criteria for success in a project management business are: vision, knowledge-base, and entrepreneurial spirit
- Your vision must clearly define what your business is all about and what you expect to accomplish
- Your knowledge-base represents the education, experience, and professional credentials that qualify you to serve client projects
- Your entrepreneurial spirit addresses the temperament and the psychological and physiological characteristics that are necessary to thrive in a project management business
- The self-assessment will help you determine if a project management business is right for you

Chapter 4

How to Get Started

Three Things You Should Not Do

If you have never been in business, starting a new venture can be a daunting and scary proposition. But I assure you that if you follow my business model it's not as complex and difficult as you may think. What I am going to recommend probably goes against most of the business self-help books out there; however, after more than twenty years of success I feel confident that my approach will position you to be equally successful.

Before you consider starting your own project management business there are three things you should *not do*:

- Do not go into business if you really want a job
- Do not write a business plan
- Do not go into debt to go into business

The first issue is obvious, but the second and third issues are contrary to most business startup books. If you follow my advice you will save yourself a lot of time and perhaps a lot of heartaches in getting your business off the ground. Let us examine these three recommendations in detail.

Don't Go Into Business if You Really Want a Job

The most important prerequisite for starting a new business is to have the right mindset. You must have a compelling dream about your business; you must desperately want to be your own boss; and you must believe that you have what it takes to be an entrepreneur.

Before I started my project management business, I had a driving desire to get out of the corporate environment. I wanted to be my own boss; I wanted to have my own company; I wanted to be in control of my destiny. I also knew I didn't want to recreate the environment I was leaving. I wanted to build a different kind of company, a small, lean, resilient company that would enable me to do interesting and challenging work and earn a good living. I was not interested in building an empire and managing a corporate bureaucracy.

I spent a lot of time thinking about the kind of business I wanted. At every free moment, I made diagrams, flowcharts, and outlines of the structure, processes, and procedures for my company. I would make lists of start-up requirements and write descriptions of the programs and services my company would offer. I also read extensively on how to start a new business, and I attended new business workshops and seminars. I got mentally energized whenever I spent time conceptualizing and designing my company.

A compelling dream provides the energy and passion to motivate you to take action regardless of the obstacles that you may encounter. I firmly believe that you must be able to visualize yourself in your business; you must get excited every time you think about your business; and you must truly feel that starting your own business is the right thing to do in your professional life. If you cannot feel the excitement and the commitment, do not go into business.

Do not go into business because of downsizing, layoffs, or termination. If you truly do not have the dream, the passion, and the vision, doesn't start a business; in the long run, you will be miserable and you will fail.

Assuming that you have the dream, the next step, according to most experts, is to write a business plan, right? Wrong!

Don't Write a Business Plan

I bought a book on writing a business plan, and I spent months trying to develop a comprehensive plan for my project management business. The business plan required me to address many things that were difficult to define. I became so discouraged that I almost gave up my dream of starting my own company.

You may have a feel for some of the requirements of your business, but at best, they may be only guesses. I believe that as an entrepreneur, you are going to capitalize on opportunities that you develop as you go along or stumble into; in many instances, these will be completely unexpected.

For example, when I started my project management business I expected to concentrate in the arenas where I had most of my experience, namely aerospace, engineering and construction. One day I got a call from an associate of mine who worked at the World Bank. I had known Bob for several years through my professional activities with the Project Management Institute (PMI). The telephone conversation went something like this:

Bob: John how you doing? Interested in getting some new business?

John: Of course, if the price is right.

Bob: Well, you heard about the revolution in Czechoslovakia?

John: Certainly, it's been on the news for weeks.

Bob: Well, we are putting a team together to go to Prague and help the new government implement American management techniques. We are going to train several hundred managers and executives on project management. How would you like to go?

John: Wow! I would love to go. How much time do we have to put together our program, a month or two?

Bob: No, we have to leave this Friday and start working Monday morning.

I thought the whole thing sounded crazy, but the following Monday, several other consultants and I stood on the stage of the Radio Palace in Prague in front of six hundred Czech and Slovak engineers, managers, and executives. We spent a week making presentations and meeting with Czech and Slovak executives to discuss American project management methods and techniques. This was the start of my career as an international project management consultant working in Eastern Europe and Russia. I tell you this story to point up the fact that in my wildest dreams, I would never have considered international consulting as part of my business plan.

As an entrepreneur, you respond as opportunities present themselves. An article in the January 9, 2007 issue of the Wall Street Journal supports my contention that you should not write a business plan. The article was titled, "Do Start-Ups Really Need Formal

Business Plans." The gist of the article was that the time spent in gathering data and writing a business plan does little to improve start-up success. Now I am not proposing that you go into business without doing any planning. Quite the contrary, you need to plan, but I recommend that you develop a project plan for your business. Later on I will address project planning for your business; however, for now keep in mind that you need a formal business plan when you want to borrow money from banks or venture capitalists to start your business. However, if you follow my business model, you will not have to go into debt to start your project management business.

Don't Go into Debt to Go into Business

I believe that it is a critical mistake to borrow money to start a business. When you borrow money, you dig yourself a hole that will be tough to get out of. You have to pay interest on your loan; you have to put up assets to secure your loan; and even if your business is successful, someone else actually owns your business until you are free and clear of debt. In the worst-case scenario, your business fails, you lose everything, and are in debt the rest of your life. I have friends who have gone down that path and are now spending their professional careers paying off creditors.

So to summarize: do not go into business if you really want a job; do not write a business plan; do not borrow money to start your business.

When should you start your project management business? The answer depends on your specific situation. Over the years I have mentored a number of individuals who wanted to start their own business. The following list identifies some of their circumstances; see which of these you relate to:

- You have a job
- You are facing job loss
- You are out of work
- You are just out of college and can't find a job
- You're a college student who wants to be an entrepreneur

You Have a Job

Ideally, the best time to start a project management business is when you have a relatively secure job. In this situation you are not under pressure, so you can take your time to conceptualize your business, develop your ideas, and build up the financial reserves you need to get started. More importantly, you can discuss your plans with those closest to you, your significant other, your family, and certainly anyone who depends on your livelihood. It is critical that you have complete support for your undertaking; otherwise, without this support you will never survive the inevitable low points of any business.

While you are working I recommend that you design your project management business, set up your corporation, develop the products and services you plan to offer, and identify your clients.

It is absolutely critical to identify your target clients before you go into business. Make a best-guess list of your potential clients; identify the products and services they may need, and spell out exactly what your company will offer these clients. In the beginning, you may not be sure about all the clients you will have; nevertheless, you should have at least one client you feel certain you can count on when you first go out on your own.

While you are still employed, build your network of associates and contacts and get exposed to the marketplace in general and your target clients in particular. You should be actively involved in professional organizations, such as the Project Management Institute (PMI) and the International Project Management Association (IPMA). Attend local and national meetings of these organizations, present technical papers, conduct seminars, write articles, volunteer for committees and work groups. Also cultivate relations with professionals in other disciplines, businesses, and industries.

Be certain to test your business ideas. Try moonlighting on your own time; provide training, consulting, or perform a service for someone outside your employer's area of interest. Be careful not to conflict with your job. As appropriate, let your employer know you have a sideline; however, if this presents a problem, don't try moonlighting. You can test your concepts in other ways. For example, take a business course at a local community college or university. Use this venue to discuss some of your ideas and concepts. Get others to critique your approach or offer suggestions. In addition, be on the lookout for resources both physical and human that you may want to use in your new venture.

Another approach is to set up discussion groups with like-minded individuals. Before I started my own company, several associates and I would gather at lunch time to talk about our business aspirations. These were unstructured bull sessions, but in retrospect they were invaluable. These discussions helped me to solidify my ideas and concepts. In some cases, I had to rethink and redesign some of my approaches after some of my critics shot my ideas down. A good critic will force you to face some issues that you did not think about or avoided because they were unpleasant.

In addition, you should take care of a number of important personal matters. First and foremost, address your and your family's health needs. Have your eyes checked, make that trip to the dentist that you have been putting off, and get a complete physical exam. You want to ensure that there are no hidden medical problems that can bite you or your family at a later date. Use your employer paid health insurance to take care of any medical issues before you leave your job. The adage, "an ounce of prevention is worth a pound of cure," is good risk management.

In addition to addressing health needs, I strongly recommend that you ensure you are in reasonably good physical condition. Starting a new business is physically and mentally demanding; therefore, if you don't have a regular exercise program, start one and stick to it; get your weight down and get your energy and endurance up. You will feel better, you will look better, and you will think more clearly. If you have trouble motivating yourself, join a gym or go to the Y; or get a personal fitness instructor if you can afford one. Consider the period between the time you decide to go into business until you give your termination notice as boot camp, and you are training for combat and survival. In order to do well in a knowledge-based business like project management, you need energy, vitality, and confidence.

When you are in good physical condition you will have the energy and vitality you need to succeed, and you will have the confidence to present yourself to any client. I cannot overstate the importance of being in good physical condition; in addition to the obvious health benefits, it also fosters good mental health. Everyone knows from experience that it is difficult to maintain a positive mental attitude if you are plagued by fatigue, aches, and pains; so be smart, get in shape.

Another important issue to consider has to do with your self-discipline and daily routine. When you have a job, your life is fairly well structured by the demands of your job. When you eat, sleep, shop, commute, work, and play are all controlled by your job. Like it or not, your job imposes a considerable amount of order on your life. When you are the owner of your own business, that overt restraint is removed, and you have more freedom than ever before. If you are working in your home office, as we recommend, you may be able to sleep late; you don't have to worry about the morning commute; you don't have to get dressed up; you can do as you please. Wow, life is great! Watch out, though, for some people this can be a trap. When you have your own business you must be more self-disciplined than when you had a job. You have to set the priorities and the schedules, and you have to command yourself to stick to them. If you have been lockstep in the corporate world for a number of years, suddenly winning your freedom can be a major pitfall.

To deal responsibly with this newfound freedom, I recommend that you first assess your body clock preferences. Some people are morning people, and they do their best work in the first half of the day. Others are night people, and they are more productive late in the day. Obviously, when working in the client's environment, you tune your schedule to the client's needs. However, when you are working in your home-based office, I recommend that you take advantage of your body clock's preference. I found out years ago that I was a night person, and I did my best work when others were sleeping. For me, there was nothing better than working on a difficult client problem during the solitude and quiet of the night. Nevertheless, when I had to make an early meeting, I would make the necessary schedule adjustment accordingly. What is important here is to understand yourself, and use your natural preference to work effectively and efficiently.

Once you determine your personal preference, you must then implement a disciplined work ethic. All the talk about the joy and freedom of being in business for yourself so you can go fishing when you want, or take time off to smell the roses when you feel like it is true, provided of course, that it is not haphazard and self-defeating. If I have a client deadline, I am not going to take time off if it will jeopardize my work. I know from experience that if I organize myself properly and work in a disciplined manner, then I will have the flexibility and the time to pursue non-work related activities. Self-discipline and good personal organization are key in reducing business stress and pressure and enjoying the freedom that owning your own business brings.

If you tend not to be self-disciplined, or if you are by nature a free spirit and don't worry too much about schedules and commitments, think twice about going into a project management business. Far too many people have failed in business because they let the little things get out of control—forgot to file a quarterly tax return, missed a credit card payment, or were late for an important meeting, and so on. Small needs and problems have a way of mushrooming into big crises. Personal organization and self-discipline is vital in a one-person operation; it is the key to having a life and not working yourself to death.

The way you leave your job is important. Make certain that you quit your job on a positive note. I have known cases where individuals have quit their job and used the occasion to vent or get even with their boss for some past hurt or injustice. Never burn your bridges because your previous employer may be an asset for your business.

When you leave your job, thank your employer and your associates for the opportunity of having worked with them and learned from them. Be positive and optimistic; let everyone know that you are starting your own company, and explain the products and services you will offer. You may find that your first client is your present employer or a vendor or supplier you have worked with. If you leave on a positive note, your employer may even recommend you to others.

You Are Facing Job Loss

If you are facing job loss, you know you are not alone. Restructuring, outsourcing, and downsizing have put a lot of jobs in jeopardy. If you are in this situation, don't panic—it may actually be a blessing in disguise. Use the stress and uncertainty to motivate you to constructive action. First and foremost, if you have had it in the back of your mind to start you own business, now is a great time to revisit your idea. Think about it; do you really want to go out on your own; is this a serious dream, or are you just reacting to the stress of potential unemployment. Over the years I have had a number of friends and associates approach me about going into business when they were facing potential job loss. I gave everyone the same advice. Unless you have a compelling desire to start your own business, don't do it. You are better off spending your time looking for another job. Nevertheless, if you decide now is the time to pursue your dream, here are a few important recommendations.

First, find out if your employer plans to offer some type of buy-out package to those being terminated. I recommend that you not leave your job until you can take advantage of every benefit your employer will offer.

Well before you leave, organize all the materials that you want to take with you. Do not take any proprietary company information; this is dishonest and could possibly lead to a law suit.

Before you are terminated, organize your personal life. Reduce or eliminate unnecessary expenditures, pay off credit card debt, and build up your cash reserve. Modify your lifestyle to conserve resources: forego dinners out, defer vacation plans, eliminate the kids' dance classes, forget the golf game, or the weekly night out with friends. If you prepare early for lean times, you will face the future with confidence and less stress.

Work systematically at setting up your project management business while you wait for your termination notice. If you have been notified that you will be terminated, do some internal marketing. Let your management know that you are starting you own company, and tell them about the products and services you will offer. I know many cases where individuals have been laid off only to be brought back as contractors or vendors. Be advised, though, that many companies have policies that prohibit bringing back former employees as temporary staff. One way to deal with this situation is to set up your own corporation. This is a relatively simple undertaking and offers many advantages. I will talk more about this later.

Follow the startup recommendations given in the next chapter and you will be able to hit the ground running when you get your termination notice. Again, as discussed above, when you leave, do so on a positive note regardless of any injustice you feel you may have suffered. Treat your employer as a resource to enhance your future business success.

You Are Out of Work

Losing your job is probably the worst situation to find yourself in. Perhaps you did not see it coming; it happened overnight; or you were doing so well you never thought it would happen to you. The result, however, is that you are out of a job and unsure of what to do next. If you are in this situation, don't despair—it has happened to the best of people. Don't panic; you have a lot of options, and if you keep your cool this horrific event may be the best thing to happen in your life.

Before you do anything ask yourself, "Do I want a job or a business?" If you have never seriously thought about going into business, then you should look for a job. My advice is to start looking on the first day you are out of work, and make it a full-time effort. Resist the temptation to take a vacation to get your wits about you or to recover from the shock of losing your job. When you are out of work you are in a negative cash flow situation, and you can never make up the lost salary. So work at finding a new job in a determined, organized, and professional manner. If your employer offers out-placement services, use these to the fullest. Don't be ashamed to be out of a job. Let everyone know your situation and what you are looking for. Finding a new job is 80 percent marketing and 20 percent selling. So work at it with all the energy you can muster.

If you have trouble finding a job, resist the temptation to go into business. Starting a business requires total commitment; therefore, if you really want a job, you must put all your energy into that effort. On the other hand, I know several individuals who became consultants or independent contractors in order to generate income while they looked for a job. Some of these individuals found full-time jobs as a result of their consulting work. Still others decided that they loved being their own boss and would never go back to being an employee.

If you are out of a job and have decided that now is the time to go into business because of your negative cash flow, you have to move quickly. Since you don't have the luxury of planning and organizing your business in a systematic manner, you will have to resort to a fast-track methodology. In short, you will have to do many things in parallel; however, you will probably have to go back and rework a number of your processes, procedures, and tools as you gain experience. Fast track is an inefficient way to start a business, but in a desperate situation, you have to employ desperate methods.

One final note; losing a job puts a tremendous strain not only on you but also on all your loved ones. I have seen families disintegrate because the breadwinner lost his or her job, became depressed, discouraged, and checked out. If you find yourself in this situation, get help; don't go it alone, you have too much talent and skill to waste in despair. Look at job loss as a new beginning, an opportunity for a new career, a new business, a new bonding and relationship with your loved ones. I have said it many times; loss of a job may be the best thing to happen in your life. Remember, you have not failed until you give up.

Just Out of College and Can't Find a Job

When I finished college in the late 50's, every graduate had at least three good job offers. Those were the heady days when America was the industrial leader of the world. Things have changed dramatically since then; virtually every nation with an educated population is in competition for America's jobs. In America today a college degree is no longer the passport for a good life. This does not mean you should not get an education; quite the contrary, you need more qualifications than ever before. But it does mean that the model for a good life and a secure future is no longer the "job."

Everyone must have a portfolio of knowledge-based products and services that he or she can offer to the marketplace. If it is not possible to offer these to an employer, then the individual must be prepared to offer them as an entrepreneur. Quite frankly, it is easier than ever to become an entrepreneur. Information technology makes it possible for an individual to do what at one time could only be performed by large organizations. Therefore, creative, self-motivated individuals without extensive work experience, like a recent college graduate, can create a viable business.

I will give you an example; a young man I know graduated from a state university with a BS degree in Mechanical Engineering. Unfortunately, the job market was dismal, and our recent graduate could not find a job. Prospects were so bad that he considered taking a job at a fast-food restaurant. However, I suggested that he look at his knowledge-base to see if there was something he could package and sell to clients. His work experience was very limited; however, he previously had a summer job with an A&E firm where he helped put together schedules for construction projects. He said he really enjoyed the work; he learned a lot about CPM scheduling, and that was probably the one area that combined his engineering education, work experience, and something he enjoyed doing. For a small investment in business cards, brochures, a Web site and some intense networking through a number of professional organizations, he was able to get a few small jobs developing project schedules for local construction companies. His original plan was to get exposure to a prospective employer in hopes of landing a job. However, after working on his own for a year or so, he decided that it was more interesting to be his own boss. Today this individual has a client list of a half-dozen contractors who are happy to give him their planning and scheduling work because he is very good at it, and also because they can demonstrate to their clients that they have a project management capability without having to build up an in-house staff.

I know a number of college graduates who have become entrepreneurs by packaging their knowledge and marketing themselves to clients. Frankly, I believe that in the reshaped economy we will live in over the next decade, college graduates will rely more on developing a business than finding a job.

You Are a College Student Who Wants To Be an Entrepreneur

When I was in college virtually everyone I knew was looking for a career with a large corporation. There were a few individuals who were going to go to work in their parents' business, but they were the exception. Today I meet college students who think only about starting their own company. The Internet has been the catalyst for many entrepreneurs, and the success of ventures like Google, YouTube, Facebook, and many others has provided the inspiration for numerous young people to pursue activities that my generation would never have dreamed of doing.

Today, many colleges and universities encourage entrepreneurship and some even provide startup support. Stanford University and the Massachusetts Institute of Technology support student entrepreneurs, arrange licensing agreements, and even take equity positions in some of the startup companies. Many universities in the United States are working to turn their research projects into profit-making companies. These entrepreneurial efforts can be extremely profitable for the university as well as the student. For example, Stanford University licensed key technologies from two Ph. D. students, Sergey Brin and Larry Page, developers of Google. There is a definite trend across most colleges and universities to offer students practical courses on starting and managing their own companies.

I find this movement particularly encouraging because it helps to break the mindset that many of us grew up with; namely, that happiness and success come from "the good job." As far as I am concerned, there is no better way to encourage individuality and leadership than to have a young person create and develop a business. It is individuality and leadership, along with determination and hard work that will ensure the economic viability of America.

To those in college I recommend that you start thinking about going into business early on. In college you have access to resources that the average employee does not. You have large well-equipped libraries, laboratories, computer facilities, and highly educated instructors and professors. Equally important, you are in a safe environment; you do not have to worry about your meals or a roof over your head; more than likely, your parents are paying the bills and taking care of your health insurance. Certainly you have your class work, but you can always carve out time from drinking, parties, and sport activities to construct the framework of a potential business upon graduation or even build a business while you are in college. Frankly, outside of the well-off retired person, I know of no one else who is better positioned to start a business than a college or university student.

If you are thinking about creating a knowledge-based business like project management, you should start by evaluating your strengths and interests. For example, if you tend to be analytical, then some aspect of project planning, scheduling, and estimating may be in order. However, if you are gregarious, a good communicator, and interact well with people then perhaps training and consulting is the way to go. I heartily recommend to every college student to start building the framework of their business while they are still in college. That way, when you graduate you are ahead of most entrepreneurs in starting a new venture. It's never too early to start a business, and it's never too late.

How I Got Started

As I noted earlier, I left a good paying job to start my own business, to control my own destiny, and to enjoy the freedom and responsibilities that only an entrepreneur can experience. And I also noted that this was not a rash decision; I spent a lot of time dreaming and planning about how I would build and operate my company. However, actually making the break, leaving my job, and going into the unknown was very difficult. I believe that I was mentally programmed by my well-meaning parents to believe that to be successful and happy in life you needed the "good job." Well, I had the good job, but I was not happy. I certainly did not feel successful.

When things went badly at work, I would say to myself, "this is it—I can't take it anymore; it's time to make the move." Then I would start thinking about the mortgage, the college tuition, the other bills, and I would chicken out. But I was lucky, because every time I suffered these episodes, my wife would say "stop worrying about everything, just go out and do it, and you will be a lot happier." I say I was lucky because I knew that when I was ready to make my move I had a good support system in my wife. Yet I hesitated to leave my job because I felt I still needed something to convince me that I had the right stuff; I felt that I needed an event, an inspiration, or some lucky break to make my dream a reality. Certainly if I won the lottery I would have enough money to back me up, and I would not have to worry about failing; however, I never did win the lottery, but something better happened to enable me to become a successful entrepreneur—I met Jack.

Role Model and Mentor

I was presenting a paper at a PMI conference in Toronto when I had a chance meeting with a person of exceptional talent and generosity. Early in the morning of the conference I went out for a long run—I was training for the Boston Marathon that year—the weather was great, the sights of the city were interesting, but I was not paying attention to where I was going and got lost. Fortunately, I saw a runner coming towards me wearing a Tee-shirt from the Philadelphia Marathon; I had on the same shirt, so I stopped him and asked him if he could tell me how to get back to my hotel. He said, "Sure, just follow me—I'm staying at the same hotel." It turned out that Jack was also attending the PMI Conference to conduct a workshop on Project Management. I told Jack that I was presenting a paper at the conference an invited him to sit in on my presentation.

Jack attended my presentation and afterwards congratulated me on an excellent delivery and a well written paper; he also invited me to sit in on his project management workshop, which I did later that day. After Jack's workshop, we got together for a few drinks, to talk, and to get to know each other; it turned out that we had a lot in common, much the same interests, goals, and values. Jack had his own company providing project management training to clients in the United States and Europe. After Jack told me about his company and the work he was doing, I said, "I would really love to be doing what you are doing." Jack replied, "Why don't you; you certainly have the skills and the credentials." I replied "I have three kids, a mortgage, and college tuition to worry about." Jack replied, "I have five kids, three in college now, a mortgage, and all the other obligations that you face. I'm sure that if you really wanted to go into business for yourself you could be very successful." I replied, "You know, I think I could make it; however, there is that little, nagging doubt in the back of my mind, or maybe its fear, but I know I'll make the move one day."

Jack and I agreed to keep in touch. I left the conference feeling pretty good about the advice and inspiration I received from Jack and meeting someone who was actually doing what I wanted to do. Despite this positive encounter, I went back to the daily grind of my job and continued to dream and plan about starting my own company. I probably would have continued dreaming, but one day I got a call from Jack who said he had an emergency, needed help, and wanted to know if I could fill in for him on a training workshop that he was conducting for a client—I jumped at the chance. I took time off from work, flew to the West coast, met Jack, got up to speed on the workshop, and spent the next two days conducting a training seminar for some thirty people. It was grueling work, but I loved every minute of it; what's more, the participants were very complimentary about my performance, and Jack was very grateful that I was able to fill in for him on such short notice. As it turned out, Jack and I entered into an informal business relationship; over the next two years I worked with Jack, using my vacation time to learn the ins and outs of the training and consulting business. Jack became my role model, my mentor, and my friend, and I developed the experience, skills, and courage to leave my job fully confident that I was ready to become my own boss.

A Good Way to Get Started

Finding a role model, a mentor, or an associate is an excellent way to help you start your business. Typically these individuals will have the experience, battle scars, and the wisdom to guide and support you. They will give your insight into the pitfalls and the highs and lows of being an entrepreneur that you will not find in most business text books. Moreover, if you can work side by side with these individuals, you will gain experience and confidence that will help you reduce the risk of failure.

The important question is how do you find the right role model, mentor, or associate? Obviously, you have to go where these individuals ply their trade. Professional conferences, seminars, and workshops are a good place to meet practitioners, observe their techniques, and evaluate their style. Over the years I have attended many conferences, seminars, and workshops, and I always make it a point to introduce myself to the presenter and to spend time talking with him or her. First, I try to determine if I can establish a rapport with the individual—I want to make certain that the chemistry is right before I get tied up with anyone—and second, I make known my interest in hooking up with a professional who has goals similar to mine. In these brief meetings you can usually tell pretty quickly if there is a basis for establishing a working relationship.

There is a number of ways you can establish a relationship with a potential role model, mentor, or associate. For example, if you are still employed, try working part time with an established entrepreneur; use your holidays, vacation, or free time to gain experience and build confidence. If you are already on you own, set up a formal or informal alliance with more experienced professionals. Make it known that you are available to augment, back up, or fill in for someone on relatively short notice. Every one-person shop or small company that I know is happy to have backup resources available.

By establishing a relationship between the experienced entrepreneur and the novice, both parties benefit from the increased depth of contacts, expanded view of their respective industries, and the synergy that grows out of the individual creativity, knowledge-base, and vision of the respective participants. One of the most important things I learned from my mentor, Jack, is that in order to grow, you must help others to grow. When you act as a mentor you deal with issues and problems beyond your own; you see things through a different lens, and you experience new and different values and emotions. As a result, you will not fall into the comfortable, well-worn groove that is the sure route to obsolescence.

Giving Back

Like many of my associates, I make it a point to advise and help other entrepreneurs. I have mentored individuals in different professions and in different circumstances, and I have freely given advice and information. In virtually every case, giving back has paid handsome dividends by increasing my range of professional associates, by expanding my understanding of other businesses and industries, and enriching my life by meeting creative people from diverse nationalities and cultures. Regardless of how busy you may be in your professional and personal life, I strongly recommend that you carve out some time to help others; in the long run, the benefits will be substantial.

I related the story of how I got started because I know how difficult it is to break the model that shapes our professional lives; however, if you can re-engineer your model, you have the potential to enrich your life in ways you never thought possible.

Summary

My goal in this chapter is to give potential entrepreneurs, regardless of their situation in life, the opportunity to consider starting a project management business. Therefore, let me summarize a few key points:

- Do not go into business if you really want a job
- Do not write a business plan
- Do not borrow money to start your business
- Identify potential clients and their needs before you leave your job

- Develop your products and services before you leave your job
- Put your business infrastructure together before you leave your job so you can hit the ground running
- Leave your job on a positive note

Chapter 5

How to Set Up Your Project Management Business

Keep it Simple and Low Cost

In the previous chapter I stressed the importance of ensuring that you truly want a business and not a job. I also recommended that if you are going to start a business, you must get organized and put in place all your processes, procedures, and tools well before leaving your job. In this chapter I define the minimum requirements for getting started. What I stress in this book is, "Don't go into debt to go into business." Everything I recommend assumes that you are setting up a one-person shop and that you want to spend the absolute minimum to get started.

To set up your project management business, you will need to address the following minimum requirements:

- Legal structure for your business
- Name for your corporation
- Corporate logo
- Place to work
- Business address
- Software tools and equipment
- Internet tools
- Insurance
- Administrative processes & procedures
- Support services
- Supplies

- Subscriptions
- Professional associations
- Professional affiliations
- Products and services

Let us review the basic requirements for getting started, keeping in mind that our strategy is to minimize startup cost.

Legal Structure

The first order of business is to set up a corporation. I will not spend any time discussing the pros and cons of a sole proprietorship, partnership, or corporation because as far as I am concerned, in today's litigant-prone environment, everyone in business needs the protection of the corporate shield. Otherwise, if you don't have this protection and you get into trouble, your creditors can go after your personal bank account, your house, car, and anything else of value that you own. Hence, be smart and set up your own corporation. Create either a Limited Liability Corporation (LLC) or a Sub-chapter S Corporation. The major difference between an LLC and a Sub-S Corporation is how taxes are handled. Income and expenses for an LLC are included on your personal 1040 tax form. The Sub-S Corporation does not pay taxes but files an information tax return stating what each shareholder has earned; the shareholder then reports the corporate income or loss on his or her Form 1040. The Sub-S Corporation may offer a tax saving since business losses can pass through to the shareholder's personal income tax return. However, in recent years the Sub-S Corporation has fallen out of favor and most startup businesses use an LLC to incorporate.

Setting up a corporation may sound like a complicated, big deal, but it is not. In fact, it is very simple to set up a corporation; you do not need a lawyer—you can do it yourself. Setting up an LLC is a matter of filling out some simple forms that you can get from your state. Go on line to your state's Web site and download the forms. To set up a Sub-S Corporation, all shareholders will need to sign and file IRS Form 2553. Check the IRS Web site for details.

If you want more guidance on this topic, go to www. Nolo.com. In fact, Nolo is an excellent source of information for most of the legal issues you will need to know to start your business. Until you become a multi-million dollar corporation, you should not have to spend money on lawyers if you follow our project management business model.

You will have to establish the appropriate corporate structure. This is simple to do, and it affords you the opportunity to give yourself and family members a corporate position and title.

An extra benefit of setting up a corporation and giving yourself a corporate title, like President or Chief Executive Officer (CEO), is that it increases your personal prestige by a wide margin. When you go to a party and someone asks you what you do, and you respond, "I am the CEO of the Management Technologies Corporation," you get a more positive reception than you would if you said, "I am a programmer at Fumpworth Consulting." You can increase your professional and social standing significantly by setting up your own corporation and giving yourself a good title. Having your own corporation involves some administrative burden, but it is ultimately well worth it.

You will also issue corporate stock. Again, this is simple to do; however, I strongly recommend that all the corporate stock be vested in the founder, namely you.

Keep in mind that a corporation provides a shield for your personal assets provided you follow all administrative rules. These involve holding an annual meeting, writing meeting minutes, and keeping corporate records. Occasionally you may have to hold special meetings to deal with important corporate decisions.

In addition to the legal protection the corporate structure affords, I found that many large companies would not do business with me unless and until I incorporated. So be professional and set up your corporation.

After you set up your corporation, be sure to get your federal tax identification number, also called the Employer Identification Number (EIN). You can get this number by filing Form SS-4 with the IRS; however, it is easier to go to www.irs.gov/to register your company and get your EIN number. Your clients will want this number before they will issue you contracts.

One final note—your personal assets will be at risk if you personally guarantee your business obligations; thus, I strongly recommend that you never make any kind of personal guarantees.

Corporate Name

I would avoid using your own name for your corporation unless you are well known in a particular area of expertise. The John Smith Corporation does not mean too much to perspective clients unless John Smith is a recognized authority in the client's business or industry.

The name of your business should tell a client the nature of your business; just as the title of a book says what it is about. A company name shouts its services to the world: International Business Machine (IBM), General Motors (GM), General Electric (GE), and Management Technologies Consulting (MTC), make clear the nature of the business. Do not confuse the client by being too cute with your corporate name, for example, Green Hills Consulting is a good name for a landscaping consulting business but not for a technology consulting business.

Identify the core services and products of your business and create a name that lets the world know what you do. For example, if you are project management scheduling experts then call yourself something like, "Project Scheduling Consultants," or "Project Scheduling Experts." When you file your corporate papers, your State Office of Corporate Affairs will tell you if the corporate name you choose is available.

Corporate Logo

I would not spend too much time on this because I've never heard that a logo brought in business. If you are creative, you may come up with a logo that really says something about your business. However, as far as I am concerned, logos of small animals, insects, vegetables, or chess pieces do not tell me much about a company and its products. Look at the big boys, IBM, GE, and GM, their logos immediately tell you who they are and what they do; hence, you can't go wrong by using the initials of your corporate name as your logo. A logo becomes valuable and provides recognition after your company does something of value and gains recognition, not before.

A Place to Work

You need a place to work that is quiet and secure. I recommend that you set up a home office for a number of reasons. A home office is convenient and cost effective provided you can find a suitable space to work. Do not try to work in the family room where the kids watch TV. You may be pressed for space, but it is important to find a quiet spot. I know one person who cleaned out a closet and made that his office. Another individual moved into the garage, while another set up shop in the basement. When I went into business, I set up my office in the loft of our farmhouse. The loft was finished with paneled walls and a hardwood floor. The previous owner, a retired doctor and his wife, a retired college professor, had used the loft as their study and library, so I was lucky to inherit a large spacious area with plenty of bookshelves.

You will need some basic furniture, a desk, table, chairs, file cabinets, and ample lighting. When you first start out you can get along with a very Spartan office; however, as your business grows you may want to invest in more up-scale décor, especially if you have clients visiting your office. On this note, let me say that many businesses operating from a home office attempt to create a facade that they are really a big corporation in a fancy office building. I for one think this is a mistake. You are an entrepreneur with a business that you built through your own initiative and creativity; hence, you have nothing to be ashamed of by operating out of your home office.

Our home office was in an older stone farmhouse in a rural area of Pennsylvania, and I found that many of our clients were happy to get out of the city and spend some time in our office. We were lucky because our house had a large deck overlooking a stream, woods, and rolling farmland. We conducted many business meetings on this deck and established a rapport with our clients that probably would not have been possible had we been working in the restricted confines of a corporate office.

Resist the temptation to lease an office. Do not let your ego get in the way of your good judgment. I collaborated with associates frequently and at one meeting, I drove into the city to meet them at their office. I had never been to their place of business, so I was shocked when I entered their office. This was a two-man firm, and they had office space for at least twenty people. They had a receptionist, very fancy furniture, and handsome decorations. When I asked my associates how they were doing, they told me they had little business, and were digging into their personal savings to keep afloat. When I asked why they had such a large office, one associate told me that he always dreamed of having a big office in the city. I asked him. "Don't you need a big income to support the big office," and my associate replied, "Yes, but that will come."

As you might have guessed, the big income did not come before my associates' cash reserves ran out. Unfortunately, my associates were stuck with a lease they could not get out of and rent they could not pay. In short order, my friends went belly up and spent the next several years trying to recover from their debts. Interestingly enough, today my friends are in business operating out of their home-based offices and doing quite well.

The experience of my friends is a lesson you should keep in mind. If you lease an office, you pay rent every month regardless of whether you generate income or not. On the other hand, with a home office, you can take a tax deduction or you can charge your project management business rent and increase your personal income.

After you nail down your business name and address, put together your company stationery, business cards, and brochures. When I first started in business, I had all of these printed on high-quality paper. If you can afford it, have a small quantity printed; however, with today's high quality laser printer you can print your own material. Since clients receive so many brochures and business cards over time, most of this material winds up in the trash can. To save money, I recommend that you design your stationery, business cards, and other documents, and save them as templates in your word processing or publication program. That way, the documents are readily available, and they can be modified quickly when things change.

Business Address

Keep your business mail separate from your personal mail; have your business mail sent to a post office box or to a mail-receiving service such as Mail Post, Pak Mail, UPS Store, or others. One advantage of using a mail receiving service is that it will give you a street address, and you can use your box number as an office suite number; in addition, they provide other services including fax, photocopying, passport photos, notary, and package shipping and delivery via UPS, Federal Express, and others.

A mail receiving service can be a valuable adjunct to your business, especially when you first start out. You can defer buying fax equipment, photo copiers, and the like by relying on this service, assuming they are conveniently located near your home office.

Software and Computers

You need only a few basic tools to start your project management business. Today, working professionals probably have most of the items I am going to recommend; if you do, you are ahead of the game. At a minimum, you will need a laptop and a printer. Get the best laptop you can afford; ensure it has a large hard drive and plenty of RAM. If you are on a tight budget, look for a used laptop. I know plenty of techies who move up to the latest and greatest gear every year, so there are some good buys out there.

Also, get a quality printer. There are multi-function printers available at very reasonable cost. These machines print, scan, fax, and make copies. In addition, some models have network and wireless capabilities.

You need a cell phone and a separate telephone line for your home office. Get an answering machine, preferably one you can use to screen calls. You can save a lot of time by screening telephone calls from vendors, sales representatives, and would-be employees.

You will need an Internet account with either dial-up access or DSL access. Initially you can probably get by with a dial-up account that is relatively inexpensive; however, as you grow your business and utilize the Internet to download large files, perform on-line research, and engage in video conferencing you will need a high-speed Internet hookup, preferably broadband.

Software tools are especially important for a project management business, and they can represent a significant investment. However, the good news is that there are plenty of quality software tools available at no cost. This software is open source and freeware, which can be downloaded from the Internet. At a minimum, you need an office suite for your laptop.

The de facto corporate standard office suite is Microsoft Office. As you probably know, MS Office includes a word processor (Word), a spreadsheet (Excel), a presentation program (Power Point), and a data base program (Access). If you have Microsoft Office, stick with it; if you can afford it, buy it because most of your clients will probably be using it. If you cannot afford MS Office, download the open source office suite OpenOffice.org; it has virtually all the features of MS Office, and it is free.

In addition, get a project management planning and scheduling package; again, the de facto standard is Microsoft Project. I have used this package since it came on the market as a DOS program, and it has increased in capabilities and sophistication with every new release. I found that it did not make any difference if I was doing business in the United States or Russia, China or Saudi Arabia—all of our clients knew Microsoft Project. Therefore, I would invest in the latest release of Microsoft Project; however, if you are budget constrained, check out OpenProj which is a free, open source desktop alternative to Microsoft Project.

Internet Tools

You should set up your company Web site as soon as you get started. There are extensive resources available on the Internet that will help you develop and host your Web site for a fee. However, I recommend that initially you take advantage of free basic editions of on-line tools available from Google, Microsoft, Yahoo, and others. For example, Google offers Google Apps (www. Google.com/) which provides Web-site hosting and can run basic office functions including document and calendar sharing, online voice chatting, e-mail, and instant messaging. Microsoft's free service is Microsoft Office Live www.office.microsoft.com/officelive. This is a web-hosted suite of services that enables you to create and share calendars, documents, e-mail, and integrate accounting functions like online banking, invoicing, and credit card processing. Of course, Google, Microsoft, and others offer these free services with the hope that as you grow your company and need more sophisticated services, you will upgrade to their fee-based advanced editions.

Also, set up accounts with all the social networks. These outlets offer unparalleled opportunities for marketing your products and services as well as for communicating with clients, associates and project participants. I will talk more about this later, but for now get started with Facebook (facebook.com), Twitter (twitter.com), YouTube (youtube.com), and Linkedin (linkedin.com).

There are many neat tools for your project management business. However, keep in mind that every time you buy a new gadget or software program there is a learning period required before you get up to speed and realize the benefit of the tool; hence, when you are just getting started, keep things simple.

Insurance

Typically your clients will spell out the insurance you need to carry in order to do business with them. You can expect that the client will require you to carry Workers' Compensation Insurance, Commercial General Liability Insurance, Automobile Liability Insurance, and perhaps Professional Liability Insurance. Generally, you have to carry insurance in amounts of one million dollars or more. However, I have found that many times you can negotiate with your client to reduce the amount of insurance you have to carry. Insurance is expensive; shop around to get the coverage you need at the lowest price.

When you leave your job, you will have to face the issue of health insurance for yourself and your family. There are companies and professional organizations that sell health insurance to small businesses. Health insurance is expensive, so get at least three quotes to determine the best value for the coverage you need. You may luck out if you have a spouse whose employer provides health insurance; on the other hand, some of my associates decided not to carry health insurance. They felt that the risk was justified since they and their family members were in good health. You can save a lot of money if you are willing to take the risk that you will not have any major health problems. At the time of this writing, the big unknown is how small business will be impacted by the new health-care legislation.

Processes and Procedures

There are a number of administrative and management processes and procedures you need to put in place for the efficient and effective operation of your business. The first thing to do is to set up savings and checking accounts for your business. It is important to keep your household accounts and your business accounts separate. You may also want to establish a money-market fund for your business which should give you a better rate of interest. Later I will talk about setting up your business retirement accounts.

Also, get two credit cards for your business. Later on I will talk about the effective use of credit cards for your business; for now, we want to ensure that you have a clear line of demarcation between business expenditures and personal expenditures. If you are careful not to mix your business money with your personal money, you will avoid a lot of hassle with the IRS in the future.

Keeping good financial records is important for the effective management of your business as well as avoiding IRS problems. Bookkeeping can be a chore if you are not an accountant. Fortunately, there are a number of software packages out there that make this job easier. For years, our company has used QuickBooks Pro, and I highly recommend this package to anyone setting up a project management business. The Microsoft package "Microsoft Money" is also a good choice. Again, if you are budget constrained, consider some of the freeware packages out there. For example, GnuCash (www.gnucash.org) and AceMoney Lite (www.mechad.net) are good alternatives to the commercial packages.

Support Services

Over the life of your business, there may be times when you will have to hire experts or specialists to address specific business needs. Support services include but are not limited to accountants, tax preparers, and lawyers; however, these services are expensive, so when you are just starting out, try to take care of routine needs yourself. Use the resources of Nolo for basic business law requirements; use Quick Books or Microsoft Money or a freeware package for your accounting needs. In addition, you should be able to do your own taxes by using any one of the off-the-shelf software tax packages. As you grow your business, you may need a tax preparer. Find someone who understands your business and is willing to work with the data you generate from your accounting package.

When my business grew and I had to do a lot of traveling, I had to enlist someone to do my taxes; fortunately, based on the recommendation of an associate, I found a competent tax preparer who handled my business and personal taxes at a reasonable rate. This is one support service where it pays to do your homework to find the right person. In addition, when you grow your project management business to a multi-million dollar, full-service firm, you will occasionally need professional legal support. Finding a good lawyer, one that understands your business, will take some work. Your best bet is to get recommendations from your associates and meet with the candidates to see if you have a good fit.

Another support service I found indispensable was printing. Our company produced large volumes of training materials for clients. Anything over a dozen or so documents was too much for our copier, so we utilized outside printers. There are many printing and reproduction services out there, but it took me a half dozen tries before I found the company that consistently produced good quality documents at a reasonable price. Price and quality vary tremendously, so you have to do some research. Talk to associates, get recommendations, and take small jobs to potential printers as a test run. When I finally found a printer I could work with, we had a business relationship for more than twenty years.

Supplies

When you start out, your office supply needs will be simple. However, as you grow you will find that office supplies can become a major expense. Get familiar with the on-line office suppliers. For example, check out www.Quill.com, www.Viking.com, www.reliable.com, and www.Costco.com. I have found that ordering on-line is more cost effective than running down to one of the national office supply stores. Ordering supplies on-line saves, time, gas and money, and typically you will get next-day delivery right to your door; also, shipping is usually free. To top it off, these on-line office suppliers usually give you a gift if your order is over a certain dollar amount. Over the years, I have accumulated a good collection of brief cases, luggage, desk clocks, coolers, pens and assorted office supplies.

Subscriptions

The business world is dynamic and ever changing, and you need to stay on top of things to remain viable. Therefore, I recommend that you invest in a few key subscriptions; take advantage of any free subscriptions that you may be offered.

It is money well spent to have subscriptions to the Wall Street Journal, Business Week, and the Economist. However, if you can't afford these subscriptions, at a minimum use the Internet to keep abreast of what is going on in the world, especially the business and financial world; as you will see later, keeping informed is vital to the long-term success of your business.

Also, subscribe to a couple of good computer magazines. I highly recommend Computer Pro, Computer Plus, PC Tools and PC Utilities. These magazines give product reviews and instructions on using various software tools. In addition, with every issue, these magazines give a CD or DVD disk with an extensive collection of Freeware, Open Source software, and demos.

It is convenient to have newspapers and magazines delivered to your door; however, if you are budget constrained, do not forget your local library which will have many newspapers and periodicals of interest to you. And of course, you can visit your favorite book store or coffee shop to catch up on your reading.

Professional Organizations

It is essential to belong to one or more project management professional organizations. These organizations provide an indispensable knowledge-base on all aspects of project management and are a meeting place for consultants and clients alike. Furthermore, the project management professional organizations are a ready resource for the project personnel you may need to grow your business.

Become a member of the Project Management Institute (PMI) and join a local chapter. You can get all the information you need at www.pmi.org.

I also recommend that you consider joining the International Project Management Association (IPMA), especially if you have an interest in working overseas. Even if you are not inclined to international work, the IPMA is worthwhile for giving you a different perspective on management issues and problems around the world.

Alliances and Affiliations

As your network of business contacts grows, you will want to establish some type of working relationship with like-minded individuals.

These relationships can be formal alliances where you draw-up an agreement to define how you will work and share revenue. On the other hand, it can be an informal relationship where you collaborate with others to pursue targets of opportunity. Over the life of our business, I have found it worthwhile to establish both formal and informal relationships. As a small operation, you soon discover that you do not know everything, and you cannot do everything by yourself, so it is good to pick up the phone and ask for help.

In creating alliances and affiliations, I found it very important to deal with individuals I know fairly well and who have the same value-base as myself. Over the life of my business I have run into only a few bad apples; however, even a few bad apples can create a rotten and expensive experience. So be very careful with whom you align yourself; ensure that they have not only a proven record of accomplishment but also a well-known reputation for ethical conduct.

Products and Services

Prior to starting your project management business, you should have developed a portfolio of products and services that you plan to offer clients. You may launch your company with a single business unit—for example, training; however, to generate significant revenue you will need to expand by adding other business units. Later on I will give you examples of how to grow your business without killing yourself or going into debt.

Your Business Life

When you are an employee, you work to make someone else rich. When you are an entrepreneur, you work to make yourself rich. When you build a project management business, you have the potential to increase significantly your personal wealth; however, you also have the opportunity to live a more fulfilling and happier life. How can this be? Well consider this. As an entrepreneur running a project management business, you are in total control; you are the architect of your destiny; you can choose the work that interests and challenges you; thus, you can apply and develop your skills, talents, and interests to the fullest. You have an unprecedented opportunity to engage in work that you truly love and work that gives you satisfaction and fulfillment.

I know from experience that when I worked on something I loved, no matter how difficult or challenging, it gave me a sense of enjoyment and satisfaction. I seldom got that feeling of satisfaction or happiness when I worked in the corporate environment; worse yet, I found myself working longer and longer hours. It got to the point where my job totally consumed my life; unfortunately, this seems to be the norm in America today.

Many people think that if you have your own business you have to work all the time. Actually, nothing could be further from the truth. Looking back over the years that I ran my own project management business, I can testify that I had more free time than I could have imagined. Sure, there were periods when I had to put in many hours to meet a deadline on some important project, but I was the sole master of my time. I could pick and choose when I would work, where I would work, and how I would work. I could create my own work environment, work in tune with my body clock, and be in complete control of interruptions and distractions. I was able to work at a level of concentration and efficiency not possible in today's information-saturated corporate office. The net result was that I generated more discretionary time than ever before.

Having a knowledge-based business like project management provides many possibilities to enhance the quality of your life. You will meet creative, ambitious, interesting people like yourself. You will have the opportunity to travel and work on challenging and exciting projects. Moreover, you will likely move in social circles that are well beyond those you would travel as an employee.

One of the significant fringe benefits of being an entrepreneur and running a project management business is that you gain considerable recognition and prestige. You will enhance your social standing significantly because you are doing something that many people would like to do but lack the initiative or the courage. When you go to a party or social gathering and people ask you about your job, you will generate immediate interest when you tell them that you are the president of your own company. They will ask you about your business, your clients, and your projects. They will also inquire about how they can get involved with you. There will be no shortage of people who want to align themselves with you and your business. As an entrepreneur, you become a model for success in your community. You also become a model for your friends and family.

By running your own business, you are breaking the age-old mentality of the "good job." You are setting an example for your children and others that show them that they have many options for earning a good living beyond working in the corporate environment. Frankly, in today's complex and competitive world, the younger generation needs as many options as possible in order to build a quality life.

Summary

Let me emphasize a few important points:

- There is a lot of work involved in setting up a project management business; I recommend that you take your time and don't try to do everything at once

- You can set up your corporation without a lawyer, implement your own accounting system, and do your own taxes. After you become a multimillion-dollar operation, you can hire these services

- Use Free Ware and Open Source software to minimize your startup costs

- Set up a home office

- Remember—keep it simple and low cost

Chapter 6

How to Generate Business

Establish Your Playing Field

The biggest problem for a new project management business is getting clients. Before you launch your company, you must define your playing field: the business, industry, government sector, etc., you plan to operate in; then, identify the clients you will target for your business, and the products and services you will offer. Do not go into business without a comprehensive list of viable clients. Be realistic; identify clients who have the resources (money) and the need (problems) to hire outside expertise. If possible, have at least one client assignment lined up before you leave your job. Above all, do not leave your job, start your business, and then spend time and money figuring out what you want to do. This can be an expensive learning process.

I had a friend who started a consulting business with a partner about the same time I launched my company. My friend and his partner opened an office, hired a secretary, and spent a year developing their business plan. Over the course of the year my friend would check in with me to see how I was doing. I was busy with a small project while my friend and his partner were still trying to figure out what they wanted to do. After about a year, my friend called and said that they had completed their business plan, and they were going to be consultants to small business. Their rationale was that because small business has a high failure rate, there was a need for their expertise. I said they were right; there was a need for their expertise, the only problem was that most small businesses could not afford to hire consultants. In fact, one of the leading causes of small business failure was under-capitalization; hence, the possibility of consulting to small businesses was limited at best. I told my friend that I was concentrating on Fortune 500 corporations because that's where the money was. In any event, I wished my friend well and went on to expand my project management business. I ran across my friend some two years later when I found him working as a purchasing agent for one of my new clients. My friend explained that they just couldn't generate enough business, so when their savings ran out, they folded their company and started looking for jobs.

Be realistic—target only clients who can afford your services.

Pick Your Game

Start your business by working at the game you know best. Your industry, company, and job are the foundation of your expertise. Stick with what you know regardless of how tempting it may be to try something new. Once you establish a successful track record, then you can transition into other areas. This is important for two reasons. First, you must have a few successful projects under your belt in order to gain confidence to venture into new territory. And confidence is important not only for talking with clients but also for dealing with problems and setbacks. Secondly, you must demonstrate success to convince new clients that you have transferable skills and experience that can help their projects. Many clients believe that their business or industry is so unique that unless you were born and grew up in that industry, you could not possibly understand their needs. It is difficult to convince clients that the principles of project management are applicable to virtually any business or industry. To get around this problem, I tell clients that if they want some fresh ideas, they have to get help from outside the box. I also quote from change management studies that show that substantial change can only be initiated from outside an established system because the natural tendency for any system is to protect itself by preserving the status quo. However, these arguments don't mean much unless you can show experience, expertise, and consistent project success in your field.

Find a Need

Identify the dynamics in your industry; what is changing and how are corporations responding to the trends and problems that change is generating. What kind of projects are corporations undertaking to meet the demands of their business environment? Keep in mind that change is not only generated by competition but also by political, economic, and regulatory forces that are in constant motion in our country and throughout the world. So keep abreast of the environmental as well as health and safety regulations that may be spawning new projects in your industry. How are changes in social programs impacting your industry? What is energy cost doing to your industry? Dramatic changes can generate unusual business opportunities. For example, I had a colleague who left his job to start a business at the height of the energy crises during the 70s. Everyone thought he was crazy; the economy was in terrible shape, business was bad, inflation was rampant, and energy costs were out of sight. It did not look like things were going to get better for a long time. My associate said this was a great time to start a business. He created an energy audit business to analyze client energy consumption and showed how to reduce energy costs. He charged the client only if he could save them money, and his fee was a percentage of the savings. His clients included factories, hospitals, schools, and office buildings. He actually had more business than he could handle; he took on staff and eventually expanded his company to include engineering, fabrication, and installation of a variety of industrial and commercial systems.

The worst of times may be the best of times to start a business. And this is especially true for project management because economic turmoil requires companies to invest in projects if they want to survive. Thus, your project management business can thrive during bad or good economic times.

We did a great deal of project management training and system development work for electric utility companies engaged in major nuclear power plant projects. However, most of these projects came to a sudden halt after the Three Mile Island nuclear plant accident. Surprisingly, our business really took off because of NRC regulatory action; some nuclear plants were shut down and others were put on a watch list. Utility companies lose significant revenue when a plant is shut down; hence, all these companies launched aggressive projects to correct their problems and get back on-line as soon as possible. This crisis presented significant business opportunities for our company and others to help utilities get back to profitability. By working hard and making important contributions to aid our clients during a time of crisis, we were able to build a relationship that provided ongoing business for a decade or more.

How do you find clients who have projects and need help? Generally, it's simple: read newspapers and business journals, talk to your contacts, work your networks and associates, and be active in professional organizations like PMI. Pay particular attention to special interest divisions or groups within these professional organizations. Special interest groups tend to give early insight to needs, issues, and problems that a particular industry faces.

Business intelligence gathering is a key component in identifying business opportunities. The payoff comes when the client seeks you out for help. This means that you have to ensure that the client knows who you are and what you can do for them.

Let Them Know Who You Are

The first order of business is to get on a client's bidders list. Identify potential clients in your industry and then contact their purchasing department to find out how to get on their bidders list. Check the client's Web site to see if you can take care of the whole process by way of the Internet. However, I recommend that you get to know the company's buyers, purchasing agents, and contract management personnel. This generally affords you a better opportunity to get to know the corporation's preferences in contractors. You should respond to all the requirements spelled out in the client's qualifications criteria for vendors, contractors, and consultants. Be sure to provide supplemental information whenever possible, not only on your credentials but also on past project successes and endorsements. If you have contacts within the client's organization, be sure to let them know you are on the bidders list.

Typically when corporations look outside for contractors, they will try to get three or more bids from qualified contractors. Often the corporation will have a list of preferred contractors for a particular type of work. If possible, use your internal contacts to get on the preferred bidders list. If you have a proven track record with a client, you may even be able to get a sole-source contract. This is a highly desirable situation because it will save you a lot of money in writing proposals. We will talk more about proposals later.

For a knowledge-based business like project management, getting clients to know you and your capabilities is critical. There are many things you can do to generate meaningful exposure. In my experience, the most cost effective ways of attracting clients are teaching, speaking, and publishing; the least cost effective ways are advertising, press kits, and electronic newsletters. Advertising tends to be a poor investment. Advertising project management services is typically limited to professional journals and Web sites. Currently there are literally thousands of firms offering project management services, and it is very difficult to find anything different or unique about any of these firms. Furthermore, a client's buyer will not pick someone from an advertisement to solicit a proposal; you have to be on the client's qualified bidders list. Save your advertising dollars for something more effective.

You should have a brochure for your company. Keep it simple and easy to read, and generate the whole package on your laser or color printer. However, don't expect that your brochure will generate any business. At best your brochure will act as a memory hook for some client you visited; with luck, your brochure may reside in their bottom desk drawer—in most cases your brochure will probably wind up in the waste basket. If advertising and brochures are a poor way to get exposure for your project management business, what about using newsletters, either electronic or print? Some businesses swear by them, but I believe they are not worth the effort. First of all, there are a lot of newsletters out there; more importantly, the busy executives that I know rarely have time to read newsletters. It takes a lot of time to put together a good newsletter; furthermore, most of the people reading your newsletter and using the information will be your competition.

Later we will talk about setting up your company Web site and using social networks. However, Web sites and social networks rarely bring in actual business; they function mainly as a signpost to let people know you exist. What you need to do is demonstrate your experience and expertise to potential clients in face-to-face encounters. One way to do this is by teaching.

For years I taught Project Management courses at Penn State University. Most of these courses were for working professionals who were getting advanced degrees or becoming certified Project Management Professionals (PMP). The benefits of teaching are many;

first, you get paid for your time; and second, you get to meet professionals from a variety of businesses, industries, and government agencies. Furthermore, you find out about the problems and projects that many of these professionals are dealing with in their respective organizations. You may get referrals from your students. Over the years, a number of my previous students have invited me to visit their company to discuss potential consulting assignments.

In addition to generating business opportunities, teaching keeps you sharp. If you are instructing working professionals, you not only need to know your subject, but you also need to keep abreast of the trends and fads that run through corporations like biorhythm cycles. We can be cynical about management fads that come and go, but in the final analysis they provide opportunities that do not exist in a static business environment. Looking back at my career in project management, I can identify major business opportunities that came out of the productivity crisis of the 70s: In Search of Excellence, the Japanese management methodology, Total Quality Management (TQM), Reengineering, and many more. I strongly recommend teaching at a college or university as a way to generate new business opportunities.

Let Them Know What You Can Do

When you set up your project management business, you must define the specific products and services that you offer. These offerings should be based on your interests, experience, skills, and expertise. You should develop two important tools to describe what you can do for clients. The first is a tender document that describes your services, capabilities, and rates; the second is a Power Point presentation of your services, experience, and expertise. You can use these tools to make presentations to prospective clients, respond to proposals, or use them on your Web site or Blog. I call these documents and presentations boilerplate tools. These tools are generic, not industry specific, so you can use them for just about any client. Organize your boilerplate documents and presentations so that you can plug in additional information to make them industry or client specific. Boilerplate tools can help you to save time and to minimize overhead costs.

The best way to let clients know what you can do for them is to show them what you have done for others. Every project you work on should be documented in your boilerplate tools along with positive endorsements from your clients.

Build on Success

Successful project engagements are powerful vehicles for generating additional business with your client as well as for attracting new clients. Every project is a learning experience that enhances your knowledge-base. You not only learn more about the industry and technology in which you work but also about the culture of the client organization. Furthermore, every engagement is an opportunity to learn how to create rapport with key client personnel and to establish relationships that can lead to long-term business opportunities. In addition, every project is an opportunity to create professional and personal friendships that can enrich your life.

I have been fortunate to have met and worked with client personnel in the United States and overseas who developed into personal friends that I have maintained a relationship with for more than three decades. These relationships have exposed me to different professions, cultures, and religions and have increased my understanding and appreciation of the world I live and work in. I certainly would never have been able to obtain this kind of personal growth and enrichment if I were still an employee in the corporate environment.

Expand Your Niche

I recommend that you start your project management business using the experience, skills, and expertise you have gained while working at your job. However, if you want to remain viable you will constantly have to develop new products and services. If you want to grow your business and increase revenue, you will have to expand beyond you own immediate experience base. This means you will have to move into other businesses and industries. For example, if you started your project management business by specializing in cost estimating or scheduling, you can expand your business by offering training or consulting.

If you focused on one industry like aerospace, you can leverage your expertise by moving into utilities or construction. The industries are different, they have their own jargon, history, and culture, but the issues around projects are pretty much the same. The key to moving from one arena to another is to demonstrate the viability of knowledge transfer and learning. Certainly, if you have worked in different industries, you can refer to your experience and show how cross-industry experience is a value-added benefit to the client. If you don't have this type of experience to show the client, then you must come up with a hot idea or innovation that the client can recognize as useful and meaningful to their projects. The way you do this will depend on the experience and personality of your client. In Chapter 7, I will discuss how to read your client and establish a rapport that provides the foundation for trust and a long-term business relationship.

Enhance Recognition

A cost-effective way of getting recognition is by speaking and conducting seminars. Many organizations hire speakers to make presentations at various functions. Typically these are after-dinner presentations that focus on some particular theme. Public speaking can be a profitable and a good marketing venue. You can expand your speaking repertory by conducting public seminars that not only generate revenue but also give you excellent client exposure and insight into problems, needs, and trends. Over the years, I have conducted seminars in the United States and overseas that invariably generated new business. In many cases, I conducted seminars at professional conferences that I attended to deliver a technical paper. Publishing is an important vehicle not only for getting client exposure but also for establishing your professional credentials.

Early on, when I went into business, I decided that I would write at least one technical paper a year. My goal was to force myself to keep abreast of business developments and get my name out in the professional arena. Over the years, I have presented more than thirty technical papers here in the United States and overseas (See Appendix A). Several of these papers have resulted in major client projects for my company. I have also written articles for professional journals and magazines, and I am a contributing author to several project management textbooks. I have also made joint technical presentations with a number of my clients. These presentations have been beneficial to my business as well as to my client's professional career. The power of the written word is well known, and it is incumbent on all project management professionals to sharpen their writing skills.

The most powerful way of gaining credible recognition is from client referrals and endorsements. When a client speaks highly about you to other clients, you are getting quality advertising and marketing that money cannot buy. If you have a good rapport with a client, make it a point to ask for an endorsement or referral when you pursue a new client. A glowing referral from a satisfied client gives you a competitive advantage that is hard to beat.

Summary

Key points to keep in mind are:

- Define your playing field—the business, industry, or government sector you will focus on and the clients you will target

- Concentrate on clients who have the resources (money) and the need (problems) to hire outside expertise

- Start your business by working in the arena you know best

- Look for opportunities generated by change and problems in a client's environment

- Gain recognition through writing, teaching, conducting seminars and workshops, and being actively involved in professional organizations

- Use referrals and endorsements whenever possible to enhance your credibility with new clients

Chapter 7

How to Build Client Rapport

All Business is Personal

They say that if you build a better mousetrap the world will beat a path to your door. However, they won't stay long, and they won't do business with you if they do not understand you, trust you, or identify with you. Project management is an intensely people-oriented discipline. When a client needs outside project help, they typically favor people and firms they can relate to, are comfortable with, and have the expertise they need. Since there are many qualified organizations in the marketplace, competitive advantage goes to the firm that can establish a strong interpersonal relationship with the client. When you have this type of relationship in place and nourish it with care, you will position yourself for a continued stream of business.

What is Rapport and Why is it Important?

By definition rapport is about relations, especially harmonious or sympathetic relations. The success of your business depends a great deal on building a strong interpersonal and harmonious business relationship with your client; this is what rapport is all about. When you establish rapport with your client, your client will trust you, believe you, understand you, relate to you, identify with you, and enjoy being with you. If you build strong rapport, your client may even become a trusted friend.

When you establish a strong rapport with your client, you will enjoy a competitive advantage that your rivals will find almost impossible to penetrate. If you consider how quickly technology and knowledge spreads around the globe, it is obvious that any competitive advantage enjoyed by a corporation or individual will be short lived.

On the other hand, strong personal relationships are hard to duplicate or penetrate. It is clear that more than technology, more than innovation, and more than a hot new product, the entrepreneur must learn how to create rapport with his or her client, especially in a project management business. However, considering the diversity and complexity of today's corporate environment and the wide range of personalities that are employed by these corporations, the question becomes, "how do you build rapport with your client?"

Getting to know and understand client personnel, especially the executive that awards the contract, is critical. However, I have found that it is even more important to know and understand oneself. Like it or not, we are all unique individuals with specific interests, values, and bias. If we are going to establish a harmonious and positive relationship with a client, we must be clear about who we are; specifically, we must know our own personality, our temperament, and our preferences.

Know Yourself

When you meet an individual for the first time, I am sure you quickly determine if you can relate to that person. After a short conversation or meeting, you may say to yourself, "I can work with this person; they think and see things the way I do." Of course, the reverse could be true; you run into someone who is your complete opposite, and you say to yourself, "This is going to be a problem because I don't understand this person." It would be great if everyone were just like us, then we could quickly establish a warm business relationship. In today's diverse workforce, the odds are that we are going to meet and work with people who are considerably different. This means that we must align our uniqueness with that of our client to build a positive working relationship. The starting point, of course, is to understand our uniqueness.

Many tools are available to help us in this regard. Perhaps the most widely known is the Myers-Briggs Type Indicator. This well-regarded tool is used to identify sixteen personality types that play a significant role in how we live and work. Based on my personal experience I can say that understanding your own temperament is critical to your professional and business success. You cannot establish a rapport with others if you do not understand your deep-seated, personal drivers. I will give you a personal example.

I left the aerospace industry where I had managed large, complex projects and joined an Architectural and Engineering (A&E) firm that was heavily engaged in the design and construction of nuclear and fossil-fuel power plants. Because of my extensive project management experience, I was hired to help the A&E Company implement a strong project management process. My first assignment was to plan, organize, and manage the design and construction of a major plant project. Because of anticipated near-term power shortages in the region, the project was to be built to a fast-track schedule. This meant that a lot of things had to be done in parallel with little margin for reworks and schedule slips.

I loved the assignment. It was exactly the type of undertaking that was challenging, rewarding, and one I knew I could accomplish.

I reported to a senior manager who had been with the company almost since its founding. I'll call my boss Dave. My boss was a highly respected engineer who had worked on many projects in the United States and overseas. He was an engineer's engineer, and he looked the part. He smoked a pipe, wore a pocket protector filled with a variety of pens and pencils, and always had his slide rule with him. When you went to Dave's office, you usually found him poring over drawings and checking calculations.

When I started my project, I wasted no time getting up to speed. I studied the contract, read the specifications, met with the client, vendors, regulators, and our own internal design and construction staff. In a relatively short time, I had my project team in place, and we developed a comprehensive project plan, schedule, and budget. I was ready to do what I had done many times before on large complex projects—hold a kick-off meeting to launch the project.

I scheduled a meeting with Dave to present the project plan I intended to roll out at the project kick-off meeting. As I started my presentation, Dave sat back in his chair, lit up his pipe, and listened attentively. As I went through the presentation, I could tell that Dave was getting excited. He started puffing aggressively on his pipe. The more I talked, the harder Dave puffed on his pipe. At one point, his pipe started to look like a coal-burning locomotive going full bore down the track. Suddenly a hot ember shot out of Dave's pipe and landed on his necktie starting a small fire. I stopped the presentation to help Dave extinguish the blaze on his tie. "Damn it", Dave said, "My wife gave me this tie for my birthday." At that point Dave said, "John, before you go any further I have some questions." Immediately I sensed that Dave was uneasy about something. First, Dave told me that they never held kick-off meetings with all involved disciplines at the same time. Instead, Dave said he met with the individual disciplines to get their inputs and then tried to build consensus. When he was comfortable that he had everyone's commitment, he would then issue a directive confirming the agreements and the schedule. They never had a formal project plan; instead, each discipline would develop their own internal task list to produce their deliverables to the agreed upon schedule. If the disciplines ran into a problem and could not meet the schedule, they would then negotiate with the project manager and the other disciplines involved to develop a new schedule.

Dave explained that was how the company had managed projects—successfully, he added—for more than fifty years. I said that process was not appropriate in this case because we had an extremely demanding schedule. Dave was unmoved. He said that if we rushed things, we were certain to miss something, make mistakes, do things over, and lose money on the job. At this point, Dave began to pepper me with detailed questions about design, construction, materials, suppliers, staffing, and many other things. I was hard pressed to answer all of Dave's questions. When I left his office, I had a laundry list of questions to answer before Dave would give me the OK to hold my kick-off meeting. When I went back to Dave with all the answers, I got another list of questions to work on. After several iterations of this, I was convinced that we were never going to be able to work together.

One day I ran into the president of the company, who had hired me, and he asked me how things were going. I told him that I thought I had made a mistake. "Oh," he said, "something to do with your project?" "No, "I said, "I think I made a mistake taking this job." He expressed dismay, but I told him that I thought you hired me to implement modern project management and change the way this company was doing business. Then I went on to explain the problems I had with Dave in getting my project off the ground. The executive said, not to defend Dave, but because of the way I started off with Dave, that he probably pegged me as a cowboy, someone who shoots from the hip. Furthermore, he said Dave was a proven performer, and I should get to know him, understand him, and learn from him. I said I was trying to do that, but I was really frustrated. Then the executive said something that surprised me; "Perhaps," he said, "you need to better understand yourself." At that point he sent me to the HR Department to talk to the OD (Organizational Development) consultant they had just brought into the company. After a short talk, the OD consultant gave me the Myers-Briggs test. I took the test and learned a few, interesting things about myself, and I also confirmed some things I already knew. Basically I was pretty much a take-charge person, totally focused on getting the job done. Furthermore, I had little tolerance for ideas and suggestions that did not fit my way of seeing things.

The O. D. consultant also gave me an overview of the other personality types. From this I learned that my boss was my complete opposite. Where I was concerned with schedules, Dave was concerned about accuracy; where I was focused on completing the objective, Dave was focused on avoiding embarrassing mistakes. It became clear that if I wanted to succeed with my boss, I had to address his concerns and fears. Thus, I decided to change my tactics and approach Dave from a different direction.

From that point on, I worked hard to ensure that whenever I had a meeting with Dave, I had all the information that he might want to see. I took time to think about the questions he might ask or the concerns he might raise. I made it a point to ensure that Dave was comfortable with the decisions we were making. At first it was frustrating to get into what I considered nit picking details; however, over time I began to realize that I was becoming a much better project manager because I was spending more time conceptualizing, analyzing, and digging into the details. It took a long time for Dave and me to begin to appreciate our personality differences and use them in the best interest of our company and our careers. I did get to hold my project kick-off meeting and get the project working to a fast-track schedule. And with Dave's intimate understanding of the organization's culture and his extensive experience in the power plant business, I was able to implement many of my new ideas and make our project a success.

As I learned from my experience with Dave, knowing one's temperament is vital to building rapport; however, you must also recognize and understand the client's temperament. The problem is that when you meet a client for the first time, you tend to evaluate the client based on impressions, feelings, or emotions. This can be dangerous, especially if the client appears to be significantly different from your model of the world.

Know Your Client

Your personal preferences are the starting point in getting to know your client. Basically, you determine how much your client is like you or different from you. We make these judgments all the time; in most cases, these are made subconsciously. Typically we get a feeling about people we meet; we develop an impression and we respond accordingly. If the vibrations are positive, we develop a warm feeling and we establish a congenial, non-threatening relationship; however, if the initial feelings tend to be negative, we become guarded, suspicious, and cool to that person.

Sometimes our initial impressions are wrong, and this is unfortunate because it can create problems and set the stage for missed opportunities. For example, once I had to take over a project that was in serious trouble. Unfortunately, I had a limited background in the technology involved, and I was not familiar with the people and organizations working on the project. Furthermore, the project was one of several that the division was working on at that time, so there was a lot of internal competition for personnel and resources. However, the Division Vice President hired a consultant to help me with this difficult project. I looked forward to getting help because, frankly, I was in over my head on this particular assignment; but when George, the new consultant, showed up, my heart sank. George was a short, portly man, barely five feet tall, with a thin pencil mustache, slicked down black hair, a well-tailored business suit, and shiny brown shoes—George looked like a cartoon character that used to be in the comics years ago called "The Little King." In fact, that became George's nickname around the office. When George spoke, his voice immediately stereotyped him as an aggressive New York salesman. And it did not help matters when George started our initial meeting by stating, "I am here to help you get your project back on track," which is what our VP told him he was supposed to do. I took this comment as a slap at my performance; as a result, our relationship was strained from the very start.

George was a highly experienced, seasoned consultant, who knew how to dig into complex problems and organize and manage tasks effectively. Over the weeks and months that I worked with George I learned a great deal about managing demanding projects, dealing with inter-office politics, and using the front office to handle situations that were beyond the powers of my position. More importantly, I started to appreciate George's style and personality which was so vastly different from mine. I slowly developed a congenial working relationship with George, and I began to employ him to break down barriers that affected my project. Over time, George became a valuable resource. I applied his knowledge and experience to ensure my success, and I tailored his techniques and approaches to my management style.

George helped me broaden my management portfolio, and he showed me how to evaluate people and interact with diverse personalities in a constructive manner. By the time George finished his assignment, we had developed a warm friendship as well as a strong professional relationship. I would call upon George for advice and recommendations many times over the years of my career.

Identifying Client Types

At the first meeting with a client, I try to estimate the degree of difference between my preferences and that of the client. I use a simple model based on the Myers-Briggs Type Indicator test. My model categorizes people's behavioral styles, or preferences, into four groups that I call the Field Marshal, the Politician, The Analyst, and the Caregiver (see Exhibit 7-1).

<u>Identifying Client Types</u>

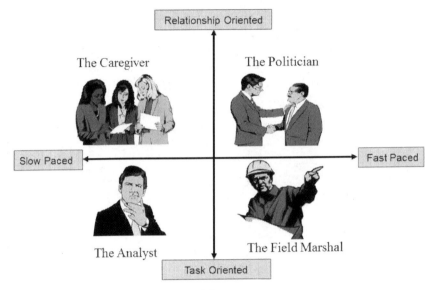

Exhibit 7-1

These are broad classifications and they are only a starting point to understanding preferences or types. It takes time, work, and patience to get to know people; hence, it is critical not to jump to conclusions about people until you have had an opportunity to interact with them in a variety of situations. Only then will you have the information that will enable you to build a long term, solid relationship. You can use my model, along with other information that we will discuss later, as a starting point to assess a new client's preference or type. Some of the characteristics of the four types in my model are as follows:

The Field Marshal—As the name would imply the Field Marshal is a take-charge personality type. He or she is a process-oriented person focused on the results of an undertaking. This individual tends to be a no-nonsense type interested primarily in productivity, action, and performance. The Field Marshall wants to be in control and has little tolerance for anything considered a waste of time. His or her communication style tends to be simple and direct; hence, it is important to get to the point quickly and to accomplish goals effectively and efficiently (see Exhibit 7-2).

Client Types - Wants, Needs, and Fears

	Wants	Needs	Fears
The Field Marshal	To be in control. A well developed process. Simple and direct communication. Little or no disagreement. Project success.	Productivity. Action. Performance. Compliance.	Loss of control. Wasted time. Failure.
The Politician	A working relationship. A variety of alliances. Firm commitments. Active participation.	Recognition. Attention.	Loss of prestige. Loss of social contact.

Exhibit 7-2

The Politician—The Politician builds relationships and alliances to accomplish goals. He or she focuses on interacting with people and managing interfaces between organizational elements. Above all, the Politician seeks attention and recognition and fears loss of prestige or social contacts. The Politician's conversation will emphasize cooperation, contacts, and interpersonal relationships over planning and control techniques (see Exhibit 7-2).

The Analyst—The Analyst has a high need for information and data. His or her goal is to get enough information and data to make them comfortable with their decisions and to avoid mistakes. The Analyst fears embarrassment and needs assurance that nothing has been overlooked in the planning and decision making process. The Analyst will ask many, detailed questions and seek facts to substantiate plans, processes, and procedures. He or she tends to have a reputation for dwelling on nit-picking details (see Exhibit 7-3).

The Caregiver—Unlike the Politician, the caregiver builds relationships to ensure tranquility and avoid conflict and confrontation. He or she is sensitive to the needs and desires of others and seeks to harmonize differences between individuals and organizations. The

Caregiver is good at team building and minimizing turf conflicts between organizations. The Caregiver's conversations will emphasize conflict-resolution techniques, morale-building programs, and behavioral modification as a process for ensuring the effective operation of the organization (see Exhibit 7-3).

Client Types - Wants, Needs, and Fears

	Wants	Needs	Fears
The Caregiver	To build relationships. To harmonize differences between people and organizations. To emphasize team building.	Stability. Tranquility. Harmony.	Confrontation. Conflict. Disagreements.
The Analyst	Detailed information. Ample data. Confirmation of facts.	Assurance and support. Time to make analysis and formulate decisions.	Making a mistake. Embarrassment.

Exhibit 7-3

I am sure that you can easily connect the four types described above with people you know or have worked with. I used this model as a starting point in determining a client's temperament or preferences; however, there are other indicators you should look for to help you assess your client.

The Initial Appraisal

When you meet a client for the first time, you need to collect quickly all the information you can use to engage in a rapport-building dialogue. Your source of information is the client's physical environment (office or work area), their appearance, communication style, and body language. By careful observation, you can use this information to tune your conversation, presentation, and interactions to connect mentally and emotionally with the client. Let us look at the information that you can access when you meet a new client.

The Client's Work Environment—The client's physical setting will give you some insight into their personality. Is the client's work area neat, attractive, comfortable, well organized? Or are there piles of documents, folders, and boxes littering the office? Are there family photos, awards placards, or sports memorabilia prominently displayed in the office; what do these things tell you about this individual? All of these artifacts help to create a picture about the client; however, you have to be very careful about typecasting your client too quickly.

Your initial impressions are a starting point for discussion; however, if you find that you are off-track, you can change direction as soon as you get additional information. For example, one time I visited a new client and I noticed a set of rather expensive golf clubs neatly stacked in the corner of his office. I immediately assumed that he was an avid golfer, so I interjected golf into our conversation; however, my client quickly informed me that he was not a golfer, and he had more important things to do than play golf. As I glanced at the golf clubs in the corner of his office, my client informed me that the clubs belonged to his son, who just dropped out of college to pursue a career in golf and socializing. I quickly assessed that my client was having serious problems with his son, so I gracefully moved the conversation around to the problems we parents face and some of the approaches I used in dealing with my children whose values were not aligned with mine. We spent quite some time discussing our challenges as parents in a modern world and our concerns for our children. This initial meeting gave me insight into my client's anxieties, values, and goals that provided the basis for building a long-term relationship.

The Client's Appearance—A client's appearance can give you some insight into their personality and preferences. Highly polished shoes, very neat dress, erect posture, and a bearing of authority might indicate a well-organized, self-confident take-charge individual. On the other hand, a neat but casual dress could indicate a more easy-going individual with an open and friendly personality, but a rumpled business suit and a food stained necktie could identify a lazy or careless individual who is not influenced by convention or authority. An individual's appearance is only a hint of their personality or preferences; however, you will get a better picture of the individual when you connect appearance with communication style.

Communication Style—Take note of how the client uses language, the extent of his or her vocabulary, use of key words, and the tone and quality of his or her voice. A commanding tone of voice, punctuated by words like, "I expect, I want, I manage," delivered in a confident, direct manner indicates a take charge, no-nonsense personality, while a low-key delivery framed by words like, "We need help, we need cooperation, we need to improve morale," probably identifies a sensitive, caring individual. Listen carefully to how the client communicates, since this will shed a lot of light on how the client sees the world. Hearing what the client says, together with seeing how they physically react to you and your discourse, will further indicate the type you are dealing with. Body language is another, but perhaps, more complex indicator of your client's temperament.

Body Language—Body language consists of posture, movement, gestures, facial expressions, and breathing. When you meet a client for the first time, you want to know if the client is interested in what you have to say and the services you are offering. In other words, are you connecting and making a good impression. Take note of the client's body language. Is the client maintaining strong eye contact, leaning forward to listen carefully, tilting his or her head to one side, and generally still and relaxed? If so, this is probably a good indication that you are in sync and making an impression. On the other hand, if your potential client gazes into the distance, lets his eyes wander, shifts weight frequently, or thumbs through papers on his desk, then it's a good bet that you are not making a connection.

Pay particular attention to facial expressions. Facial expressions can mirror a person's feelings and interests (see Exhibit 7-4). At one meeting with a potential client, no matter what I said, it was clear that I was not getting through; however, about the time I was getting ready to give up, I happened to mention the name of an executive I knew at another firm. It was as though I hit a hot button; the client's face lit up like a Christmas tree, he sat erect in his chair, and peppered me with questions about the services I was offering to this executive. In short order I obtained a consulting assignment which positioned me to work in many different areas of the corporation. It was not until much later that I discovered the reason my client showed so much interest in the work that I was doing at the other firm—he was trying to get a job at that company.

Facial Expressions: Powerful Nonverbal Communication

Exhibit 7-4

Body language can be very revealing, so it is important to be alert and observant and not get carried away by your own voice.

It is especially important to not focus on just one observation but to take in what you *see*, *hear*, and *feel*. Collectively, the client's work environment, appearance, and communication style can reveal a wealth of information about the client's preferences. However, to make good use of this information you must document your findings and impressions while they are fresh in your mind. It is critical to get information down on paper (or in your computer) as soon as possible. I find that if I do not document this information quickly, I soon forget some of the subtle but important details about my client, and I wind up focusing on those things that are especially annoying. Timely and comprehensive documentation is the foundation for objectively evaluating your client and setting the stage for building rapport.

Evaluating the Client

After I document my meeting with a client, I identify the most significant personality attributes that I observed and I develop a gap chart to compare the client's preferences against my own. The gap chart helps me to be objective and avoid making emotional judgments about the client. If the gap chart shows that the client is a lot like me, then it is easy to start building rapport. However, if the chart shows that the client and I have significant differences, then I have to decide if I can accept or adjust to these differences.

If I see value in our differences, I start thinking about how I might build a relationship with this client. But, if I do not see value in the differences or if the differences are too great for me to accept, then I may decide not to attempt to cultivate a relationship with this client. After I had been in business for a number of years, I decided that if I felt really uneasy about a client I would not work with that client. This may sound like an idealistic philosophy especially during lean economic times, but I learned that the stress of dealing with difficult or toxic clients is not worth the wear and tear on my mental and physical well-being. What is more, there are too many good clients in the marketplace to waste time on a few bad apples.

After every client meeting, I enter my contact information and impressions in my client database. It is important to document your impressions and observations over time. As I noted earlier, it takes time to build rapport, so you must regularly evaluate your client against your personal emotions and biases. All of us have emotions and well-developed likes and dislikes which color our decision-making responses. By documenting these, we avoid or reduce internalizing our biases and letting our emotions overly influence our decision-making process. When I look back at the client profiles I developed over the years and review my personal reactions to each profile, I am amazed at how many of my impressions and perceptions changed over time. Sometimes these changes were positive and constructive, and sometimes they were not. In all cases, the information helped me to make business decisions that were in the best interest of my company. My goal was always to invest in building rapport with a good client that would lead to a profitable long-term business relationship and to avoid toxic, dead-end clients.

Basis for Building Rapport

To build rapport, you must look for opportunities to meet and interact with individuals. We interact with people in the work environment, social environment, and at places of worship, civic and political events, clubs, and sporting events. Every venue is an opportunity to interact with someone and to get to know him or her better, to build rapport. However, you will never really get to know and understand a client until you have interacted with them under a variety of conditions and circumstances. As you work with your client during periods of stress, you will discover personality attributes that are not apparent under normal conditions. In addition, the client may be a totally different person outside the work environment. Hence, to build rapport and establish a long term working relationship, you must be keenly aware of the different facets of your client's personality under different circumstances.

Years ago I won a very lucrative contract with a major corporation to design, develop, and implement a computer-based project management system. The system was to improve planning and control of the client's construction programs. The project manager, Frank, (not his real name) and I hit it off at the very first meeting; professionally, we had similar backgrounds and interests, and Frank's vision for the new system was right in line with mine. As a result, we got the project up to speed quickly. We put together an integrated team of client and consultant personnel; we developed the project plan and studied requirements, developed the system specifications, and initiated system design. Frank did a great job of ironing out internal corporate conflicts and getting enough funding to keep the project moving forward on a fast track. As we ran into problems and setbacks, and there were many, Frank always maintained a positive attitude and never engaged in faultfinding or blame fixing. Frank was the type of client you wished you had on every project; he did everything possible to ensure his project was a success, and most importantly, to ensure my company was successful. I greatly admired Frank's work ethic; unfortunately, Frank played as hard as he worked.

Frank and I would meet every few weeks to assess project progress and problems. These were daylong meetings. At the end of the day, Frank made it clear that I should take him out to dinner. Furthermore, he would suggest the restaurant that in most cases was on the very expensive side. At dinner Frank would pick out the wine, and I have to admit that Frank knew his wine; however, cost was another matter. When I hinted at my concern about the cost of these outings, Frank said, "Don't worry, just charge the expense to project team building; I have plenty of money in the budget."

After dinner and several bottles of wine, Frank was always in the mood to explore nightspots. Our trips to various hot spots usually took us well into the early morning. As the evening wore on, Frank got more energetic, louder, and cruder. He had a habit of making loud comments about the attributes of various females we would see in the nightclubs we were visiting. On more than one occasion, an outraged boyfriend or husband would confront Frank about his crude remarks. However, Frank was a big guy, so there were not many who were willing to take him on. Furthermore, Frank had a gregarious personality, and he often would mollify the offended individual with a joke and a drink. I hated those evenings out with Frank; they were very stressful and it usually took about two days to recover.

Frank's idea of fun was the complete opposite of mine; in most cases, I would avoid people like Frank. However, I adjusted my personal preference to accommodate Frank, as long as it did not approach what I considered an unacceptable limit. Later on I found out that Frank's management was well aware of Frank's personality and tolerated him because his projects were always successful. Frank was eventually promoted to a senior position, and his management sent him to an executive charm school. As a result Frank modified his social behaviors to some extent. This was fortunate for me because our company received a steady stream of assignments and I found it less stressful to work with Frank.

An important question is what to do when you determine that your client and you are 180 degrees out of sync. I have worked with clients I did not especially like, and clients I never really got to understand; however, I would never work with a client who's moral and ethical values were not in line with mine. I have run into clients who were blatantly dishonest and tried to manipulate their consultants for personal gain. I have met clients who were running their projects to promote their own side business or to get a job with another corporation. Regardless of how lucrative the assignment might be, I made it a policy to walk away from any client I considered unethical or dishonest.

How to Build Rapport

To build rapport you need to evaluate, item by item, the similarities and differences between you and your client. Note the positive and negatives, then build on the positive; accept, avoid, ignore, or adjust to the negative differences. Do not try to change yourself or the client.

If you are unable to build a reasonable level of rapport with your client, you will find that your performance, no matter how outstanding, will never quite fulfill the client's expectations. When you build a solid foundation of rapport with your client, you will have an invaluable resource that can sustain you during the inevitable ups and down of any client engagement. There are many straightforward ways to go about building rapport.

Look for Common Ground—The best way to get started is to look for areas of interest that both you and your client share from a business, professional, and social point of view.

What is the client's business or professional needs or problems? What is the client trying to accomplish, what is the client emphasizing, what are the problems, concerns, and fears? If you can understand and relate to what the client is discussing and if you have the expertise and skills to address their needs, you can start building a relationship with the client. But, you and the client have to see the same things in the same way. If there is a significant divergence of views, you will have a problem.

For example, I responded to a client request to develop a project management system for their business which was growing at an explosive rate. The client was having problems keeping up with all their projects; as a result, deliveries were late, costs were out of control, and quality was beginning to suffer. From what I heard about the client's problem, I was confident that I could help because I had experience with this type of problem in other industries. However, I did not have experience in the client's specific business; I assured the client that project management was applicable to a wide range of business, industry, and government undertakings, and I gave him several examples to back up my claim.

But, the client insisted, their business was so unique that unless you grew up in that business, you could not possibly understand the problems. I was rather amused to hear the client say that their business was so unique—it was not. Since the individual I was talking to had never worked any place else, I could not convince him otherwise.

If you can't connect with a client on a business level, try to connect on a social or interpersonal level. Is the client an avid golfer, interested in Little League, involved in community affairs, cultural activities, political, or professional organizations? Usually it does not take too long to get insight into a client's outside interests. If you and your client share a common interest, then you have a natural link for building rapport. In working and communicating with a client over time, you will better understand their beliefs, values, perceptions, expectations, and attitudes. And of course, the client will also discover the same about you. If there is a good fit, there is a high probability that you can build a positive professional and personal relationship. However, if there are significant differences, you can expect that you will not build a harmonious relationship; in fact, significant differences can produce negative or hostile results. In this case, it may be prudent to walk away from this particular client.

Strive for Mutual Success—As a provider of project management services your mission is to help the client accomplish their project objectives on time and within budget. A subtler, more overarching objective is to help your client to be successful. Your client may seek recognition, advancement, prestige, personal growth, and development. If you can be an enabler or a catalyst to help the client realize personal and professional goals, you are well on your way to establishing strong rapport with your client. Better yet, if you can find ways to assist the client in the quest for success in concert with your own goals, you will create professional and personal bonds that will enrich your life and enhance your business growth.

Over the years, I have worked with young project managers who were striving for recognition and advancement in their corporation. Gaining recognition in a large corporation is difficult; the competition between professionals is intense and senior management has too many problems to deal with to get to know any individual project manager very well. Therefore, I have encouraged many project managers to get actively involved in professional organizations like PMI, to write technical papers, and to make presentations. This is one way for young professionals to get head-and-shoulders above the rank-and-file of the corporate organization.

I make it a point to write a technical paper on every client project of significance. This is important for my professional development and growth, for the advancement of project management, and for the growth of my company. Furthermore, I encourage my clients to co-author papers with me. This gives the client recognition, helps enhance their professional portfolio, and broadens their experience. Over the years I have had a number of my clients move up the ranks of the corporation into senior management positions; consequently, I have enjoyed a steady stream of business with these corporations as well as endorsements with new clients.

Appreciate and Learn from Differences—One of the advantages of a project management business is the diversity of organizations, peoples, and cultures you will encounter. This was not obvious when I worked in my professional field in the United States, but when I started working overseas I became aware of the significant differences in values, beliefs, and cultures between myself and my host. As an American, I felt that everyone else was out of touch with the modern world; however, over time I began to appreciate views that were completely different from mine. I began to develop a broader outlook and an appreciation for things that I had not been exposed to before. I feel that my life was enriched considerably as I became exposed to new and different foods, music, art, literature, and attitudes. I now look at every encounter with a new client as an opportunity to broaden my knowledge-base and enhance my professional, social, and cultural experience; as a result, I have found it easier to build client rapport. Nevertheless, there will be times when despite your best intentions, you will find it difficult to relate to the client; for whatever reason, you just will not get a good fit.

Dealing With a Bad Fit—Building rapport is easy when you meet people who are like you, but what do you do when you run into the individual who is your opposite? How do you deal with someone you find difficult to work with or in an extreme case, someone you cannot tolerate? A lot depends on your model of the world, your flexibility, and your interpersonal skills. Over the years, I have developed positive relationships with individuals that encompassed diverse personalities, cultures, and nationalities. These relationships have enriched my life and in many cases advanced my business. I have worked with people that I never did figure out, individuals who remained a complete enigma, and people I did not especially like. In most cases I was able to interact with these individuals and conduct business in a professional manner.

So, what do you do when you are not in alignment with your client? Here are a few pointers:

Be clear about the differences between you and the other individual. Certain values and beliefs, such as religion and political ideologies, cannot be reconciled and in most cases are topics you should avoid when dealing with your client. Identify all the significant disconnects between you and the client, try to avoid these disconnects, and still establish a working relationship. Avoidance is one strategy for dealing with a bad fit; the other is to accept the differences, tolerate the differences, or learn from the differences and enhance your tolerance or wisdom in the process.

Dealing with people who are significantly different from your model of the world depends largely on your flexibility and openness. Many of us believe we are tolerant and open-minded; however, the truth is that from birth we are programmed with certain beliefs, values, and perceptions that drive our interactions and relationships with everyone we meet (see Exhibit 7-5). Any belief, value, or perception that is significantly different from our own will be a threat and we will respond overtly or covertly. However, we can reduce this feeling of threat if we can train ourselves to look at the interaction as a learning experience. If we can convince ourselves that every experience is a learning opportunity that we can use to our advantage, then we can grow in tolerance, and eventually accept the differences we see in others. However, most people will not accept differences that are totally contrary to their ethical and moral foundation. There are situations where it is wise to avoid certain people and relationships.

Programming Your Mental Model

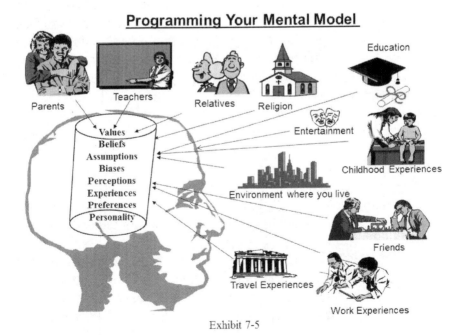

Exhibit 7-5

Toxic Clients—Every time you meet a new client, you hope it will be a positive experience and that it will lead to a mutually profitable business relationship. Certainly, this is what I strive to do with every client encounter; however, I have had clients that I never did figure out, yet I still managed to do business with them. On the other hand, occasionally you will run into a client that is so out of sync with your values and beliefs that it is not only impossible to establish any type of meaningful relationship, you just want to get away from this individual as quickly as possible. Fortunately, over my business career I only had one encounter with what I will call a toxic client.

A senior executive had retained me to work with one of his more experienced project managers to, as he put it, "unscramble one screwed-up project." When I looked at the resume of the project manager in charge, I found an individual who was well educated, highly experienced, and had many successful projects under his belt. I was mystified as to why this seemingly experienced project manager could be in such deep trouble. My first meeting with the project manager was an experience I never want to repeat.

I introduced myself to the project manager and explained that the senior executive assigned me to help him with his project—I got no further. The project manager snarled at me and stated flatly that he knew what was going on, that I was there to undermine him, and take his job. No matter how much I insisted that I was not a threat only made him more aggravated; eventually, he did cool down and sent me to talk to his project team. After meeting with the project team, I concluded that the project was in a state of chaos—it was well behind schedule, the budget was totally blown, the scope had expanded well beyond the contract requirements, and the project team was totally demoralized and dysfunctional.

After a brief study, I met with the project manager and made a number of recommendations to address the project's problems. The meeting was brief; the project manager flew into a rage, and let loose with a string of insults, punctuated by profanity. I said nothing and left his office. I could not decide if the project manager was burned out, had a mental health problem, or if he was just an odious person. I decided I was not qualified to deal with a mental health problem, and I was not about to deal with a loathsome individual, no matter how lucrative the assignment. I gave senior management my recommendations, submitted my invoice, and left.

Key Factors in Building Relationships—There are certain fundamental principles that are important when it comes to building rapport. First, do not try to change your core values and beliefs, and do not try to change your client's. Core values and beliefs are ingrained in your mental model of the world and can't be changed without some severe mental reprogramming; however, you can enlarge and enhance your core values and beliefs as well as your attitudes, perceptions, and expectations—after all, this is what learning is all about.

Second, building relationships takes time. Do not expect instant rapport. You have to work at building trust; you have to prove that your ideas, plans, and recommendations are sound; and you must demonstrate your accomplishments. You build trust by doing what you promised; you provide remedies, not excuses, when things do not work out. You must be honest in your analysis and recommendations, even when you have to tell the client things they do not want to hear.

Third, you must establish mutual respect. You gain respect when you are steadfast in your principles and integrity and you understand and are congruent with the client's principles and integrity. You will have clients that may not agree with you, perhaps not even like you, yet they will do business with you because they respect you. Respect is a key building block to rapport.

Finally, you must communicate effectively so your client understands and believes what they see, hear, and feel. Effective communication involves more than words. Effective communication is eye-ball to eye-ball interaction; that is, tone of voice, body language, and words that create pictures that the client can visualize, internalize, and understand. To demonstrate purpose, sincerity, and honesty your communication must be in harmony with the client's model of reality (see Exhibit 7-6). You build rapport through face-to-face communication, and not by e-mail or any other electronic or written means of communication.

Project management requires people with diverse skills, expertise, and experience to accomplish complex undertakings to meet demanding schedules and budgets; hence, project management is intensely people oriented. Therefore, competitive advantage goes to the individual or firm that can establish a high degree of rapport with the diversity inherent in today's projects.

Communication Must be in Harmony with Client's Mental Model

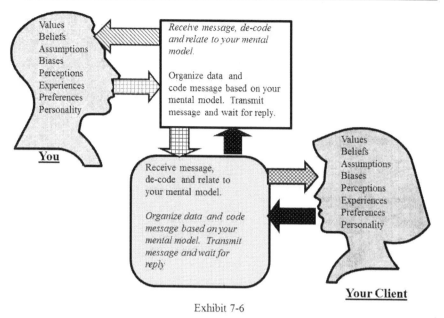

Exhibit 7-6

Summary

- By definition rapport is about relations, especially harmonious or sympathetic relations

- The success of your business depends a great deal on building a strong interpersonal and harmonious business relationship with your client

- It takes time to build rapport; however, you must start at the first encounter with your client

- Be certain that you know your own temperament and then determine the client's temperament

- Build rapport by focusing on common ground, understanding, accepting, and learning from differences

- Do not try to change yourself or your client

- No matter how attractive the business opportunities, avoid toxic or unethical clients

Chapter 8

How to Deal With Clients: The Good, the Bad, and the Ugly

Know Your Client

When you have a number of project management assignments at a large corporation, you will have several different clients. These may include senior executives, division managers, project managers, department managers, or specialists. As a project management provider, you will have clients who, despite working in the same corporation, will have different interests, motivations, and values. Many of your clients will be highly professional, hardworking, ethical individuals. Others will be inexperienced or even incompetent individuals who have little or no interest in their job other than to collect a paycheck. Still others will be nefarious individuals who will steal from you or try to manipulate you to accomplish their own ends. In order to succeed in your project management business, you must be able to identify the type of client you are dealing with and formulate strategies that will enable you to provide your services effectively and efficiently.

I put clients into three broad categories: Good, Bad, and Ugly. I guarantee that, over the life of your project management business, you will run into all three types.

Good Clients

Good clients are ethical and honest, and in most cases these characteristics permeate the organization from top to bottom. Furthermore, the organization tends to be well organized and highly professional; employees know their jobs, they carry out their responsibilities effectively, and they treat their contractors, vendors, and consultants with respect. Good clients understand that you, like them, are in business to provide a product and/or service to make a profit; hence, they set the stage for you to accomplish your assignment successfully.

Good clients know why they need outside support, and they are clear about their requirements and expectations—there are no hidden agendas. Good clients help you to succeed by providing the necessary support, people, facilities, information, and time; what is more, ambiguities, misunderstandings, or disagreements are resolved quickly and professionally. Good clients give feedback and resolve organizational roadblocks in a timely manner. Most importantly, good clients act on your advice and recommendations and they pay your invoices promptly.

Good clients may go out of their way to ensure that you do not fail. For example, early in my career I worked with a client on a fixed price incentive contract. I had a small team housed in the client environment performing equipment installation and acceptance testing. It was relatively straightforward work, but as we neared the end of the project I found that there were a large number of punch-list items— tasks that had to be completed. It turned out that even though I had assembled a team with the expertise to do the work, I failed to consider that other contractors working in the same area might impact us; hence, when there was interference between contractors, certain tasks had to be pushed off until later; in other words, put on the punch list. As my team struggled to complete all the open items, I saw my incentive fee go out the window and my contract slide into the red. The situation put me under considerable stress because if I did not find some way to clear the backlog, my business was going to fail.

When I gave my client a progress report, I did not hide the fact that I had underestimated the amount of cleanup work involved in the contract, and as a result, I was in trouble. My client was a senior engineer of some thirty years' experience, so I knew that he knew I was in trouble. Instead of letting me sink, which was certainly his right, my client said, "I have money in my budget for training; I'll bring my people over now to learn the system, and in the process help you close out some of the punch-list items." My client went out of his way to create a win-win situation that literally saved my company.

When you find clients like this, you must value them, cultivate them, and do your best to establish a long-term relationship. When you perform well for a good client, you will enjoy a steady stream of assignments, work in a stress-free environment, and build rapport that will make working with your client an enjoyable and rewarding experience.

Bad Clients

Bad clients are not evil; they are just bad because they make your life difficult and stressful for a variety of reasons. I find that bad clients tend to have dysfunctional organizations usually because of downsizing, outsourcing, mergers, or restructuring. In the dysfunctional organization, morale may be poor, leadership weak or nonexistent, and the organization may be plagued by internal strife and conflicts. In many cases, a bad client may have inexperienced, incompetent, or over-worked staff. In this type of environment, client needs and expectations will be poorly defined, support and direction will be fragmented, and it will be difficult to accomplish your assignment effectively and efficiently. This type of environment may be a gold mine of opportunity for new business; however, you will be subjected to stresses, strains, and setbacks. In some cases, bad clients may cost you money, or the engagement may be so uncertain that it is not worth the trouble.

I had a client, whom I'll call Bob, who was a good example of a "bad client." Bob had obtained a major contract for his firm, mainly because of his technical expertise and salesmanship; however, it turned out that Bob was more salesmen and less project manager.

I'll never forget my first meeting with Bob to present my qualifications in hopes of getting a contract to provide him project support. At 9:00 a.m. sharp, his secretary, Sue, escorted me into his office and said, "Bob is tied up in a meeting; he knows you are here, and he will be down shortly. Can I get you a cup of coffee?"

At first I thought that I had been escorted to a stock room; Bob's office was a collection of file boxes, piles of report folders, and stacks of computer print outs. The office walls were decorated with family photos, photos of Bob with political figures, celebrities, and sports figures plus certificates and plaques for various awards from civic organizations near and far. In one corner of the office was a pile of running clothes, shoes, and rain gear. In the other corner was a computer with a screen-saver showing fish swimming about and eating other fish. I entertained myself by assessing the chaos of Bob's work environment. At regular intervals, Sue would come into the office to offer me more coffee, apologize for Bob's tardiness, and assure me that he really did want to talk to me, but was delayed because he had been called to the front office; but, she said, "Bob wants to buy you lunch."

Bob showed up at lunchtime and said, "We can't go out because I have another meeting right after lunch, so Sue will get us some sandwiches; now, tell me how you can help me." I think I got through three complete sentences about my capabilities, before Bob, interrupted me, and started telling me about his project, his management, his project team, his wife, his kids, his golf game, and a lot of other things. About the time that I decided this meeting was a lost cause, Bob got up and said, "I have to run to my meeting—can you start today? O.K.", "See Sue, and she will cut you a Purchase Order." Amazing, I thought, no presentation, no proposals, no contract negotiations, and I got the job. What a lucky break—boy, was I wrong!

Working for Bob was the classic, "good news, bad news," story. The good news was that Bob's project was in chaos, and he needed a lot of help. I was able to add on-site staff support quickly, but getting paid was another matter. My invoices sat in accounts payable for months awaiting Bob's approval. In addition, Bob offered little direction, so I was on my own to figure out what the project needed. When Bob did need help, he would call at the last minute. For example, Bob called me at home around 11:00 p.m. one night; he needed me to put together a presentation he had to make to his management at 9:00 a.m. the next morning. I worked through the night putting together a Power Point presentation; when I delivered it to Bob the next morning, he said, "Great," and invited me to sit in on his presentation. Bob made the introductions, offered a few jokes, and turned the presentation over to me—working for Bob was never dull.

In time, I learned Bob's idiosyncrasies, and was able to anticipate his needs. Nevertheless, I had to develop a lot of administrative procedures and safeguards to ensure that my staff was constantly informed of project requirements and that work requests were documented in detail. In addition, this detailed information had to be included in my invoices, so I would be paid without undue delay. All of this extra administrative and management effort added to my overhead cost and diverted me from projects that I had with other clients. It took almost two years, but I was finally able to establish a degree of sanity with Bob, and get his project operating to an acceptable degree of efficiency. More importantly, I was able to build a high level of rapport with Bob and his project team that helped me to become a preferred contractor with Bob's company.

The lesson learned here is that bad clients can be good for your business provided you have the opportunity, the skill, and the patience to deal with the client's shortcomings. On the other hand, there are clients who are evil and should be avoided at all cost.

Ugly Clients

Every entrepreneur I know who provides some type of consulting or support services has run into at least one client that I define as the "Ugly Client." They are out there; they exist, and they can do you a lot of harm—so be wary.

Ugly Clients are nefarious individuals who want to profit at your expense. Ugly Clients will try to manipulate you to accomplish their own agenda; they will cheat you, steal from you, or malign you in order to protect their own interests; they may even try to make you fail because they resent you or envy you.

I have found that ugly clients tend to work in companies where the moral and ethical fiber is compromised right up to the highest levels of management. Often, these companies think it is fair game to take advantage of their consultants, vendors, and suppliers; they usually have implicit strategies for extracting extras from their providers. I had a run in with one such company, which was a learning experience that no small business can afford to repeat.

Quite unexpectedly I received an RFP (Request for Proposal) to develop a project management system for one division of a major corporation. I found out later I was put on the bidders list because of a paper I presented at a national project management symposium. I was rather flattered when I won the contract over other bidders, which included several nationally known consulting firms.

The first phase of the project was a fixed-price contract to study the division's project management capabilities and make recommendations for the development of new or revised project processes and procedures.

The second phase would involve actual development of the processes and procedures; this phase would be priced out later depending on what the division wanted to implement. For me, this was a straightforward assignment; I had several of these projects under my belt (which was the subject of the technical paper I had presented at a national symposium), so I submitted a very competitively priced proposal backed up by testimonials from other clients. I won the competition and received a purchase order for the work.

My first meeting was with the Division Vice President who was funding the project. The VP said to me, "I want to design and build a world class project management organization; I want people, tools, processes, and procedures that will enable my project organization to take on any kind of project and deliver that project on time and on budget, every time." I was impressed with the VP's objectives and sponsorship, and I firmly believed that we would have no difficulty in fulfilling his goals. It was not until we were well into the study that I realized the magnitude and complexity of the challenge.

I assembled a study team to assess the client's project management capabilities. We evaluated staff education, experience, skills, motivation, and morale. We reviewed the division's process, procedures, tools, and techniques. We assessed past project accomplishments, and we examined on-going projects. In addition, we talked to the division's customers and stakeholders. After several weeks of intensive effort, we were able to develop a comprehensive analysis of the division's capabilities to accomplish its project management responsibilities; unfortunately, it was not a pretty picture.

The project management organization was dysfunctional. It was a diverse staff of men and women, a few experienced professionals, and many struggling, inexperienced people. Most of these employees seemed to be unhappy, bitter people who were preoccupied with looking for other jobs. If there was any consistency in the project staff, it was their universal dislike of their boss, the division manager, a middle-aged woman who had worked at the firm since she had graduated high school.

Marge (not her real name) started work at the firm as a billing clerk. She was well known for her dedication, hard work, and desire to get ahead. She would start work an hour earlier than everyone else and stay late every day. Frequently, she could be found in the office on weekends; all of her bosses loved her and counted on her. Marge moved into supervisory positions in the billing department and later when she learned to use a computer and could develop spreadsheets, she moved into the accounting department. Apparently, Marge got into the project management department because she could set up project budgets and track project expenditures in time to alert senior management of emerging project overruns. Marge became manager of the department when her boss left to take a higher-level job at another company.

Marge soon established a reputation for strict cost oversight by identifying and tracking project cost in microscopic detail. Her fifty-plus page project cost reports were renowned. On the other hand, when it came to project management, Marge was totally clueless; she knew it, and she admitted it. However, she believed that if you worked hard you could master anything; therefore, she continued her long established habit of working ten to twelve hours a day, and she expected all her people to do the same.

Marge directed that her detailed cost tracking and reporting procedure be used by all her project managers; otherwise, the project managers were free to use whatever project planning and control techniques they believed appropriate. Most of the inexperienced project staff used spreadsheets to plan their projects and identify major work tasks and milestone dates. The experienced project managers knew how to develop detailed project plans and schedules; some actually took the time to plan their project in detail; however, most did not.

In our study, most of the experienced project managers told us that they knew how to plan projects but had little incentive to do it. As one manager told me, "The only thing important to my boss is her spreadsheets; we spend an enormous amount of time tracking the cost of paper clips, but project deliverables are late because we do not develop detailed schedules; specific tasks are missed because we do not employ a Work Breakdown Structure (WBS); and contractors get paid for extras because we do not have a change control process—I could go on, but it's not worth it because my boss has no clue about what is important in managing a project."

When we completed our study, we developed recommendations and a plan for the Phase II effort. We also developed a detailed cost estimate for the development and implementation of the processes, procedures, and training programs needed to improve the Division's project management capabilities. Finally, we scheduled a meeting to present our findings to Marge and her boss, the Division VP.

Client meetings of this type usually involve a Power Point presentation followed by questions, followed by discussion if all goes well, followed by decisions to move to the next phase of work—but not this meeting. I was only part way through my presentation identifying the deficiencies in the division when the VP stopped me and said, "We know all that. What does it take to make us world class?" Therefore, I jumped ahead and described the processes and procedures that needed to be developed, the schedule for development and implementation, and the training programs to enhance the staff's project management capabilities. I finished my presentation with a cost estimate for the Phase II program.

Without hesitation, the division VP said, "We don't have money to do all that, just give us copies of stuff you developed for your other clients, and we will build our own system." I was stunned. I had not run into this type of situation before, and I was not sure how to respond. After a long pause, I finally answered by saying, "I cannot give you copies of the processes and procedures that other clients have paid us to develop; this would be unethical, and furthermore, we have confidentiality agreements with all our clients." Marge responded by saying, "there is a fine line between ethical and unethical; just change your client's processes and procedures a bit and no one will know the difference." The VP jumped in and said, "We work with other consultants who give us stuff this way, and we've never had a problem; for example, we just completed an engagement with XYZ consultant, and he gave us a lot of his other client's information." I happened to know the XYZ consultant, and I found it hard to believe that he was involved in this unethical game.

The division VP went on to say, "We have a lot of business for you in our company if you help us on this project; right now I am in a budget crunch, and I can't afford to spend money to improve our project management capabilities; clearly we need to make improvements." I left the meeting in a complete state of shock only promising Marge and her boss that I would get back to them.

I agonized over the situation; however, I knew I was not going to compromise the confidentiality agreements that I had with my other clients, and I knew I was not going to compromise my ethical standards. After a while, I called Marge and told her that I could not and would not give them material from my other clients; furthermore, I stated, "Your request is outside the scope of our contract." Marge said, "It was our expectation to get this material in some form; my boss wants me to get this material; if you don't give us what we want, we will not pay you, and we will take you off our bidders list." I was left with two alternatives, take legal action, or walk away; after looking at the cost benefit of the situation, I decided to walk away and eat my loss.

In looking back, I probably had a sense that this client had a hidden agenda, but I was wrapped up in the excitement of starting a project with a new client and could not see the handwriting on the wall through the façade of professionalism that the division VP displayed at our first meeting. What's more, I did not verify the credibility of this client through my network of consultants and professional associates.

Sometime later I contacted the XYZ consultant that the VP said had given them a lot of free information from other clients. My consultant friend verified that he indeed did give Marge a lot of free information. I said, "Aren't you compromising your confidentiality agreements with your other clients?" "Hell, no," he replied, "I just dummy up some crap and feed it to them, and they love it." "You actually get away with this?" I said. "Yes," he replied, "why do you think that organization is so screwed up; believe me, I am not the only one playing this game." Apparently other consultants had caught on to this client and were treating them in kind. Perhaps if I had played the game I could have made a lot of money; I would have had to compromise my ethics, and I am certain that the stain would soon become apparent to others.

A number of my associates and I have noted that in recent years there seems to be an increase in the tendency of clients to extract extras from their consultants. I suspect that this may be due in part in how companies award bonuses, or it may be due to desperate individuals trying to survive layoffs by showing that they can save the corporation money. My experience with an Ugly Client was an expensive but valuable lesson. As a result, I am more cautious and analytical in evaluating a client's culture, ethics, and motives.

Knowing your client before you start work is critical to the success of your business. This can be difficult if you have never worked with a particular firm; nevertheless, there are some simple things you can do to better prepare yourself before you get deeply involved in a particular engagement.

Identify Your Client

You can determine if you are dealing with a Good Client, Bad Client or Ugly Client fairly quickly by taking the time to do some simple things. The easiest thing to do is to tap into your network of contacts and professional associates. Vendors, suppliers, and other consultants are an excellent source of information about a client. Former employees and even current employees can give you an indication of the ethics and mode of operation in their company; other clients can also provide information. If you want to be a successful project management provider, take the time to use your contacts to investigate and understand your client before you accept a contract. This will help you to smoke out hidden agendas and develop a more precise scope-of-work definition that will minimize unwritten expectations and misunderstandings.

Now, if you are just getting started and you do not have an extensive network of contacts there are other things you can do to identify your client type. Stay up-to-date on business news, read the Wall Street Journal, Business Week, Fortune Magazine and on-line news briefs. Is the client facing laws suits, labor disputes, product recalls, or are they receiving accolades for business, technical, or professional achievements? Also, check on-line resources and send out queries to the multitude of Internet outlets that are available. Make an effort to get to know your client before you get locked into a contract; this will help to reduce the potential for problems later on.

Strategies for Dealing with different types of Clients

It takes time, money, and hard work to win a client contract. Thus, when you take on your assignment, you not only want to fulfill all your contract obligations, but you also want to generate additional business. Once you get your foot in the door, it is a lot easier to generate additional business than looking in from the outside. However, your ability to generate more work will depend to a large degree on the type of client you are working with. So let us consider some strategies for generating additional business with our three types of clients: good, bad, and ugly.

CULTIVATE GOOD CLIENTS

When you get a good client, you want to do everything in your power to cultivate that client for a long-term business relationship. As I stressed in the previous chapter, the success of your business depends a great deal on building rapport; that is, creating a strong interpersonal and harmonious relationship with your client. In addition, you must do an outstanding job. Doing an outstanding job means that you successfully fulfill all contract requirements and that you meet client expectations. Bear in mind that sometimes the client's expectations may be different from your contract.

Early in my career, I had a complex and demanding project that I accomplished on time and on budget despite a number of unexpected technical, organizational, and political issues that developed over the life of the project. I was quite pleased to have completed my project successfully in spite of all the unforeseen roadblocks. However, when I gave my final report to my client they acknowledged that I had done a good job; however, they said that they did not want to do business with me again. After I recovered from the shock of this statement, my client informed me that even though the project was a success, they did not want to go through that kind of experience again.

I was working for a very conservative company whose management was not comfortable confronting issues and making the decisions that I forced them to address in order to keep the project moving forward. My client's expectation was that I would take care of everything, and they would not have to be involved in the details of the project. From this experience, I make it a point not only to define the client's role in the project but also to understand their personal expectations. Many times it is difficult to ferret out a client's personal expectations; however, you must be sensitive to any hints or suggestions that you get from your client and respond accordingly.

Even though the personal expectations of an individual client may be difficult to determine, there are certain things you can be sure about. For example, the individual you are working for will more than likely want recognition and opportunity for advancement. Furthermore, they will not want to be associated with a failed project, will not like surprises, and will not want their boss to know things about their project before they do. Also, they will not want to have doubts about your trust and integrity. Much of this is common sense, but it is easy to overlook the obvious in the stress and strains of a demanding project.

Some clients may want to get into the details of the project or they may only want to see the big picture. They may be using the project as a stepping-stone to another job or a different career, or they may be totally indifferent to the project and want you to shield them from the turmoil. Helping your client fulfill legitimate expectations will enhance your business opportunities in the long run.

Working inside a client's organization provides the opportunity to identify problems and make suggestions for improvements. Frequently these suggestions will lead to additional work. For example, on one project I worked with a team that clearly did not have the expertise to address the demands of their project. I suggested to management that they have some of their personnel take project management courses at a local university. I was teaching project management at Penn State University at the time, and I was happy to see some of my client's project personnel show up in my class. The courses helped my client's project personnel to better carryout their responsibilities; furthermore, through the interaction with other students from other businesses and industries, they generated ideas for improving their project management practices. My students made suggestions to their management for project improvements, and as a result I received several sole-source contracts to develop project processes, procedures, and systems. In addition, I received glowing referrals from this client that were invaluable in getting work with other clients.

COACH BAD CLIENTS

As noted above, bad clients are difficult to work with for a variety of reasons; however, they can be good for business. The first step is to recognize that you are dealing with a bad client and ready yourself for the challenge ahead. Avoid saying to yourself, "this is one screwed up organization; I don't know how we will ever get the job done." This will only create a negative framework, and it will make your job ten times more difficult. Instead, say, "I can do a lot of good work here to help turn this organization around." By doing this, you mentally program yourself for a positive encounter with your client from day one.

In my experience, working with a bad client requires a two-prong effort. The first part is to accomplish the client's project objectives while dealing with the shortcomings inherent in the client's organization. The second part is the on-going coaching you must provide to help the client recognize and resolve their shortcomings.

You can coach your client on a daily basis as you go about providing the services defined by your contract. This coaching may be performed in a variety of ways: you can take the role of expert, instructor, mentor, advisor, or trusted friend. In all cases, you must engage your client in a constructive, professional, and non-threatening manner. Coaching a client is a slow, on-going process that requires patience and tolerance for setbacks. However, if you are successful you may establish a long-term relationship that pays handsome dividends over the life of your business.

AVOID UGLY CLIENTS

Earlier I defined ugly clients as nefarious individuals who will do you harm in some manner. Avoid this type of client at all cost. Do not try to work with them in hope that you will change them—you will only fail and be hurt in the process. The most important thing is to identify this type of client as quickly as possible. Sometimes this is difficult to do as I found out in my encounter with an ugly client. A con artist can take in even the most diligent of individuals. What is most frustrating is that sometimes these individuals do not believe they are doing anything wrong. As one executive said to me, "it's all part of getting ahead in business." When you run into this type of individual, I suggest that you formulate an exit strategy as quickly as possible. You will save time, money, and aggravation in the long run and avoid the possibility of having your reputation tainted by being associated with an ugly client.

Summary

- Over the life of your business, you will run into many different types of clients: most of these can be classified as good, bad, or ugly

- Good clients are a pleasure to work with, pay their invoices on time, and enable you to be successful

- Bad clients are dysfunctional in some manner and hence difficult to work for, but they may provide the potential for a lot of business

- Ugly clients are nefarious and will harm you in some way. Ugly clients are always bad for your business; avoid them at all cost

Chapter 9

How to Get Paid On Time, Every Time

Billing Your Client

You would think that once you have completed a job for a client all you have to do is send them your bill and they will pay you. Not true. There are many reasons why a client will either not pay its contractors or delay payments for a long time. Quite often the problem relates to poor invoicing procedures on the part of the contractor; however, occasionally you will run into a bad client or an ugly client who will give you a hard time. Most clients, however, do pay their contractors promptly if they are billed properly.

Keep in mind that your client's accounts payable department must ensure that your bill is for services that have been authorized and funded, is accurate, and payment has been approved by the person in charge of your project. The accounts payable department must also make certain that they are paying the right contractor, that there is no duplication of payment, and that there is no fraud involved in the billing. Therefore, it is incumbent upon you to do everything necessary to make the accounts payable job as easy as possible.

There are three essentials to effective client billing: the contract, the invoice, and billing management.

THE CONTRACT

The starting point for getting paid on time, every time, is the contract agreement you have with your client. This agreement must be in writing in the form of a letter of agreement, a purchase order, or a formal contract. I have had occasions where I initiated work for a client based on verbal authorization; however, these were instances where the client needed emergency support, I knew the client well, and the client followed up the verbal authorization in a timely manner with a written contract. In all other cases, I would never do work for a client without a formal, written contract.

It is important that the contract spell out as clearly as possible the work to be performed, the duration of the effort, the rate or fees to be paid, and the basis for payment. This last item is critical. If you are to be paid a lump sum upon completion of a task or submittal of a deliverable, be certain that you and your client are in complete agreement as to what constitutes a completed task or a deliverable. Furthermore, if you are to receive progress payments, be sure to define how progress will be determined—by milestone accomplishment, percent complete, or passage of time. I often have found that client contracts are not as precise as they should be to facilitate your billing process; therefore, I recommend that whenever you receive a contract you immediately follow up with a letter to your client confirming your acceptance of the contract, your readiness to start the work, your summary of the key points of the work you will perform, as well as the duration of the effort, the rate or fees you will charge, and the basis for payment. Make a point of writing this letter every time, because in any contract dispute, the last written word on a contract carries the most weight.

THE INVOICE

The format and details of your invoice will determine to a large degree if you receive payment on time. Your invoice must give accounts payable and your client—the person who has the funding to pay you—all the information they need so they can pay you without having to call you for clarification or additional details. Poorly constructed invoices will face endless delays; furthermore, it is unreasonable to assume that everyone in the client's organization knows you and what you are doing and that they will pay you without question. A well-crafted invoice will save you endless hours of frustration (see Exhibit 9-1). At a minimum, your invoice should consist of the following:

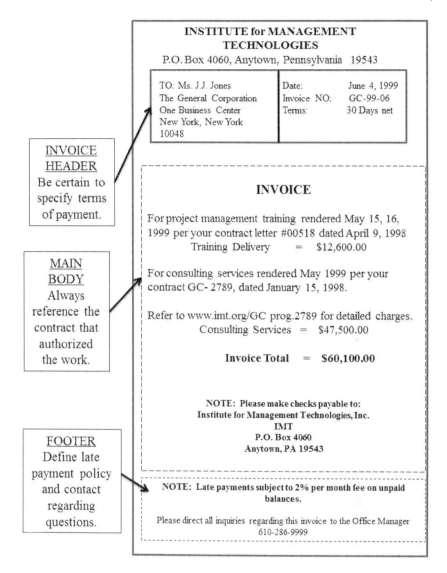

Exhibit 9-1

The Header—The header must provide all the information to identify accurately who you are and where you are located. Give your company name, address, telephone number, e-mail, web URL, and any of your social networking sites.

The header must also give the invoice date, invoice identification number, and the terms of payment (when the invoice is to be paid). In most cases, you want your invoice to say, "Payment due upon receipt." In some cases, a client may require payment to be net thirty days; some clients require longer payment periods, sixty or ninety days. In the old days, BC (before computers), when accounting was a laborious, manual process, there was some justification for a long billing cycle; today there is no excuse for any billing cycle longer than thirty days. Be certain that your client understands that you are a small company operating strictly on a cash basis and you can pay your bills and your people only after your clients pay you. I have found that most clients will understand your needs and will try to accommodate you, provided you give them the information they need to process your invoice in a timely manner.

Main Body—The main body of your invoice must define the period of time the invoice covers, the contract name and number that authorized the work, the name of the client project manager responsible for the contract, their telephone number, office location, department, and any other information. Spell out in sufficient detail what your invoice is for and for how much. Provide all supporting or backup information needed to substantiate your charges. In most cases the client will define the details they need in order to process your invoice, so be sure to provide the required information without fail. Occasionally you may have to hit the client with unexpected charges; in these instances, you must provide all the supporting information necessary to justify your bill. When you run into this situation, be certain to advise your client of the charges before you submit your invoice—clients hate surprises.

Your invoice must spell out how you want to be paid, i.e., make checks payable to XYZ Corporation or make your deposit to XYZ Account number, etc.

Footer Information—The footer information should define fees for late payment, i.e., 2 percent per month on the unpaid balance. Do not hesitate to advise your client that there are penalties for late payments. This is good business practice and will do much to head off future problems. Also, identify the contact for inquiries regarding your invoice.

BILLING MANAGEMENT

If you want to receive payment on time every time, you must actively manage your billing process. The starting point for this is to know your client's accounts payable process and the people involved in this process. Over the years I found it useful to draw a flow chart of the steps involved in getting my client to pay my invoice and the client personnel involved in every step. Most important, make it a point to get to know the people who actually process your invoice. Frequently, the manager in charge of the project is too busy with day to day fire drills to worry about your invoice, and it is usually a secretary or contract administrator who will actually review the invoice and send it off to accounts payable for payment. Get to know these individuals on a first-name basis, let them get to know you and your company, and why it is critical to your cash flow to be paid promptly. This streamlines the process and avoids a lot of heartburn. A small investment in a cup of coffee, donuts, or a lunch for these people can lubricate the corporate bureaucracy to keep your cash flow in black for the life of your engagement.

If a client is late paying, don't delay a call to find out if there is a problem; also, submit a revised invoice with the interest penalty charges added. If there is a valid reason for the delay in payment and the delay is not too long, you can always drop the penalty charges.

Billing management is an on-going process, and there are times when you will have to make some extra effort to get paid depending on the type of client you are dealing with. Let us consider the three types of clients we discussed in the previous chapter: Good Clients, Bad Clients, and Ugly Clients.

Good Clients

As I said in the previous chapter good clients tend to be well organized, professional, and pay on time. However, there are occasions when you may have a problem getting paid. For example, the person you are working for gets sick, is transferred, or leaves the company and your invoice is stuck in limbo. If you know your primary contact is leaving, get your invoices in before they leave, find out who the replacement will be, and start cultivating and educating that individual. Also, be certain that you know the key personnel in accounts payable to talk to about your invoice and how to get it approved if your primary contact leaves the company or is out for an extended period. I have found that well organized corporations are resilient and know how to deal with disruptions. If you employ good invoicing procedures, you will rarely have a problem getting paid by a good client.

Bad Clients

Bad clients are not evil—they are just bad because they tend to be dysfunctional, disorganized, or demoralized usually as a result of reorganizations, mergers, or layoffs. Often the people you work with in these organizations may be inexperienced, incompetent, over worked, or just plain lazy. Whatever the case, I can guarantee that you will have problems getting paid. In this type of environment, you will have to implement additional invoicing procedures, get to know and cultivate more people, and establish a rapport with senior management.

ADDITIONAL INVOICING PROCEDURES

It has been my experience that getting paid by bad clients has a lot to do with preempting questions about your invoice. Typically a bad client will hold up an invoice with questions like, "What is this charge for?" or "Who authorized this task?" or "Why did you charge so many hours this month?" or "Is your billing still within our budget?" It may be that your client is spread too thin to keep track of what is going on in his or her project, or you may have a project where there are several client task managers giving direction to your project staff. Whatever the case, you need to implement processes and procedures to document and track who, what, why, where, when, and how much you charge for the work you perform for your client on a day to day basis. The complexity and level of detail you need to invest in setting up these processes and procedures will vary; however, once I developed a system for a particularly difficult client I tended to use my system for all clients.

I set up a Web site for each client project. One section of the project web provides details on contract requirements, scope of work, schedule, and budget. All approved contract amendments, changes, or additions are documented as well as any pending changes. In addition, new client requests are documented to show *who* requested the change or addition, *what* work is required (task definition and scope), *why* this change is needed, *where* the work is to be performed, *when* the work is to be accomplished (schedule details), and *how much* the additional work will cost.

It is important that this information be documented in detail because, in many cases, your client project manager will need to get additional funding for scope changes to his project. If your project manager cannot get additional funding, you probably will not be paid. This is why I have a strict policy of not taking on additional project tasks without an approved contract change from my client. Occasionally I will work to a verbal authorization from a very good client, but this is the exception to the rule and applies only to clients that I know well and trust based on past performance.

Defining your contract requirements in detail and tracking all contract changes is paramount to effectively managing your project, getting paid on time, and keeping all project participants informed and up to date. I advise all client personnel to check the Web site if they need information, and I tell my project staff to be certain to verify that changes have been approved before they start work on any new task.

My project staff is required to input the project web each and every time they get a client request for additional work. This information is documented, reviewed, and if found to be out-of-scope, a formal contract change request is presented to the client. On some especially dynamic projects I found it useful to sit down at regular intervals with the client project manager, contract administrator, and accounts payable clerk to review the project web page and assess the status of all contract changes. Once all of the client participants were comfortable with the project Web site, they found it to be a tool that made their job easier; as a result I was paid on time every time.

The project Web site also provides project status information. For some projects, a simple Gant chart schedule and spread sheet budget will be sufficient. For more demanding projects, we may employ CPM for detailed task scheduling or use earned value for tracking and reporting. Project status reporting is an important part of your invoicing process. Your client needs to ensure that they get what they pay for; hence, it is incumbent on you to give your client all the necessary supporting information with your invoice so they won't have to call you for additional information or clarification. A well-organized invoice, supported by easily accessible backup information, will minimize delays in payments.

One final note; even if you are a one-person shop, you will find that it is time well spent to set up a project web page, use Facebook, or some other social network, to track your project activities. These can also be powerful tools for influencing clients who may not want to pay you.

CULTIVATE CLIENT PERSONNEL

Putting computer-based processes and procedures in place will do a lot to enhance and streamline your billing process; however, there is no substitute for establishing rapport with the right client personnel. In today's volatile business environment, change is constant and personnel turnover is a way of life. The relationship that you cultivated with a particular manager or executive may be useless because they may be fired, laid off, or forced into early retirement. When you deal with organizations that are being reorganized, merged, or down-sized, you can bet that all normal processes and procedures will be disrupted. Hence, the project manager who must approve your invoice is gone; the administrator who normally processed your invoice has been laid off; and the accounts payable department is being merged into another department on the other side of the world. Do you think you will be paid in a timely manner? What can you do? The truth of the matter is that unless you have an extensive network of contacts in the organization, you're out of luck.

I have been in this situation, and the only thing that saved me was the fact that I had contacts up and down the organization. Some of these contacts were a direct result of the work I was doing for the company. Other contacts came about because of my involvement in professional, political, and social organizations. Even though I did not know some of these people well, I did not hesitate to introduce myself and ask for advice or help with my billing problems at their company. Many times these individuals could not provide direct help, but they could refer me to someone else who could. During times of turmoil and confusion, do not hesitate to ask for help. In most cases, you will eventually track down the right person and you will be paid. This assumes, of course, that you are dealing with an ethical client; however, if you are dealing with an ugly client, you have to resort to a different set of tactics.

Ugly Clients

Previously I defined ugly clients as nefarious individuals who are out to hurt you. One way they can really hurt you is not to pay you for the work you have done for them. An ugly client can find numerous excuses for not paying you; "We can't find your invoice," "Your invoice is in error," "The person you worked for left and we have no record of your deliverables," or, "You did not meet our expectations," "We did not like the result." When the ugly client runs out of excuses they will stop talking to you and you will not get paid.

If you are a small shop or an independent contractor, you are not covered by most employment laws as is an employee. If an employee does not get paid, they can turn to federal or state labor departments to bring legal action against the offending employer. The self-employed entrepreneur has little protection outside of the courts in dealing with a client who refuses to pay. You may threaten to sue, but this can be a time-consuming and expensive process. Even if you win your case, the courts will not help you collect—you have to do that on your own. So how can you protect yourself against an ugly client who refuses to pay you? There are three things you can do to prevent or minimize financial loss; these are: detection, prevention, and persuasion.

DETECTION

The best way to avoid not getting paid by an ugly client is not to work for them. As I recommended in the previous chapter, always check out a new client, use your network of professional and business associates to find out if you are dealing with an ethical client. There are also resources available on the Internet like RipoffReport.com, blogs and professional and industry discussion boards that you can consult. A small amount of research up front can prevent a lot of heartburn and financial loss later on.

One final note; if things are tough and you really need the work you may be tempted to take on a job for a client that has a very bad track record of payment. You may think that things will be different for you—forget it. My experience has been that Ugly Clients keep screwing their small contractors because they can get away with it.

PREVENTION

First and foremost, never give your client a legitimate reason not to pay you. If you do the job you were hired to do, and you follow the billing techniques I defined above, the client should pay you as defined by the contract. However, if you find yourself working for an ugly client who may have slipped under the radar of your initial screening, there are a few things that you can do to minimize damage.

Know the management structure of the client organization. Get the names, telephone numbers, and e-mail addresses of the senior executives and board members. If you have a billing dispute with a low-level manager who is trying to look good by coming under budget at your expense, you may need to elevate your problem to the highest levels of the organization. Do not hesitate to raise your billing problems to senior management; many times this level of management is unaware of the tactics used by the lower echelons of the organization.

Even if your invoice is for a small amount, continue sending the invoice, and apply the interest penalty with every submittal; also, start sending copies of your invoice to senior management with a letter requesting help. I have found on more than one occasion that senior management was totally unaware of the problems that their organization was having in paying contractors on time.

If you have a project of more than thirty days duration, insist on some type of progress payments; avoid lump sum payments at the end of the project. Also, withhold any critical final deliverable until you have collected at least 90 percent of the total contracted amount. Even then, if an Ugly Client tries to screw you out of the last 10 percent, you will have minimized the damages somewhat; however, I do not believe in letting Ugly Client take bread off my table and there are some effective tools you can use to convince them that they should pay you.

PERSUASION

If you are certain that you have fulfilled your contract obligations, invoiced properly, called all the right people, and you still have not been paid, then it is time to take more drastic action. When I started in business in the pre-Internet age, the only recourse we had to deal with Ugly Clients was to sue or turn over our unpaid invoices to a bill collector. For a one-person shop, lawsuits are expensive, time-consuming, and frankly very problematic. Collection agencies, if they are interested in your business, will take a big chunk of the money they collect. Today, however, the Internet offers some very powerful tools that you can use to persuade an errant client to pay you or suffer the consequence. These tools include social networks, blogs, forms, and business and government Web sites that you can use to inform, advise, cajole, persuade, or humiliate an Ugly Client into paying what they owe you. A systematic invoice collection program would employ all your social network resources to do the following:

Get Information—Use Twitter, Facebook, and other social networks to determine if anyone else has had problems getting paid by your client. Get the facts: names, dates, and circumstance; compile the information, create a client profile and post it on line.

Ask for Advice—Find out what others have done to get paid, solicit ideas, and suggestions.

Ask for Help—Request help from your circle of friends, business associates, or others to suggest to your client that it is bad business not to pay their contractors. Encourage everyone to be professional, business-like and civil when communicating with your client.

Give the Ugly Client an Ultimatum—Let the Ugly Client know that you will not give up; be certain that throughout this process you submit your invoice with accumulating interest charges. Throughout this process do not malign, insult, or slander your client. Stick to the facts, and be professional and constructive.

Strive for Maximum Humiliation—Notify, suggest, or recommend that all contractors, suppliers, and vendors, insist on getting paid up front before doing business with this client.

Last Resort—If they threaten to sue, let them; then hit them with a counter suit.

At every step of the process, be certain that the Ugly Client knows they are being exposed on the social networks. Very few companies will want to suffer the negative publicity that you can generate by using the social networks. Just be certain that your claim is valid and be very business-like in pressuring the Ugly Client. Stick to the facts and never defame, malign, or insult the client. If the client threatens to sue you, tell them to go ahead and that you will counter sue.

It is very expensive for a client to sue. The client does not need the negative publicity and has more to lose than you. If they do sue, I am certain that in today's environment you can find an out-of-work lawyer who will take your case to gain experience, or will work on contingency. However, unless you are dealing with a very stupid or arrogant client, they will realize it's cheaper to pay what they owe rather than run the risk and expense of confronting you in court. Even in a worst-case situation where the client might win, just fold your corporation and start over.

CASE HISTORY

Whenever I get together with my fellow entrepreneurs, we eventually wind up talking about our most difficult clients, especially those who try to short-change their contractors. I have heard many stories but none better than the one I am going to tell you now. I have to admit that I have not been able to verify the accuracy of this story, but it is just too good to pass up.

The story has to do with Walt and his client the MJW Finishing and Dying Mill located in an economically depressed area of Pennsylvania. The company MJW was operated by two brothers, Mark and Jerry Weasel (not their real names), but the company was owned by Mark's father-in-law who was retired and lived in Florida. Mark and Jerry lived in New Jersey, but worked at the mill in Pennsylvania six days a week. All the workers at the mill referred to Mark and Jerry as the two Weasels from New Jersey.

The mill itself was in a rundown, 19th century, brick factory building—large grimy windows, equally grimy skylights, wooden floor, large roof fan for ventilation, steam heated dye vats, dryers, and row after row of three-level storage bins. Working conditions at the mill were deplorable and wages were low; however, since there were no other jobs in the area, the union had little power to change things. Mark was quick to squelch any dissension by threatening to move the operation to Mexico.

Every morning, tractor trailers would line up at the receiving dock where workers would manually unload bolts of fabric and stack them in the receiving storage bins. Material was pulled from the storage bins and run through the various dye vats, then dried and stacked in the outgoing storage bins for shipment to customers around the country.

Old Charley was in charge of shipping, receiving, and inventory. When all the trucks were unloaded, Old Charley would go to the front office and log the bin location of the new inventory on a big blackboard. Jerry was in charge of scheduling and production, and he would select the fabric from the bins and designate the vats they were to go to for the various dying operations. Jerry kept track of production and scheduling on his big black board. Mark was in charge of finance. When the fabric was dyed and ready for shipment, Mark would bill the customers and release the material for shipment. Old Charley was responsible for getting the material loaded on the trucks for shipment to their customers.

It was a straight-forward, simple, and quite profitable business; however, Mark and Jerry did have to work very hard in that hot, crummy mill, and Mark's father-in-law did not pay them very well. Nevertheless, Mark and Jerry adapted and made the best of the life they were living. Mark relieved his stress and boredom by checking the office supply room every noon with his secretary. Jerry, who was openly gay, dealt with his frustrations by snorting a line of coke at lunch time. Life was good for Mark and Jerry until one day Jerry had an emotional breakdown—his partner left him.

Jerry was so upset he had a double snort of coke to ease his pain; unfortunately, in his mental haze, Jerry scheduled material into the wrong dye vats. No one noticed the mistake, so Mark billed the customers, and Old Charley shipped the material. When customers called screaming, Mark and Jerry realized that they had a catastrophic financial problem. Mark's father-in-law threatened to fire both of them, but Mark protested saying the problem was that the business had grown, and they needed to get a computer system to stay on top of everything. They convinced the old man to put up the money to get a computer management system. Mark was put in charge of getting the system installed with the stipulation that it would not cost too much.

After rejecting a dozen proposals for a computer system as being too expensive, Mark was advised by his nephew, who was attending a local community college, to contact Walt who taught computer science at the community college. Walt was retired from IBM and he now had his own consulting practice. He taught at the community college because he enjoyed teaching and because the community college gave him exposure to small businesses in the area.

Walt met Mark and Jerry at their office to review the operation and determine their requirements. Mark made it clear that they wanted something simple and not too expensive. Walt submitted a proposal for a simple computer-based scheduling system, which Mark accepted with the stipulation that they pay Walt a lump sum after three months of successful operation of the system—as Mark said, "To be sure we are getting what we paid for." Walt said, "I am sure you will be happy with the results because I have designed and installed many systems for clients."

True to his word, Walt installed a computer scheduling system that Jerry could operate with ease and was very happy with; however, after three months Mark called Walt and wanted to know if they could expand the system to handle inventory control and billing. Walt said he could do that and quoted a price for the system enhancement. Mark advised Walt that they would not pay his invoice until the new enhancements were installed and operating for three months. Walt was reluctant to agree to the new terms; however, he now had a sizeable investment with this client and wanted to see the project through to completion. As it turned out, there were several iterations of enhancements to the MJW management system, and Walt had still not collected a single dime.

In the meantime, Mark streamlined operations at the mill. He fired Old Charley, scrapped the blackboards, got rid of all the old paper files, and advised all his customers of their enhanced management process.

Three months after the final enhancement to the MJW management system, Walt submitted his invoice for the total job. In short order, Walt got a call from Mark saying that the cost was too high; he had no idea how the project had gotten so expensive; he was completely in the dark about all the changes; and quite frankly, the system did not meet their expectations. After several communications back and forth, Walt was convinced that he was not going to get paid, so he called Mark and said he was going to sue. Mark replied, "Go ahead and sue; you will have to get in line."

Walt got the impression that MJW was on the verge of bankruptcy and even if he sued, he probably would not collect anything. However, when Walt was attending a trade show he happened to hear Mark bragging about their new management system and how they were making money selling copies of their systems. Walt did some digging and found that Mark got his nephew to modify and package the system that Walt had developed and sell copies to other companies. Apparently, Mark was pocketing the money from these sales to supplement the paltry salary he was getting from his father-in-law.

One Monday morning Jerry came into the office and fired up his computer and waited for the program to load—he got a blue screen and nothing else. Jerry wasn't especially computer literate, so he unplugged the computer and started again. This time the computer booted up to a green screen with a big black hole in the middle. While Jerry was staring at the computer screen and scratching his head he heard a loud screech and suddenly a weasel burst from the black hole and started racing across the computer screen, then another weasel came out of the black hole, then more weasels rushed out; the screen was filled with screaming weasels racing around, then suddenly the screen when blank.

Jerry did not know what to do. When Mark came into the office they both tried to get the computer working—no luck. They called their nephew in a panic; he said that it sounded like some type of virus, and he would get to the mill as soon as possible to look at the computer. Meanwhile, work came to a halt; trucks waited at the receiving dock to be unloaded; dye vats were cooking, but no material was being processed; workers sat around or played ball in the parking lot. After several hours of playing with the computer, Mark's nephew said that some kind of virus had wiped out all their files, and they had to reload everything from the backup files. Unfortunately, since Mark and Jerry were computer illiterates, there were no backup files. On top of this, companies that had purchased the MJW management system started calling and screaming that their computers were being attacked by weasels. Mark called Walt and accused him of sabotage and threatened to sue. He demanded that Walt come right over and fix the problem. Walt did not say a word; he just hung up the phone.

The MJW Finishing and Dyeing mill never recovered, filed for bankruptcy, and closed their doors forever. Jerry dropped out of sight and Mark wound up living in a small room at the YMCA. Apparently some of the union guys had put a secret camera in the stock room to record Mark's lunch breaks with his secretary and then posted copies on the Internet—they also sent a note to Mark's wife to check out the pictures on the Internet.

Walt never did get paid, but for years after, among his consultant friends, Walt was known as, "Walt, the weasel killer."

Summary

Getting paid on time, every time, is critical to your survival and you can eliminate most of your invoicing problems if you:

- Ensure that your contract defines clearly how you will be paid and the basis for getting paid
- Produce a well-crafted invoice that gives your client all the information they need in order to pay you
- Establish systems and procedures to define and track progress, changes, and additions to your contract
- Get to know and establish rapport with all the key people involved in approving and processing your invoice
- Make certain that your invoice defines a penalty for late payments
- Do not knowingly work for ugly clients
- Use the power of social networks to cajole errant clients

Chapter 10

How to Grow Your Business

Why Grow Your Business?

If you earn a good living you may not be inclined to think about growing your business. However, there is a risk in getting too comfortable. Success breeds complacency, things change, your services can become obsolete, your client may change jobs, retire, or die. Furthermore, competition is always knocking on your client's door. Hence, you need to grow your business to keep energized, engaged, and make money.

If you earn your living by selling your services, there is a limit to how much money you can make. If you are in great demand, you may be able to bill about 2000 hours per year. Multiply 2000 by your hourly billing rate and you get your peak earnings. However, you can improve your earnings by increasing your billing rate. The billing rate you can command will depend on the arena where you work, the skills and expertise you offer, and your ability to market yourself to clients.

For most solo practitioners just starting out, as rule of thumb, you will spend 50 percent of your time on job-chargeable work, and the other 50 percent on marketing and business development. As you grow your business and build a solid client base, you will tend to spend less time on marketing and business development. It is even possible to become a full-time provider to a client. An associate of mine gets a steady stream of assignments from one client year after year. This is a very comfortable relationship, but there is no potential for growth, and there is always the risk of losing your sole source of income. I recommend that you build a base of three preferred clients. These clients should have a portfolio of active projects, need your services, and have genuine rapport with you. When you have a solid client base, you should be able to achieve your maximum yearly billing potential.

You can also generate revenue by selling project management products. Products can encompass training materials, software applications, utilities, tools, and how-to-do-it books. Some project management providers I know have had considerable success in selling products in conjunction with their project management business. In some cases, a successful product gives the creator wide recognition and enhanced acceptance as a project management expert. This is especially true for those who have published project management books. However, based on my experience, the half-life of most specialized project management products is relatively short, so at regular intervals you need to improve your product or develop something new.

Most successful solo project management providers tend to operate within a specific industry, business, or government arena. However, if you want to increase your earnings, you must expand your business beyond your comfort zone. You need to develop and provide a greater range of products and services to more clients in a wider array of businesses, industries, or government organizations. This can be a problem if you have developed a comfortable solo practice and are earning a good living. You may decide that you enjoy your work and really don't need more money. Nevertheless, I recommend that you consider how much money you need to accumulate for a secure and comfortable retirement.

Most people believe that if you amass a million dollars for retirement you will be well off. The truth of the matter is that a million dollars is not what it used to be. Most experts recommend that you have at least three million dollars available at retirement. In a later chapter, I talk about what you should do in order to build up this level of wealth. However, one thing is clear—it is very difficult to amass three million dollars by working as a one-person shop. If you want to live well and have a comfortable retirement, you must grow your business.

Typically, to grow any business you have to borrow money, hire staff, lease office space, buy equipment, and aggressively market your company. In our project management business model, we are not going to do any of this. Instead, we are going to grow our business horizontally and vertically by enhancing capabilities, forming alliances, and exploiting change.

Enhancing Capabilities

To grow, you must enhance your business capabilities. You can do this by adding new business units to expand horizontally and by adding staff to each business unit to grow vertically. (see Exhibit 10-1). For example, I started my business as a project management training company. Later I got into consulting, then expanded into client support and ultimately took on major projects. I grew my company into five business units or divisions: training, consulting, client support, specialized products, and special assignments (see Exhibit 10-2). Each of these divisions or business units generated revenue and provided the opportunity for growth. You should organize your company based on your interests and skills; however, consider some of the ways you can achieve business growth by adding and expanding business units.

Project Management Business Units

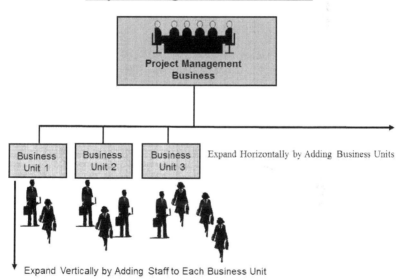

Exhibit 10-1

TRAINING

I got my start by helping an associate who ran a management training company. I worked for a few years as an independent contractor, taking time off from my regular job. When I felt I was ready to go on my own, I started my business specializing in project management training. In a later chapter, I will discuss why you should have training as one of your business units and how to set up and manage a training business.

My training business exposed me to many organizations that were dealing with project management issues and problems; quite often I would receive requests to consult to these organizations. As I took on more consulting assignments, I began to retain independent contractors to handle my training work load.

As I stated at the outset of this book, I designed a business model to run my company like a project. I put together teams for specific client projects and disband the team when the project is complete. In all cases, I use personnel who are interested in working on projects— typically these people are referred to as independent contractors, consultants, or free lancers. In the next chapter, I will talk about independent contractors in detail, but for now it is sufficient to say that the independent contractor is not a full-time employee but a person who contracts their services for a fee.

I used the experience and knowledge I gained consulting on client projects to create innovative training programs. My new programs focused on specific issues and problems that my clients faced in managing their projects. Eventually, I had a portfolio of training programs that I could offer in the United States and overseas. I assembled a cadre of independent contractors that I could count on to conduct my training programs when needed. Thus, I grew my training business vertically by developing new training programs and recruiting staff to conduct these programs. This strategy enabled me to increase my revenue and freed me to take on more consulting engagements.

CONSULTING

Consulting is a worldwide multi-billion dollar industry dealing with every facet of human endeavor from aerospace to zoology. My business model focuses on consulting as it relates to client projects. Clients are not inclined to spend money for consulting services without good reason. When it comes to projects, clients have many motives for retaining consultants. Projects are expensive, involve risk, and divert internal resources from on-going revenue generating operations.

Project failure not only cost the client money but also represents lost opportunity—the opportunity to roll out a new product to beat the competition to market; the opportunity to streamline operations or increase efficiency to enhance profits; and the opportunity to remain competitive and viable in a changing global environment. Thus, if you have a skill or knowledge resource that can help to ensure client project success, you will be needed.

Project Management Business Units

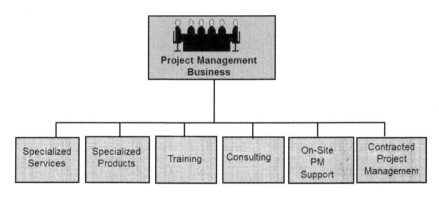

Exhibit 10-2

For clients, the cost of your consulting services will be small when measured against the cost of project failure. Project failure results when a project does not meet its defined cost, schedule, and technical objectives. Research shows that the failure rate for projects is very high, and this is one of the main reasons why project management consulting is a premiere business arena for the twenty-first century.

If you analyze a project life cycle, you can identify opportunities to sell consulting services to your client. The phases of a typical project life cycle are:

Pre-Project Phase—Astute clients will make an effort to ensure that they have all the capabilities needed to accomplish a project before they commit resources to the undertaking. Hence, clients will retain consultants to evaluate their projects and their capabilities including:

- Risk assessment—what are the risk issues in this project and can we deal with them?

- Bench mark studies—what can we learn from the leaders in our industry?
- Skills, capabilities, resource availability—do we have what we need to be successful?
- Processes and procedures—do we have prudent controls in place?
- Templates, models—does our team have the right tools for the job?

Project Startup—To bring project teams up to speed, clients retain consultants for:

- Team skills assessment
- Training and mentoring
- Team building
- Team-based planning, scheduling, and cost management
- Project sponsor assistance
- Staff augmentation

On-Going Projects—Consulting relative to all aspects of the on-going project includes:

- Audits and reviews
- Problem identification and resolution
- Team building and team revitalization
- On-going resource support
- Progress analysis
- Specialized training
- Lessons learned

Completed Projects—To assist clients in closing out a project consultants:

- Collect and analyze lessons-learned data
- Develop recommendations for future projects
- Assist in reassignments for team members
- Organize celebrations and rewards

The above is just a small sample of the opportunities to sell consulting services to clients.

I find that project management consulting is interesting and rewarding work. Consulting also provides opportunities to expand your business presence with a client. For example, I was working for a client on a project that was beset with a number of management and technical problems. The cause of most of the client's problems was that they simply did not have the people resources needed to accomplish their overly ambitious goals. Furthermore, because of a hiring freeze they could not get additional staff. I suggested that I augment their project team with some of my staff. The client readily agreed; thus, I brought in several of my people who were highly experienced project managers.

As it turned out, my staff was able to ease the burden of the overworked client project personnel and resolve some of the knotty technical problems that were hampering the project. Our successful integration into the client's project team created a model that the client used on other projects. I received many requests to provide project staff to this client on numerous projects. Over the years, I worked with other clients to augment their project teams with my personnel. As a result, my business and my revenue grew beyond my wildest dreams.

CLIENT SUPPORT

Another way to grow your project management business is to provide on-site support to client projects. You can use independent contractors to supplement client project teams. You generate revenue by the markup you put on your contractors' rate. This markup will depend on the skills you are providing, the arena you are working in, competition, your operating expenses, and profit objectives. Markups typically run from 1.5 to 2.5; however, keep in mind that everything is negotiable. In recent years there has been an increased opportunity to sell on-site support services. Many clients are reluctant to hire full-time employees because of the temporary nature of projects. In addition, the unfortunate trend seems to be that corporations are eliminating full-time jobs in favor of temporary employees for a number of reasons. Corporations want the flexibility to respond quickly to changing market conditions, and they are willing to pay a premium rate to avoid paying not only employee benefits but also the cost of hiring, firing, or layoffs. There is a significant trend to lean, corporate structures and more reliance on virtual organizations, resulting in plenty of opportunity to sell support services to client projects.

It is kind of ironic that the worst of times may be the best of times to sell project support services and grow your business and enhance your bottom line.

PROJECTS

Another way to grow your business is to bid on client projects. If you are on the client's bidders list, they may send you a request for proposal (RFQ). If you are not on a bidders list, you will have to scout all the normal advertising media for proposal requests. It is important that you be very selective in pursuing contracts to bid on. Proposal preparation can be an expensive and time-consuming process, and you want to be sure that you have a reasonable chance of winning a contract before you decide to respond to an RFQ.

In my experience, the key to winning competitive bids is to convince the client that you will make them successful. This is more important than a glossy proposal package, compelling narrative, or price. A low bid does not guarantee winning the job; in fact, if your bid is too low, you may lose credibility. Clients want the solid feeling, that by selecting you, they will be secure in their job by demonstrating that they made the right decision in picking you for their project. The only way to give clients this feeling of confidence is to show them your successful track record.

Over the years I have beat out some of the largest consulting companies on competitive bids for client projects. I was able to do this because I had the hands-on experience the client was looking for. If you are just starting out, you may not have the portfolio of projects or track record of experience to beat out the competition. If this is the case, then you probably should not bid on the job; on the other hand, you may want to consider aligning yourself with another firm. I will talk about forming alliances in the next section.

There is a world of business opportunities in pursuing client projects. All client projects have a specific objective which is to be accomplished by a certain date for a certain amount of money. I like to put projects into two broad categories: traditional projects and contemporary projects. Traditional projects are deterministic in nature such as engineering, construction, or manufacturing. Usually these projects produce physical deliverables such as power plants, factories, bridges, highways, aircraft, electronic devices, or anything that you can see, touch, and use. Contemporary projects, on the other hand, tend to be esoteric and more problem solving in nature. Contemporary projects typically focus on software, information technology, business processes and related issues; hence, these projects tend to produce deliverables that are not easy to define or visualize. When I started out most projects were traditional in nature; therefore, most of my early experience was in aerospace and construction. Today there is an explosion of contemporary projects which opens up almost unlimited opportunities for your project management business

This can be a very exciting time in the growth of your project management business. The challenge of developing proposals, winning contracts, organizing your teams, and working on client projects will not only energize you but will set the stage for continued growth and enhanced earning power. However, keep in mind that as you grow your company by adding or expanding business units, you will have to take on more administrative responsibilities. You will have to submit more invoices to more clients, pay contractors, insurance, bills, taxes, and address a host of other non-revenue producing activities. One way to deal with this increased burden, without hiring outside staff, is to get your immediate family involved in your business.

In the opening chapters of this book I stressed the importance of having your spouse or life partner completely on board with you when you start your business. This is absolutely important in order to endure the invariable ups and downs of any business undertaking. In addition, your spouse or life partner can be an important resource in the operation of your business by helping you with the day to day administrative demands of your company. When I was totally consumed with consulting and managing projects, my wife managed the day to day operation of our company. In fact, she designed and implemented processes and procedures that enabled us to take on more work while addressing the increased administrative demands of a growing organization.

Involving your immediate family is important from several standpoints. Every member of the family must understand the challenges and demands of your business in order to appreciate the benefits and rewards being generated. In addition, it is important for your children to realize that the path to a rich and rewarding future is not necessarily "the good job." Therefore, I believe that you should have your children help you run your company. Giving children the opportunity to participate in your company enhances their real-world learning and enlarges your personnel resources without having to go outside to hire full-time personnel. Children can perform a wide range of useful tasks from data entry, answering telephones, copying and collating reports, and running errands. Our children were very helpful in assembling and packing orders for the training materials we produced in our Special Products Division.

SPECIALIZED PRODUCTS

You can grow your project management business by selling a specialized project management product. I know a number of individuals that do well selling specialized products in conjunction with their consulting or training practice. Specialized products tend to fall into two categories: publications and software. Most publications are of the "how-to variety," and usually include project management books, training manuals, user guides, and test preparation materials. Software products usually deal with some aspect of project management including but not limited to planning, scheduling, estimating, cost control, and risk management. Recently there has been a proliferation of publications and software dealing with the Project Management Institute's Project Management Body of Knowledge (PMBOK) and the Project Management Professional (PMP) Certification Program.

Early on in my business I generated revenue by publishing and selling a variety of project management training manuals. Later I got out of the document publication business and instead licensed my materials to clients for their internal use. Licensing your specialized products is another way of generating revenue, and if you can tie your license in with some type of product maintenance contract you may be able to supplement your income for an extended period.

Whenever I think the market for specialized project management products has been saturated, someone comes up with a new twist or slant and carves out a respectable return for their effort. One of the most successful developers of specialized products I know is a fellow named Paul who works for me from time to time as an independent contractor. When I asked Paul how he got into his business, he told me the following story:

> I started my career as a software developer for a big tri-alpha corporation where I worked on many projects for more than twenty years. I thought I was an important member of the corporation until one day I found out that I was just so much surplus resource. Getting laid off was the shock of my life, but after I picked myself off the floor I decided that I had too much ability to waste on feeling sorry for myself, and I decided to go out on my own. As it turned out, it was the smartest move of my life. Now I teach courses at a local university, I do consulting for you and others, and based on what I learn about client problems during my consulting work, I develop unique project management applications and tools. I am making a good living, but more importantly, I have more satisfaction and more enjoyment in my work and in my life than I ever had when I worked for a large corporation.
>
> When I was an employee, I spent endless hours in meetings, was constantly side-tracked by phone calls, e-mail, and text messages; worse yet, everything I did was subjected to endless review, discussion, and critique. By the end of a typical day, I was exhausted, stressed out, and had very little to show for all my hard work. Now I work in the tranquility of my home office and I am in complete control of my time and my environment. I am free to create and work without interruption. As a result, I produce a hundred times more than I ever did working in the big corporation. Also, I can see how the result of my work helps clients. For the first time in my life, I feel that I am in complete control of my life and my future.

Paul's experience is typical of the many independent contractors that I work with, so always be on the lookout for an opportunity to package your experience, skill or knowledge into a product or a service.

SPECIAL ASSIGNMENTS

I set up a separate division to deal with business opportunities that were unique, different, or unexpected. I did this as a way to experiment and test new concepts and to manage risk. My goal was to have a way to think about and develop future services and products without diverting attention from on-going business activities. For example, I had an opportunity to bid on a pay-for-project contract with a client who was looking for a way to contain project cost. In this situation, the client would pay a fixed fee to manage their project from start to finish. I was intrigued by the idea, and I concluded that it would be possible to realize a significant profit for a well-run project. However, the risk involved in this type of project was significant, so it was important to establish a protective shield between this undertaking and the rest of my operations.

In another case, I had an opportunity to do some consulting in Eastern Europe. This led to joint ventures with some Eastern European firms. Before I knew it, I had become an international project management consulting organization. Since the work and the people involved were different from the arena I knew well, I decided to manage this activity as a separate and distinct entity from my other business units.

I had a number of ventures that I pursued over the years. Some turned out to be very successful, and set the stage for future business. Others were not so successful, but provided valuable lessons-learned experience. Because I employed a project management approach to all my ventures, I had the flexibility to build and dismantle organizations quickly and to align myself with other organizations to create a competitive capability. Teaming with other firms is another way to grow your business.

Forming Alliances

You can leverage your business by establishing relationships with other firms. There are many advantages for doing this. You can get into other business areas, integrate and expand your portfolio of expertise and skills, take on more challenging assignments, reduce the cost of marketing and business development, and spread technological and business risk. You will find that there is no shortage of people who will want to team up with you. However, your challenge is to align yourself with the right organizations and people who can do you the most good.

There are many ways you can associate yourself with other organizations. The most basic way of forming alliances or coalitions is by: networking, teaming, or partnering. I have used all three approaches over the years and have found that forming some type of relation with other firms can provide a variety of advantages. Keep in mind that in any alliance you will be bound by certain obligations and limitations, formal and informal, and you must address a wider range of administrative and management issues. Let us consider the advantages and disadvantages of each type of alliance.

NETWORKING

Networking can be an informal or formal relationship. Over the years I found that it was invaluable to call someone when I was stuck on a problem or needed help on short notice. I had an informal network of people that I knew and had worked with over the years. These people were from academic, civic, and professional organizations, as well as fellow entrepreneurs and specialists I knew in various corporations. My informal network represented a vast talent pool that I could access free of charge.

There are unwritten rules of conduct in any informal network. Violate these rules and you will be quickly locked out of the network. Basically, everyone in the network is obligated to be helpful when possible, discreet, and ethical in all matters. Everyone in a knowledge-based business should have some type of informal network. If you are just starting out, you can build your informal network by keeping in touch with former coworkers, becoming active in professional and civic organizations, and introducing yourself to fellow entrepreneurs at every opportunity.

Be sure not to restrict your network to your industry or profession; strive for maximum exposure in any venue that comes your way. For example, one time I was invited to speak at a meeting of chiefs of police—I suspected that they needed a quick replacement when their scheduled speaker got sick—an audience I was certain would not be interested in project management. However, I was surprised to find that the audience was quite responsive to my presentation; not long after my speech I got a call from a corporate vice-president who was referred to me by one of the police chiefs. I always made it a point to get exposure to and maintain contact with as many organizations that I could work into my schedule.

There are times when it is worthwhile to belong to a formal network. Formal networks are usually small groups of entrepreneurs bound together by common interests. Generally, these groups will share business leads, provide help when needed, and collaborate on issues and problems related to their business or industry. Formal networks may have formal as well as informal ground rules or protocols for their group. For example, some groups will expect a finder's fee for business leads they give to another associate; or, they may collaborate in developing a proposal in return for billable work later. Groups may network to reduce their overhead expenses by sharing office space, equipment, and support personnel.

You must exert caution, because formal networks can become cliques or elitist groups that exclude outsiders and lose the synergy that really makes a network worthwhile. Also, some groups become self-serving. For example, I was invited to collaborate on a major proposal effort by one group that indicated that they had the inside track for getting a big project, especially if I provided my specific experience and skills. I was flattered and agreed to participate, whereupon the group sent me the RFP and copies of their resumes, and asked me to put the proposal together for their review. Since proposal preparation is time-consuming and expensive, it was obvious that the group was attempting to minimize their overhead cost by getting me to do the bulk of the work. I promptly advised the group that I was not interested in participating. However, there are times when you should collaborate with other firms in pursuing new business opportunities and one of the best arrangements for doing this is teaming.

TEAMING

In teaming, you enter into a formal contract agreement to accomplish a specific business objective. Teaming is by definition a temporary arrangement usually crafted to target an opportunity. Generally, organizations will team to develop a proposal to win a major contract. If the team wins the contract, it shares the work, expenses, and income based upon the teaming agreement. Teaming is a powerful way for organizations to enhance their capabilities to take on larger assignments, reduce financial and technical risk, and grow their business and experience portfolio.

I have used teaming to obtain projects well beyond my company's capabilities. Since I worked on projects in the nuclear industry for a number of years, I had established a network of nuclear experts in various corporations across the United States and overseas. When I decided to pursue an upgrade project for one nuclear plant that I knew well, I assembled several well-known nuclear experts, a cadre of vendors and suppliers, a major nuclear manufacturing corporation, and an internationally known consulting company to participate in developing the proposal and performing the work. We developed a teaming agreement that met the needs of all the participants and satisfied the owners of the nuclear plant that we were a viable bidder.

You might wonder how a small firm such as mine could convince major corporations to work under my banner. It is quite simple: when you have a proven track record, a viable business opportunity, and business is tough (as it was during this particular period), even the big guys will participate with you in order to generate revenue. I structured several teaming arrangements over the years and as a result, significantly enhanced my bottom line and my portfolio of experience.

It is important to stress that managing a diverse team for a major project is not for the inexperienced practitioner. Successful teaming arrangements usually involve organizations that have a solid base of rapport and have complementary skills and capabilities. In addition, teaming works best when you have seasoned, mature professionals involved. This is important in today's global marketplace because teams may be composed of organizations of different cultures, values, and beliefs.

Teaming agreements must be precise in spelling out who does what, when, and for how much; otherwise, the team can quickly resort to nitpicking and bickering especially when problems surface in the project. I have developed three page teaming agreements that satisfactorily addressed all the team's requirements; however, when lawyers became involved in some projects, the teaming agreements ballooned to thirty or more pages. Fortunately, when you work with seasoned professionals, you can relegate these legal monstrosities to your bottom desk drawer.

Teaming is a temporary arrangement designed to win a specific job; however, if you're just starting out it may be appropriate to enter into a more permanent relationship with others in order to grow your business beyond its present boundaries. Thus, you should consider partnering.

PARTNERING

In partnering, you enter into a formal business agreement with other firms to work together in some fashion. You may decide to work together to develop opportunities in a specific business, industry, or government sector. Therefore, your partnering agreement will spell out how you will collaborate with your associates in marketing, advertising, presentations, and performing the work. You may partner to develop a new product or service, or integrate your respective organizations to create enhanced capabilities for existing and new clients. Partnering provides many opportunities for the small firm to grow its business; however, to be successful, partnering requires you to give up certain freedoms you have as an individual entrepreneur.

When you partner with others, you have to respond to the will of the majority or engage in negotiations or compromise. This can be a positive experience, especially if you have a congenial personality; however, if you tend to be fearlessly independent, you may find it grating to bend your will for the benefit of the group. In this case, I recommend that all your partnering agreements have an appropriate escape clause.

I found that partnering is especially useful when you venture into unfamiliar territory. When I started doing work overseas, especially in Eastern Europe, it was invaluable to partner with local firms who knew the clients, culture, and laws. In addition to enhancing business growth in new areas, partnering can expose you to new ideas, enable you to meet new people, and challenge some of your concepts and perceptions about the world you work in.

Successful partnering requires trust and integrity; therefore I recommend that you partner with people you know well, people who have a good reputation, or people who are highly endorsed by well-regarded associates. I stress this because I have heard of cases where unscrupulous individuals used partnering as a way to gain access to proprietary information that they exploited for their own gain.

Managing Teaming and Partnering Arrangements

If you are diligent and carefully evaluate those you want to align yourself with, then things should work well. However, this is not a perfect world, and quite often—especially on complex projects—the unexpected will happen, usually at the worst time. It is during these stressful periods that you discover the true nature of your associates and the relationships between you and others in the alliance. The issue you must deal with then becomes how to manage people and activities when things go wrong, and you are a lone player in a multi-organizational venture. Basically you have only four fundamental courses of action which are: control, influence, accept, or retreat.

Control—If you have a new client, then you can invite others to join you in some type of teaming or partnering relationship. Those who join with you must agree to abide by the terms and conditions of the teaming agreement. You define the strategies, activities, and conduct of all participants. In short, you have the power to directly control all the participants.

Influence—If one of the alliance partners is in control, you may influence their conduct and decision-making by virtue of your experience, expertise, and role on the team. If you provide expertise and resources (people, tools, processes, and money), then you may be able to exercise sufficient influence over other participants. However, keep in mind that influencing is a two-way street and that you may also be swayed by others on the team.

Accept—Very often in a teaming or alliance arrangement, the role, contributions, and conduct of all the participants are spelled out in detail. In most cases, all the participants accept the plans, programs, and decision-making if there are no major departures from the contract that everyone accepted. In cases where events present an unexpected situation, the participants should exercise rational judgment to determine if the course of action being proposed is acceptable. Nevertheless, if you find that you cannot accept the proposed solution, you have some tough decisions to make. You may even find it expedient to terminate the alliance.

Retreat—In the previous section I stated that you should always have an escape clause in any agreement you develop with your alliance partners. You need a way to quickly bail out of any relationship that does not live up to stated requirements and to your expectations. This is especially relevant if you find yourself in a situation where one or more of your alliance partners are engaged or attempting to engage in unethical behavior. It is not untypical that when a business gets into a performance or financial bind that the owner is tempted to bend the rules just a bit to save his company. The problem that I have witnessed over the years is that when an entrepreneur bends the rules just a bit (in their mind), it soon becomes a strategy for everyday business. My advice is don't fall into that trap; when you see one of you alliance partners moving to an unethical position, no matter how seemingly minor, walk away as quickly as possible. You will save yourself a lot of grief in the long run.

There are many advantages to participating in a partnering alliance of some type. In addition to the obvious business advantages of moving into new markets, making more money, and sharing the risk, partnering made it possible for me to meet new entrepreneurs and learn from them, travel to different areas of the world, and be exposed to a wide range of cultures, religions, and political ideologies. In addition to growing my business, this experience enabled me to mature and develop as an individual.

If you partner with the right people you not only create synergy to enhance you and your partner's capabilities, but you also enhance your level of courage to experiment and try out new and different things to meet the challenges of an ever changing global business environment. Change generates opportunities, and you can grow your business only by exploiting the opportunities that change brings.

Exploiting Change

Consider how management has changed over the last forty years. Traditional management concepts, such as the hierarchical corporate structure based on subdivision of work and specialization, has given way to team-based management where planning and decision making is driven down to the level where the work is performed. Computer and information technology have made it possible to plan, organize, lead, direct, and integrate business activities across national boundaries, time zones, and political ideologies in ways that once only science fiction writers could have conceived. Over the course of my career, I have learned that there is minimal opportunity for business growth in a static environment. Dramatic change, both good and bad, provides the best opportunity to generate new business and make money.

New laws, regulations, competition, social, political, cultural, and conceptual change provide opportunities to generate revenue from studies, analysis, design, and implementation of process, procedures, systems, tools, techniques, and training. Corporations constantly strive to determine the impact of change on their business; they undertake projects to minimize the negative impact of change or to capitalize on the opportunities that change generates. There are always opportunities to grow your business during any kind of change, good or bad.

In the early part of my career, I worked primarily on brick and mortar projects, like the design and construction of nuclear power plants. After the Three Mile Island nuclear accident, many nuclear plants were shut down and many nuclear construction projects were terminated. The whole industry was brought to a standstill, and it looked like my project management business would never get off the ground. However, there was a proliferation of safety-related projects at a number of the nuclear plants. I was working on one such project when senior management implemented a company-wide reorganization with the express objective of changing how they operated.

One of the major objectives of the reorganization was to change the culture of the company. To do this, senior management retained a number of Organizational Development (OD) consultants to implement a change management program. I was completely intrigued by the change management process, and I decided to learn more; consequently, I became a certified change management consultant. I grew my traditional project management business to encompass consulting and support for change management, reengineering, and process improvement projects. As it turned out, the addition of these new services more than doubled my company's income.

In order to thrive in a knowledge-based business like project management, you must keep abreast of change, you must understand the impact of change, and you must formulate products and services that enable your clients to deal with change. Social, political, economic, and technological changes impact every organization in every country, directly and indirectly. In change there are dangers and opportunities; however, the trick is to let the fear of the unknown motivate you to find opportunities and use them to your advantage. I saw a perfect example of this when I worked in Eastern Europe.

I was teaching project management techniques to Czech and Slovak managers and engineers who were striving to adjust to the transition from socialism to a market-based economy. Here were well-educated professionals who spent their careers working in state-owned enterprises. They had secure jobs, never had to worry about cut backs or layoffs, and if they followed the party line, could look to a comfortable retirement with a modest pension. Suddenly their world fell apart, the government changed, socialism was dead, and all their security was gone. Can you imagine the shock, the insecurity, the fear?

As part of my training program I invited a Czech engineer, Andrew, to come to the States to live and work with me for a short period. More shock. Andrew had never been outside Czechoslovakia, had never seen an American supermarket, had never experienced a freeway traffic jam, and had never worked in an office where everyone had a computer. It took a few weeks, but Andrew adjusted to the new environment and quickly absorbed American management techniques and ideals. When Andrew completed his assignment with me, he returned home to find a job. During that time I was very busy, so I did not keep in touch with Andrew, except for a Christmas card or two. Two years later I was in Prague, and decided to look up Andrew.

When I met Andrew, I asked him how he made out in face of all the changes in his country and his life. Andrew told me the following story:

> When I left you to return home, I was apprehensive about the future, but based on what I saw in America and learned from you, I was full of ideas. The first thing I did was to get together with some of my fellow engineers and tell them about my experience with you and the ideas I had for a business. We pooled our money and ordered computer parts from Taiwan and built personal computers to sell to local companies. Then we set up computer training programs for our customers, and eventually started to develop software programs specifically for Czech and Slovak users. One thing led to another and today we have our own engineering and consulting company and employ several hundred people. I would never have accomplished all the things I did had it

not been for all the traumatic changes that took place in my country and in my life

Today, when I listen to the news and read the Wall Street Journal about the terrible state of our economy, the job losses, and the social and economic impact on families, I can't help but wonder about how many Andrews are out there who will find opportunity in the adversity we now face.

Summary

Finding ways to grow your project management business is vital to enhancing earnings, keeping you energized, and ensuring the long-term viability of your company. You can grow your business by:

- Creating new business units to include but not limited to: training, consulting, client support, projects, and products
- Adding new services or products to existing business units
- Forming alliances through networks, teaming, or partnering arrangements
- Entering into alliances with others that you know are competent, professional, and ethical
- Managing the alliance relationship to *control* events and activities if you are in charge, or *influence* participants if you have the resources, or *accept* decisions, activities, and events if they meet the alliance agreement, or *retreat*—terminate your alliance relationship
- Exploiting opportunities generated by change

Chapter 11

How to Staff and Manage Your Projects

Build Staff to Enhance Business Capabilities

When I started my company, I knew that I did not want to create an empire. I was not interested in building a large corporation, I did not want to manage employees, I did not want to deal with all the human resource issues involved in creating a bureaucratic organization, and I did not want the stress and strain of downsizing and layoffs when things got tough. In short, when I left the corporate world, I did not want to reproduce that environment in my own company. What I did want was to be my own boss, make all the decisions, take responsibility for my successes and failures, and control my own destiny. Most importantly, I wanted to apply my education, experience, and skills to the utmost on work that was interesting, fulfilling, and financially rewarding. This, in a nut shell, was the specification that I used to design and build my project management business.

The dilemma, of course, is how to grow a business if you don't build an organization of people with the experience, training, and skills needed to perform the work involved in your enterprise. Clearly, a business that deals with repetitive tasks, such as manufacturing, must retain a relatively permanent workforce. However, a business that is seasonal, such as farming, hires only when needed, and a business that works on specific projects, such as construction or consulting, also employs personnel only when needed. A project management business works on undertakings that by definition are life limited. Each project is a different, unique, one-of-a-kind undertaking that requires skill sets appropriate to the specific needs of the venture. Thus, a project management business must recruit and hire temporary workers for the limited life of a project.

These temporary workers are the new breed of knowledge workers who represent a sizeable portion of the American workforce. An article in the February 8, 2010 Wall Street Journal reported that 20 percent to 23 percent of workers operate as consultants, freelancers, free agents, contractors, or micropreneurs. And by all projections, the numbers will increase in the coming years. This is good news for a project management business because it means that you will have a reservoir of talent to draw upon for the diverse needs of your projects. However, there are legal, tax, and management issues that you must address when using independent contractors.

Who is an Independent Contractor?

An independent contractor (IC) is any person who is in business to sell their services to others. By definition, the IC is not an employee, and therefore does not have the same legal rights and protection of an employee; hence, the IC does not qualify for benefits under the Fair Labor Standards Act (FLSA), and is not entitled to employee or workers' compensation benefits. Also, the IC is not covered under the Equal Employment Opportunity laws.

Since the IC provides all the resources needed to operate his or her own business, they bear the cost of their office, furniture, computers, software, supplies, and anything else they require. In addition, an IC does his or her own marketing and sales and is responsible for paying all taxes and expenses related to their business.

Legal Definition

Federal, state, and local government agencies prefer employees over ICs because it is easier for these government agencies to collect payroll taxes and income tax withholdings from employees than from ICs. However, there are companies who have misused this classification because, as we shall see later, there are financial advantages to classifying someone as an IC. As a result, government agencies have implemented aggressive audit programs to clamp down on hiring ICs. Unfortunately, the criterion for classifying an IC is complicated and confusing.

Check out the Government Web site (http://www.irs.gov/businesses/small/article/) for the criteria for determining if an individual can be classified as an IC. The criteria—some twenty-five requirements—may seem onerous; however, the fundamental issues boil down to control of the IC's work. You can tell the IC what you *want,* but the IC determines *how* the work will be done. Furthermore, you must have a formal contractual agreement with the IC, and you must issue Form 1099-MISC to report the IC's earnings. Also, you pay the IC only the fees agreed to in the contract. The IC is responsible for all his or her own expenses and taxes. Typically, if you adhere to these rules, you will have fulfilled your legal obligations; however, this does not mean you will not be audited—any Government agency can audit you at any time for any reason. But do not let the possibility of using ICs deter you since the advantages of using an IC outweigh the possibility of an audit.

Benefits of Hiring Independent Contractors

There are three primary benefits of using ICs for your project management business. The first is flexibility. Projects are temporary undertakings that require a diversity of expertise over the life of the project. Hence, you may need a project planner in the early phase of the project to develop the framework for the project's strategy. Then, you may employ an estimator to develop the initial budget. As the project gets up to speed, you may bring on board schedulers to schedule and track progress. At some point you may need trainers and facilitators to provide team building and conflict resolution programs. On projects of any significant complexity, you may cycle in and out numerous specialists to address the myriad issues that develop over the life of a project. By using ICs you have the flexibility and the speed to address the varying requirements of your client's project. Clearly, it would be expensive and difficult to provide the diverse skills and expertise needed to support a project with full-time employees. More importantly, when the project is over, you do not have to face the agony of finding your employees jobs or subjecting them to layoff.

The second benefit of using ICs in your project management business is cost savings. There are two types of cost saving: Overhead and Administrative.

When you hire an IC, you do not pay for office space, equipment, supplies, and benefits. You don't have to make contributions for workers' compensation insurance, state unemployment compensation insurance, and Social Security and Medicare taxes; typically you will save 30 percent or more by not having to make all these payments.

When you hire employees, you must address a number of administrative requirements that do not exist when dealing with an IC. When you have employees, you provide Human Resources (HR) functions to ensure that you comply with all the legal requirements defined by the Fair Labor Standards Act (FLSA), the Equal Opportunity Act, OSHA, the Americans with Disabilities Act, and all the other regulations that our modern society demands. When you contract with an IC, you do not deal with these legal and administrative requirements. Furthermore, even though you have the right to fire an employee, you know that in our litigant-based society it is not that simple. When dealing with an IC, you can terminate the engagement based on the terms specified in the agreement. In most cases, this is a lot easier than trying to fire an employee. Also, when you no longer have work, the ICs leaves; however, with an employee, you have to find them other work or resort to layoffs and absorb all the costs involved in downsizing your staff.

The third benefit of using ICs is experience and expertise. When you use an IC, you select an individual who has the specific experience, expertise, and skills to address the needs, issues, and problems of a project at a particular point in time in the life of the project. The ability to assign critical skills when, and only when, they are needed is an advantage that the typical organization of generalists cannot match in effectiveness and efficiency.

Certainly, there is a strong argument for using ICs in your project management business; however, there are some limitations to using ICs that you need to take into account.

Disadvantages of Using Independent Contractors

First and foremost, keep in mind that the IC is in business for himself or herself. ICs need a backlog of projects, they need to make a profit, and they need to market themselves for future assignments. Also, they want to take on assignments that are challenging and rewarding, and they want to be treated with respect. In some situations you may not be able to provide enough work to attract an IC, or you may not be able to afford their rate, or the assignment may be routine, boring, or located in an undesirable location. It is even possible that your client has an odious reputation that scares off potential ICs. There will be times and conditions that prevent you from getting the personnel you need. When the economy is strong and the job market is good, you may have problems getting the people you need. But when the reverse is true, you will have a surplus talent pool to draw upon.

The other disadvantage of relying on ICs is the loss of lessons learned. When you work on a number of projects, you accumulate a data base of experience that cannot be duplicated. In many cases, this reservoir of experience gives you competitive advantage. When ICs leave your projects, they take their lessons learned on the project with them, and it is difficult to build the experience base you would with regular employees. You can offset this limitation to some extent by having a core of ICs that you call upon project after project.

Since the IC has the right to determine how to do the work, you may not interfere in his or her effort, even if you believe there is a better way of getting the job done. You can suggest or advise, but unless your IC is not fulfilling his contract commitments, you cannot and should not interfere.

One last note, it is important to draft a contract agreement that provides you with the protection you need and which the IC can agree to and live with. I have found that overly complicated contracts tend to turn off ICs, and in most cases you are better off keeping it simple, straight forward, and aligning yourself with ethical, professional people. Keep in mind that no contract agreement, no matter how well crafted, will prevent someone from engaging in unethical activities if they so desire.

Assessing Project Manpower Requirements

When you become involved in a project, you must determine the type of staff you will need (skills, experience, expertise), the length of time they will be needed, and the rates you will be able to pay for their services. In general, when you augment a client's project team, the client will tell you the type of people they want, the duration of the assignment, and the rates they will pay. When you have the total responsibility for a project, you have to determine the human resources you need to successfully accomplish the project. The best way to do this is through the application of project management methodology.

First, review or develop a scope of work for the project and ensure that the client is in complete agreement with your definition of what is to be accomplished on the project. Then develop a work breakdown structure (WBS) to define the specific work task that will be accomplished by an individual with the necessary skill set. Next, estimate how long it may take to accomplish this work. Then total the number of people you will need to do all the required work. If the total duration for doing the work is too long, you may have to increase the number of individuals working on a particular task. Use the WBS to develop a responsibility matrix where you identify a skill set (person or persons) with every task defined in your WBS.

When you have completed your responsibility matrix, develop a rate estimate that you expect to pay for the staff you contract to work on your project. Calculate the rate times the number of hours you expect it will take to accomplish each task, apply your markup, total all the WBS items, and you will have the estimated project cost. Again, review this with your client to be certain there is no misunderstanding about project cost. The real challenge will be to recruit the specific expertise you need, when you need them, at the rates you plan to pay.

Recruiting Project Staff

Getting the best possible people to work on your projects will be the single most important factor to the success of your project management business. When I first started in business, I recruited only people I knew well. In most cases, these were associates or coworkers I knew when I was an employee in the corporate world. Later, as I increased my professional network, I got to know people through professional organizations and the academic world. Many of these individuals were moonlighting or freelancing part-time from their regular employment. However, over time I found that more and more people were becoming full-time free lancers, consultants, or independent contractors. In large measure, this reflected the changing job market in the United States and in other industrialized countries. A relatively large population of well-educated knowledge-workers has been laid off or forced into early retirement at the peak of their professional careers. For some individuals, this has been a traumatic change; for others it has been a positive new beginning. The result of all this change is that there is a ready pool of talent available that you can draw upon for your projects. Furthermore, there are many easily accessible outlets you can use to draw upon this talent pool.

HOW TO RECRUIT

There are two basic avenues for recruiting people: personal contacts and the Internet. Personal contact is done simply by calling someone you know, telling them about the job, and asking if they are interested in the assignment. The great thing about a project management business is the speed and flexibility you have to build staff, especially if you have an extensive network of associates. I have met with associates in restaurants, in shopping malls, and on the golf course, to discuss and explain an assignment, the duration, the pay rates, and my performance expectations; if my associate was interested, I would have him or her sign my contract agreement on the spot. This was possible because, in most cases, I dealt with individuals I knew fairly well. However, if you do not have an extensive network to draw upon, you will have to use the various resources of the Internet.

Internet avenues for finding and recruiting project personnel include the dedicated job sites, Monster, CareerBuilder and Yahoo!, Hot Jobs, and the social networking sites, Linkedin, Doostang, Ryze, and Facebook. Of course, you can also advertise for people on your Web site. When you use the Internet for recruiting, you have the challenge of screening candidates and verifying their credentials, especially those who promote themselves on the social networking sites.

Keep in mind that there is considerable creative writing on these networking sites. For example, I had hired a junior scheduler; after he left me, his resume appeared on one of the social networking sites where he portrayed himself as a senior consultant with extensive experience. What was really humorous was that he had testimonies from a senior executive, who in reality was a technician who serviced the copiers for one of our clients.

Regardless of the avenue you use to find the people you need, it is important to take the time to ensure that you are getting the best people possible.

Characteristics of Good Independent Contractors

I worked as an independent contractor off and on for a number of years, so I have first-hand knowledge of what it takes to be successful. When I recruited independent contractors(IC) for my projects, I looked for a number of important characteristics. First, I looked for experience. My ICs had to know their stuff; they had to be able to go into a client's project and start contributing from day one. There was no on-the-job training; what's more, they had to know more than the client's personnel, they had to have seen it all before, and they had to apply their skills and experience to the client's situation.

This brings us to the second point—initiative—they had to hit the ground running from day one, they had to determine what needed to be done, and had to start doing it immediately. In most cases, no one was going to tell them what was needed, what the problems were, or where they should focus their efforts. I needed self-starters, people who did not need management or direction. I also needed confident people.

Most of my engagements involved projects that were in trouble, behind schedule, over budget, and beset with technical issues. I looked for people who could go into a chaotic environment, see through the smoke and confusion, and start to establish a sense of order and direction as to what should be done next. I have had IC's who have gone into a troubled project, and because of their experience, knowledge, and professionalism, have evaluated the situation, established priorities, and initiated work on the truly critical tasks. For clients, these people are worth far more than the fees they command.

In addition to a strong portfolio of experience, skills, and work habits, I looked for people who had a solid ethical foundation. For unethical people, it is easy to look like they are working hard when they are not; it is easy to pad their invoices for work they did not do; and, it is tempting for them to try to take over the business you have with your client, despite the non-compete agreement that they signed. Unethical ICs can create a lot of problems, and I have found that they usually have a track record of nefarious actions; hence, it pays to research any IC before you bring them into your project management business.

When I recruited an IC, I looked at educational credentials and professional certifications. Much of my business was in technical arenas, so I looked for people with appropriate education and certifications: engineers with advanced degrees, registered professional engineers (PE), and certified Project Management Professionals (PMP) were always at the top of my list. But I must point out that academic badges by themselves are not sufficient. I have had MIT and Harvard graduates who were poor performers that I had to remove from my projects. Success for an IC has more to do with experience, initiative, and personal self-management than academic achievements. When you're working on a demanding, troubled project, you soon realize the answers are not in the back of the book.

Also, when I evaluated ICs of equal capabilities, I gave preference to those individuals who were incorporated. An IC who has his or her own corporation will conduct their affairs in a business-like fashion, and you will not spend a lot of time explaining how to submit invoices or what their obligations are relative to taxes, unemployment compensation, insurance, and other administrative issues. In most cases, IC's who have their own corporation are in business for the long haul, and I can count on them for future services.

One final note—in today's severe economic environment there are many knowledge-workers who have resorted to consulting, training, or contracting in order to make money while they are looking for a job. I have no problem with this, so long as their intention is clear from the start. I have had a number of ICs work for me who eventually were hired as full-time employees by my client. You might think that I gave up part of my business as a result of this policy, but nothing could be further from the truth. Having people find employment inside a client's environment gave me ready access to current problems, needs, and upcoming projects. In addition, I received referrals and recommendations that gave me an advantage over my competition.

Characteristics of Bad or Evil Independent Contractors

Over a span of more than forty years, I have worked with professional men and women on a wide range of projects in the United States and overseas. About 93 percent of these individuals were hard working, serious, and trustworthy. The remaining 7 percent presented problems ranging from irritating to criminal. As a result of my experience, I evolved a check list or profile of things to look for when recruiting ICs for my projects. This list covers the disorganized, the lazy, the fanatic, the troubled, the hooked, and the criminal. Let's take a look at this list and identify the types of people you want to keep out of your project management business.

THE DISORGANIZED

Typically the disorganized are those who, for some reason, cannot get their act together. They forget appointments, are late for meetings, always lose their keys, security badge, or computer. They may work hard, display flashes of brilliance, and have a pleasant disposition; however, their productivity is low because of sloppiness or disorganization. Often they become the brunt of team jokes which tend to produce a negative professional image. If you hire this type of individual, get them off your project team quickly; however, they may be useful as an individual contributor working in their home office doing research or software development on a fixed-price contract.

THE LAZY

I am always amazed when I run into this type of person. I wonder how they ever got through college. But these individuals constantly conceive ways to avoid doing work. I had a project with many office and plant locations, so my ICs worked in different locations depending on the activities that were critical at a particular location. One of my ICs was always between locations; thus, he was absent when assignments were being handed out, and his tasks were never quite completed. If you run into this type of individual, don't try to figure them out or motivate them—just terminate their contract as quickly as possible.

THE FANATIC

These are individuals who are totally preoccupied with some issue or belief. It could be religion, politics, the environment, or just about anything else. The problem is that these people will bring their personal crusade into the workplace and at every opportunity try to convert their associates to their way of thinking. Religious beliefs, political preferences, values, and culture are highly personal and typically generate a negative response when someone is trying to impose their view. I have had some very competent and hardworking ICs that I had to terminate because, periodically, they would start lecturing, preaching, or ranting about their burning beliefs. I have found that fanatics cannot see the difference between polite discourse and abrasive opinion-mongering.

THE TROUBLED

Individuals with serious personal problems can present a variety of situations that you may not be able to deal with and, more than likely, should not get involved in. Individuals with serious emotional issues, marital difficulties, or money problems may, in one way or another, bring their problems into the work place. They may be constantly preoccupied with their problems such that their work performance is severely impacted; on the other hand, I have had ICs with heavy personal burdens that they carried without anyone's knowledge or without any effect on their performance. All of us would like to extend a helping hand to those who need help; however, keep in mind that in most cases, these people need professional help. As an engineer, I quickly learned that I was totally unqualified to help people with emotional, marital, or money problems.

THE HOOKED

Years ago, when I started recruiting people, I would on occasion run into a guy with a serious drinking problem. Today, I see men and women with addictions that run the gamut from alcohol, drugs, porn, and other things I don't want to know about. Since I had a number of nuclear power plant and government projects, it was necessary to have my ICs pass drug tests and background checks. Occasionally, one of my ICs would fail to pass a drug test or background check. I could not understand why seemingly smart and well educated people would jeopardize their livelihood and their careers by engaging in activities they know to be illegal. I feel sorry for people who are hooked; however, I have a strict no-tolerance policy, and I will not do business with these individuals no matter how insignificant they think their addiction may be.

THE CRIMINAL

Yes, if you are in business long enough you will run into individuals who will break the law for personal gain. These people may breach your contract agreement, steal your proprietary information, sell drugs, or engage in child porn while working on your projects. In almost all cases, these individuals are consummate con artists, hard to spot, equally hard to uncover, and quite often not apparent until the damage has been done.

I have a strict policy to hire only people I know, people who were recommended by others that I know and trust, and people with solid and verifiable references. As a result, for most of my career, I have been associated with ethical, trust worthy people who accomplished their contract commitments in a professional manner. The rare occasion when I violated my policy I suffered the consequences.

For example, I was approached by a young man who wanted to work for me as a consultant. He was recently laid off and desperately needed a job; times were tough, jobs were scarce, and since he seemed like a clean cut, honest individual, I decided to take him on for some routine project support task. The young man adapted well to the client's environment, and made worthwhile contributions. I was pleased when I received positive comments from the client about his performance; however, sometime later I ran into a former coworker of this individual who expressed dismay when I mention that I had this person on my staff. The coworker was blunt and said, "let me warn you, you cannot trust that guy; he cheats on his wife, he lies, he steals, and he will double cross you." I was shocked to hear this, so I resolved to get more information. When I called his former employer they would not tell me anything other than he had worked there and was laid off as a result of company downsizing. When I informed the young man that I had received some negative comments from one of his old coworkers, he explained that it was simply a vendetta because he had beaten out this individual for a promotion years ago. I felt uneasy about the situation, but since I had no other information to go on and his performance was excellent, I dismissed the matter, much to my regret.

Sometime later I was informed by one of my senior ICs that this young guy was having an affair with one of my client's female executives. When I queried my young IC, he merely laughed and said it was all talk because of the long hours he spent working with this female executive on her critical project. I advised him that I would not tolerate any improper conduct, and I would immediately terminate his contract if I found any such action. Again, he assured me that there was no truth in the stories, and he was conducting himself in an ethical manner. I was greatly troubled by the stories I was hearing, but not having any tangible evidence, I could do nothing about it. However, I knew this individual's wife and children, and it was inconceivable to me that a man with such a beautiful family would have an affair. But as things turned out, I underestimated the capacity of people to do stupid things.

Not long after I confronted my IC about the rumors that were circulating about him and the female executive, he called me and told me he was leaving to take another job. Shortly, I found out that he had received a sole-source contract from the female executive in question, and he and a few of his friends were now in business with my client. I immediately contacted my attorney and filed a breach of contract law suit. The result was that this individual spent two years making payments for damages.

There are many things you can do to ensure that you are dealing with ethical people; however, keep in mind that no contract and no law will prevent a crime if someone is inclined in that direction. The only thing you can hope for is justice after the crime has been committed.

Managing the Independent Contractor

Managing the IC is significantly different than managing an employee. When you hire employees, you define their position, their duties, and the time and place where they will work. In addition, you provide direction as to what they do, how much they do, and how they do it. You also provide the processes and procedures, equipment, facilities, and supplies they need to do their work. Thus, there is a large investment in computers, copiers, offices, desks, chairs and supplies. When you have employees, you supervise, direct, and correct their activities. When you retain independent contractors, you do none of this.

As I explained above, independent contractors are in business for themselves; hence, they provide their own tools or equipment, maintain their own offices, acquire their own benefits, and pay all taxes. What's more important, you do not supervise an independent contractor; instead, you contract with them to provide a service or accomplish a task, by a certain date, and for a specified amount of money. Experienced independent contractors know how to do all these things, and this is why I emphasize the importance of contracting with experienced professionals who have the expertise to address your project needs and know how to manage their businesses. However, independent contractors need to be managed to ensure that they will fulfill your contract requirement. There are actually two modes of managing independent contractors depending on whether your IC is working out of his or her own office or if they are working on a project in your client's office or facility.

MANAGING THE IC WHO WORKS FROM A HOME OFFICE

Typically the IC will work in their own office when you contract with them to provide a specific deliverable. You may require them to design a process, develop a software application, write a procedure, edit a document, develop a presentation, or some other deliverable.

Thus, the first thing you must do to ensure you can effectively manage your IC is to develop a mutually acceptable contract agreement. You can find sample independent contract agreements on the Internet; however, I would recommend that you get a copy of the Nolo book: "Hiring Independent Contractors, The Employer's Legal Guide," by attorney Stephen Fishman. This book is an excellent resource for your project management business; it covers most of the legal and administrative issues in dealing with independent contractors and provides a selection of Independent Contractor Agreements.

In general, all contract agreements must specify the following: the task or deliverable to be accomplished, the completion date, the rate or fees to be paid, the requirement that the IC provide his or her own tools, a place to work, and pay all their own taxes and fees. Furthermore, the contract should spell out how and when the IC will submit invoices and when they will be paid. The contract should also specify any special requirements; for example, not-to-compete provisions, ownership of materials developed by the IC, rework requirements, and contract termination provisions.

Your obligations in managing the IC are to make clear your performance and quality expectations as well as the ethical standards and code of conduct you require. In addition, you must pay the IC on schedule and issue a Form 1099-MISC at tax time. Again, if you retain experienced, professional independent contractors, most of these requirements and obligations will be straightforward and routine. Even though the IC manages his or her own activities and performance, you should exercise a certain level of management oversight to ensure that the IC will meet all your expectations and contract requirements.

Keep in mind that the IC, like you, is in business to make a living. Thus, the IC may be working for others while he is working for you. The IC may be juggling several contracts at the same time, which should not be a problem. However, even the most experienced IC can run into unexpected problems, and your contract may be delayed, cancelled, or result in an unacceptable deliverable. To avoid this situation, you have to lay out specific ground rules, and you must exercise active contract oversight.

It is my policy to advise all my ICs that I must be informed of any problems, road blocks, or unexpected events that may jeopardize their ability to fulfill my contract. I tell all my ICs that I know stuff happens, and if they identify the situation soon enough, we can develop work-arounds. I also tell them that it is unacceptable to wait until the last minute hoping that they can crash out the task. I also insist on regular progress reports. I like eye ball to eye ball meetings. If the IC works nearby, I visit their office, or set up breakfast or lunch meetings. These are generally brief, informal gatherings to smoke out any problems. If the IC is not nearby, then a brief Internet video or Skype conference is in order; otherwise, phone calls, e-mail, or Tweets will do. The frequency and level of detail of these progress reviews are based on the importance and risk issues involved in the task that the IC is working on. Obviously, the greater the importance and the higher the risk, the more frequently you must hold these meetings.

If the IC is not meeting expectations, you must take corrective action. I have had occasions to cancel an IC's contract when it became apparent that they were not going to deliver as scheduled. There have been times where I have had to break up the contract and farm out the work to other ICs in order to keep on schedule. And there have been times when I modified the contract to address unexpected issues that developed, either in the IC's area or mine. The point is that if you maintain prudent oversight of your IC's effort, without interfering in how they are doing the work, you can manage the contract to mutual advantage. Since you are paying the bills, you have a lot of leverage to ensure contract success.

In most cases, I pay the ICs only upon receipt of an acceptable deliverable. Once in a great while, if I contract with an IC for a major effort that may span several months, I might agree to some type of progress payments. These progress payments are based on some defined tangible accomplishment, i.e., detailed outline, first draft, second draft, conceptual drawings, screen layouts, etc. I also refuse to make progress payments based on percent complete estimates. From my years in project management, I learned that the last 10 percent of the schedule or budget usually takes another 50 percent to complete.

One last comment about managing the IC who is working in his or her office; never allow the IC to farm out the work; if he or she gets behind schedule, redo the contract and take back some of the work. Otherwise you will lose control of your contract. I had an IC who sub-contracted some of the work when he got into a bind; unfortunately, his subcontractor also farmed out part of the work and the end result was a communication nightmare.

MANAGING ON-SITE STAFF

Managing ICs that work in your client's environment presents a different set of problems. In this situation, the issues have more to do with personality or cultural misalignments than administrative or process issues. Typically your ICs will be part of a client project team. The client project manager will define the objectives, make the assignments, and define his or her performance expectations. For you, the main issue will be to ensure that your ICs have the skills required for the project, are able to meet the client's performance expectations, and fit in with the rest of the project team. If you do a careful job of evaluating the client's project requirements, recruit qualified candidates, and coach them on the client's requirements, then you can be confident that you will satisfy the first two client needs; however, as to how well the IC will fit into the client's environment is another matter.

You might assume that if your IC worked on a similar project, say a power plant up-grade project for another client, they should do well with your new client. Unfortunately, nothing could be further from the truth. Each organization has a personality, culture, and a political dynamic that sets it apart from others in the same industry or business. In addition, most of the independent contractors that I have worked with over the years tend to be confident, strong-minded individuals who take pride in their work and have little patience with superficial, inexperienced, or arrogant individuals. This can set the stage for unexpected confrontations. Let me relate just one experience I had with my ICs working in a client's environment.

Several other organizations and I provided personnel to a new project that was headed by a young female project manager. The company in question was making a major push to promote females into management positions. I for one was happy to see this effort because it meant that my daughters and other young women would have opportunities that were not available to women when I first entered the workforce. Unfortunately, in some cases these young women were thrust into management positions totally unprepared—often they did not have the experience, skills, or temperament for the job. Some of the women recognized their shortcomings and were smart enough to rely on the recommendations and counsel of their more experienced staff; others took the "I will fake it until I make it" attitude which usually resulted in dumb decisions and blame fixing; still others resorted to modeling their superiors' style of management.

In the company I was supporting there were a number of nuclear-sub veterans in key senior management positions. Their style of communication was simple, blunt, and accented with frequent bursts of profanity. Frankly, the style seemed to fit the background and personality of the individual executives. However, when some of the newly-appointed, young female managers started to emulate this style of management, it did not work and was not accepted, especially by more experienced staff. In most cases, the women that copied this blunt, tough-talking style only succeeded in making themselves look juvenile and undermined their credibility.

I can recall sitting in a project kickoff meeting that was presided by a young, tough-talking female who laid out the ground rules for her project. When she was done, one of the other contractors who was also providing support to the project said, "we are happy to be part of the team," that was as far as he got with his statement when the project manager interrupted him and said, "You are not part of my team, you are a contractor. We hire you for a service just like we hire janitorial services. I expect my contractors to meet their contract obligation without fail or I'll get rid of them." To say that these comments had a chilling effect would be an understatement.

Every contractor on the project resorted to a very protective mode of operation. Each time the project manager gave directions, the contractors documented the request and evaluated it against their contract, and as appropriate, issued a contract change request. No work was done until the change requests were approved and funds were authorized. As a result, in a relatively short time, the project ground to a halt, and the budget went out of sight. For my part, a crisis developed when the project manager started to berate my lead IC in front of the whole project team during a progress review meeting.

My lead IC was a quiet, self-composed, soft spoken individual, highly experienced, with a proven track record of accomplishments on a number of complex projects. He was also a highly decorated combat marine who, while serving in Korea, personally led a bayonet charge to stop a Chinese attack which was about to overrun his unit's position. He rarely talked about his personal life or combat experience, so most people were not aware of this individual's strength of character. When the project manager started to berate my IC, she soon learned that she had made a major mistake. My IC pointed out in a clear, concise, and polite fashion why she was wrong, and then he proceeded to flame her in a way that only a United States Marine could—making clear that he was not providing janitorial services and informing her where she could file her services contract.

When the project manager called me it was clear that she was in a state of shock. I advised her that she could cancel my contract, or I could look for a replacement that would better fit her project team. Since the project manager was desperate to keep her project moving forward, and because she recognized that she had made some serious mistakes, she agreed to interview the replacement candidate I was proposing. I was lucky because at that time I had an IC who was wrapping up a project at a local steel mill and was looking for another assignment.

My IC was an older woman who, early in her career, was a nurse but later decided to move in a different direction and eventually got an advanced degree in computer science. She was astute at managing projects because, as she would say, when she learned how to manage arrogant doctors, everything else was easy. When I aligned my IC with the struggling female project manager, it was a case of instant rapport. My IC showed the young woman how to exercise power and authority without emulating management styles that did not fit.

Managing ICs in any client environment requires a combination of strategies. First, you need to assess the client's environment and identify the unique issues that your ICs may deal with. Organizations that have been downsized, merged, or reorganized will present the IC with client team members who are unhappy, bitter, resentful, shocked, and confused. In addition, processes and procedures may be in shambles, and new managers may be learning on the job. After you assess the client's environment you need to recruit ICs who can function effectively in that kind of environment.

The second thing you should do is institute a change management strategy for the client. Recruit ICs who, in addition to applying their technical skills to the project, can act as change agents and mentors. Look for ICs who have been in a dysfunctional organizational environment before. Many of my experienced ICs had been laid-off or downsized from this kind of environment, and many had experience consulting to dysfunctional clients. I used these veteran ICs to implement change management tactics and provide mentoring to my clients. In many cases this approach paid handsome dividends in obtaining follow-on work, building rapport, and creating a long term relationship with the client.

The ICs who do best in a client's environment are those who can quickly understand the culture of an organization and adjust their behavior and management style to the accepted norms and standards of the organization, while coaching and mentoring their project associates in a non-threatening and constructive manner.

Summary

You can enhance your business capabilities by:

- Recruiting Independent Contractors (IC) to staff your projects
- Contract only with ICs that are experienced, productive, and ethical
- Ensuring that your IC contract agreement spells out what you need, when you need it, the rate or fees to be paid, and any restrictions needed to protect your client and your business
- Managing your ICs performance without interfering in how they do the job

Chapter 12

How to Manage Training Programs

Why Do Training

You should always provide training as part of your project management business. First, training can be very profitable. I have several associates who make a handsome living as full-time trainers. Jack, a friend of mine, has been doing training in the United States and overseas for years. Jack says that training enables him to meet new people, travel to interesting places, and live well.

Second, training is also a cost effective way to advertise and market your products and services. When you provide training, you demonstrate your experience, skills, and expertise to a wide range of people and organizations, thereby giving credibility to your products and services as well as to yourself.

When you interact with diverse organizations and personnel in your training sessions, you learn about their problems, concerns, and needs; thus, you are in an ideal position to propose solutions and services. You also gain insight into emerging trends, changing business conditions, and new management issues that these organizations are facing. This insight gives you a head start to develop new products and services to offer to clients. As I look back at the years when I conducted training programs, I can identify changes in the business environment, from the productivity crisis of the 70s, the emphasis on TQM in the 80s, and process improvement, (Reengineering) of the 90s that provided my company with new business opportunities.

Third, you can also expand your network of associates and contacts by offering training in different venues and in conjunction with other organizations. It is possible to team with colleges, universities, professional organizations, and other trainers to expand your training curriculum and circle of influence. Hence, you can enhance your revenue stream and ensure the continued viability of your company through volatile business cycles. Networking and keeping in tune with the changing world is paramount to business survival.

Finally, training keeps you sharp. When you train a group of professionals, you will be tested every minute of the program. You must know your material, know your audience, and know how to deliver value-added material in a well-organized and engaging manner. Every trainer knows that when you train you as well as your participants learn and grow in the process.

Types of Training Programs

There are numerous ways to deliver project management training that will provide the opportunity to generate revenue and lock-in new or existing clients. The type of program you offer will depend largely on your training skills, subject matter, and client needs. Training programs can include customized client programs, train-the-trainer programs, product training programs, professional seminars, public training, and contracted training. You can also offer self-study Internet-based training programs; however, to use training as a vehicle for client contacts and business development, I recommend that you focus on training programs that offer maximum client contact.

CUSTOMIZED TRAINING PROGRAMS

As the name implies, you develop these programs to fulfill a client's specific or specialized training need. Generally, you get these assignments through competitive bidding or by way of ongoing client work. Over the years, I have responded to solicitations from corporations and government agencies and have won a number of contracts to develop and deliver a wide range of project management training programs. In many cases, when you develop and deliver customized training, you will meet a large cross section of client personnel. If your program is well received, you may conduct training for your client at regular intervals, perhaps for several years; hence, you will have a steady stream of revenue.

When you work with existing clients, you often uncover opportunities to suggest customized training to address specific problems or to improve project performance. Often these training programs will enable you to maintain a solid client business relationship for many years.

There are many advantages in providing customized training. You can conduct your program in the client's facilities, at off-site conference centers, or at local colleges or universities. In most cases, the client will make all the arrangements, provide the meeting rooms, audio-visual equipment, support materials, and refreshments. In addition, the client will set the meeting dates, line up the participants, and take care of administrative requirements. The client may print and distribute your training manuals, workbooks, and handouts prior to the meeting. The result is that you save money by not having to advertise, rent meeting rooms, or take care of the administrative details that are necessary if you offer public training programs which we will talk about later.

In my experience, customized training tends to center on project performance, team effectiveness, project planning and control, and application of specialized project tools and techniques. The program you develop must not only address the client's specific issues or problems but must also fit the client's business, industry, and culture.

Also, your program must be interesting, engaging, interactive and value-added. The most successful programs are those where the participants learn by doing and leave the program with knowledge and products that they can immediately apply to their job.

In many of my customized programs, I develop case studies or simulation exercises to focus on specific client problems. For example, I worked with a dysfunctional project team with an out-of-control project. I developed a case study of a fictitious project with scheduling, budgeting, and resource problems. I had the participants analyze the project and develop corrective action plans to get the project back on track. Over three days of intensive work, the participants—working in five-person teams—learned how to employ team-based project planning, control techniques and action plans.

At the end of my training program, the participants gathered all their materials and said, "We have been struggling for months to get our project back on track; now we have ideas and plans we can take back to our office to use on our project." When your client can immediately apply what they have learned in your program, you have delivered "value-added," training.

Customized training programs require creativity, imagination, and hard work; in addition, these programs must be delivered with energy and enthusiasm; hence, the trainer must be well versed, flexible, and able to connect with the participants. Most importantly, customized training must provide activities and exercises that challenge and engage the participants. Case studies and simulation exercises are great tools for customized, client training, but they must look and sound like the client's environment in all aspects; otherwise, participants will say, "this is all interesting, but it won't work here."

Also, room arrangement is important for a successful customized training program. Participants should be organized into small teams and positioned so they can see and interact with the instructor and all the other participants (see Exhibit 12-1 for a typical room setup). In addition, disruptions and distractions have to be strictly controlled; thus, ground rules concerning cell phones, extraneous conversations, start times, breaks, and anything else that will sidetrack the proceedings must be defined in advanced and enforced during the training sessions. Good trainers must also be good meeting managers.

Room Arrangement

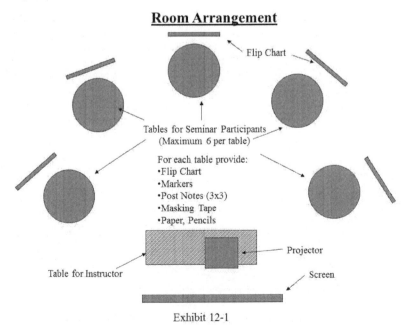

Flip Chart

Tables for Seminar Participants
(Maximum 6 per table)

For each table provide:
•Flip Chart
•Markers
•Post Notes (3x3)
•Masking Tape
•Paper, Pencils

Projector

Table for Instructor

Screen

Exhibit 12-1

There is always a demand for customized training, and the demand increases as clients seek to remain competitive during troubling or volatile business conditions.

In summary, customized training programs provide the best opportunity for generating revenue, building relationships with new and existing clients, and increasing your knowledge-base. In addition, you can always enhance, repackage, and use the intellectual knowledge gained from your customized programs to support other clients; therefore, I strongly recommend that you make customized, client training a major component in your project management business.

TRAIN-THE-TRAINER

Train-the-trainer is another version of a customized training program. In this type of program, you develop a training program for a client with the objective of turning the program over to the client who will train their own personnel. It may sound like you are putting yourself out of business with train-the-trainer programs; however, I have had several such programs and I have found all of them to be profitable and rewarding.

When a client wants a train-the-trainer program, it is for some major training initiative that the client expects to offer for a number of years. Hence, the program-development effort can be extensive and may require several iterations of presenting the program, training the presenters, evaluating feedback, and making improvements before the program is finalized and turned over to the client.

In addition to developing the program and conducting the first few sessions, you will be busy mentoring the client's trainers and you will always be in demand as a backup trainer when needed. I also found that when I got involved with a client on this type of program, I was usually retained to provide support to on-going projects. Often the client's projects identified new issues and problems that should be addressed in their train-the-trainer program; hence, the programs had to be updated in order to remain viable. The net result is that the follow-up work to these training programs helps your revenue stream.

PRODUCT TRAINING PROGRAMS

If you are selling some type of project management product, you must offer training on how to use your product. You may offer free training as part of the initial sale of the product, or you may have follow-on training for a fee. In addition, you may expand your training offerings if you are able to integrate your product with other applications.

I know several project management providers who have developed specialized planning, scheduling, estimating and reporting tools that integrate or plug into Excel or Microsoft Project. So, in addition to providing training on their own tools, they also offer training on the Microsoft programs.

The life of product training programs can be extended every time Microsoft releases the next generation of its software. In addition to offering product training programs to clients who have purchased your specialized product, it is possible to offer training on your products at professional conferences and seminars.

PROFESSIONAL CONFERENCES AND SEMINARS

Many professional organizations offer training programs or workshops at their conferences and seminars. If you belong to one of these organizations or you plan to attend their conference, you can submit a proposal to conduct a training program. Frequently, the professional organization will have a theme for their meeting; thus, your proposed training program should be compatible with the focus of the conference.

Over the years I have presented a number of training programs and workshops for the Project Management Institute, the International Project Management Association, and other professional organizations. The great thing about these seminars is that they attract professionals from all over the world from virtually every type of business, industry, and government agency, thus the exposure for yourself and your company is priceless; however, don't expect to make a lot of money by doing this type of training.

Most professional societies will pay you a modest honorarium for your training program, but you will be responsible for your travel and living expenses, and you may even be required to pay the admission fees if you attend the conference. However, the professional societies will advertise your training program in their conference announcements and will take care of all the training facility arrangements and administrative details; thus, the only thing you have to do is show up with your training materials.

Professional conferences and seminars may not enrich your bottom line but I strongly recommend that you actively pursue these training opportunities as a way of keeping yourself and your company in the main stream of current trends and events. Professional organizations, like the Project Management Institute and the International Project Management Association, work hard to respond to the issues and problems of their members and the businesses, industries, and government entities that employ them. Thus, if you attend a professional conference and conduct a training session or workshop, you will gain new insight into the trials, tribulations, and needs of participating organizations.

In addition to getting timely business insight and intelligence, working at a professional conference is your opportunity to contribute to the advancement of your profession as well as to expand your own professional and intellectual development. I always feel refreshed and renewed after I attend a professional conference and conduct a training workshop.

PUBLIC TRAINING

If you want to generate significant revenue from training, consider offering training to a large audience. That is, instead of focusing on a specific industry, company, or profession make your programs available to the public. You need a timely topic and you need to do some creative advertising and marketing to attract a large number of participants. I have worked with associates who conduct seminars in major cities across the country in rapid-fire succession, presenting some twenty seminars in four to five months. Personally, I do not recommend such an arduous schedule; however, the revenue may make it worthwhile if you have the stamina to keep up the pace.

Apart from the money, public training programs offer the potential to meet people, companies, and industries outside of your normal arena. So if you have trouble breaking out of your niche, or if your industry or client is in a slump, try expanding your offerings to the community at large. Keep in mind that this type of training requires considerable planning, marketing, and administrative details that may be beyond your capabilities.

When you offer training to the public, you will have to ensure that you have a topic that is timely and has wide appeal. During the 80s, there were companies crisscrossing the country offering one-day seminars on project management; in the 90s, reengineering and process redesign were the hot topics, and in the last few years, project management certification training is the topic of choice. Certainly, training on infrastructure projects and other initiatives funded by the federal government may have a strong appeal in today's market.

If you have an interesting topic you can deliver to a large and diverse audience, your challenge is to promote, organize, and conduct your program at a time and place that will attract enough participants to make the whole venture profitable. Some of the issues you have to address are:

When to offer your program—The timing of your program is critical; take into consideration holidays, school schedules, local events, and weather conditions. It is important to select training dates that make it convenient for participants to travel, especially if families may be traveling together.

Where to conduct your program—The location for your program is important, and it may be the main reason why people will consider attending your program. This is why major tourist areas are popular sites for seminars and conventions. People often look for an opportunity to combine their professional development with a bit of recreation or vacation time. In today's world, you have a wide range of training venues including resort areas, convention centers, cruise ships, country clubs, universities, and churches. Most facilities that cater to seminars and conventions provide training rooms and equipment and will be up-to-date relative to safety, handicapped accessibility, rest rooms, restaurants, and other amenities. However, you should inspect any facility that you plan to use before you sign a contract.

Administrative and management issues—There are numerous administrative and management details that require your attention including advertising, registration, billing, cancellations, no-shows, shipping, logistics, travel arrangements, evaluation, feedback, and follow up.

If you are not an experienced seminar organizer, I suggest that you associate with someone who is. Work as a contractor or volunteer to get firsthand experience; otherwise, consider hiring a professional seminar organizer. Hiring a professional will cut your profits, but it will reduce your workload and minimize stress so you can concentrate on what you do best—delivering a solid, professional training program.

CONTRACTED TRAINING PROGRAMS

You can work as a trainer for professional organizations and universities. The advantages of this type of work are many. In most cases, the pay is reasonably good and you do not have the headaches of organizing and promoting the program. In addition, you will meet new people, travel to different locations, and gain exposure that may position you for opportunities with new clients. The sponsoring organization may limit you in marketing and promoting yourself or your products; however, your expertise will be apparent in the training you provide and this is usually sufficient to attract clients in need of your services.

I have worked as a contract trainer for the Project Management Institute, Penn State University, and other organizations and I can testify to the value of this type of work as a complement to your project management business. I know several individuals who do only this type of work; however, I personally believe it is risky to rely on one source of income, especially in today's volatile economy. However, if you want to pursue this type of work, I recommend that you carefully evaluate the organization that wants to hire you and the restrictions in their employment contract.

For example, after I delivered a paper at a PMI Symposium, a representative from a prestigious New England university approached me about working for them as a trainer. I was flattered by the offer, and after a brief discussion about the proposed program, I said I was interested and looked forward to receiving their contract. I was excited about working with this prominent institution and was certain that the relationship would lead to new business opportunities.

However, after I read the university's contract, my heart sank. The pay rate was modest at best, and the limitations and restrictions imposed on the trainer were the most severe I had ever seen. It was clear that I was not going to gain any business benefit from the relationship with this particular organization other than being in the reflected light of their fame and glory.

When I talked to the university administrator in charge of training programs, he expressed shock that I turned down their offer. The tone of his voice denoted indignation when he implied that I did not recognize the value of his institution's reputation and prestige. I agreed with him that his institution was well known, but I told him that I felt that his contract was one notch above indentured servitude. The conversation went downhill at that point; nevertheless, this experience highlights an important issue that you must address as you grow your project management business. You have to decide what your experience and expertise is worth and how you want to run your business. If you agree to work under a very restricted contract, you are not a business person but an employee; if you hire yourself out at a low rate, you relegate yourself to the ordinary. When clients need help, they seek the exceptional, not the ordinary.

Characteristics of a First-class Training Program

Over the course of my professional career, I have attended more training programs than I care to remember. Many of these programs were offered by the corporation with the hope of improving staff effectiveness and efficiency. Far too often, the challenge in attending these programs was staying awake. The instructor may have been uninspiring, the material poorly organized, or the topic of little interest. Whatever the cause, poor training programs cost the corporation money—not just the cost of the program, but also the loss of productivity while personnel are in training sessions.

The American Society for Training and Development (ASTD) has developed volumes of material on developing and delivering training programs; however, based on my years of teaching at the university level and conducting training around, the world I have determined that the most important elements of a first-class training program, especially in project management, include the following: value-added, challenging, learn by doing, relevant, minimum lecture, maximum participation, and safe environment. Let's briefly consider each of these elements.

Value-Added—At the end of your program, participants should be able to go back to their job and apply what they learned to do things faster, better, smarter. If participants can't apply what they got out of your program, then you have only provided entertainment.

Challenging—Participants must engage in analysis, planning, scheduling, and problem solving related to their in-house projects and organizational needs.

Learn by Doing—Study after study shows that students learn more and retain more of what they learn by doing than any other method of teaching. Make extensive use of exercises, case studies, simulations, role play, and team projects.

Relevant—All the discussions, materials, and exercises must fit the business, industry, values, and culture of the organization you are working with. Otherwise, participants will say, "This is interesting, but it's not us; it will not work here," or something to that effect.

Minimum Lecture—Avoid becoming a talking head; introduce a topic, explain the concept, then set the stage for a problem or exercise.

Maximum Participation—Strive to involve all the participants in discussion and exchange of ideas, experience and use of methods, techniques and tools.

Safe Environment—Ask questions, challenge the status quo, and recommend changes in pursuit of improvements, all in the protected environment of the class room.

No matter how well structured the training program; it all boils down to the ability of the instructor to deliver a good program.

Attributes of a Good Trainer

To be a good trainer, first and foremost, you have to love what you are doing, you have to be comfortable talking in front of an audience, and you have to be able to think on your feet. Of course, you must know your audience and your material.

Training is hard work. To run a good program, you have to engage everyone, ask questions, pose problems and situations, relate your experience, and cite examples from other organizations, businesses, or industries. You have to make it interesting and enjoyable while moving the participants out of their well-worn groove to consider new ideas and concepts. I advise everyone who attends my training programs that, "No one ever falls asleep in my class."

If you find it difficult to do training, if you are not comfortable in front of a group, and if no matter how hard you try you don't get better at it, then I recommend you partner with someone. Perhaps you can breakup your training program into segments where you handle a part that you are comfortable with, and delegate the rest to your partner. You should present at least some of the training material in order to be identified with the product, service, or expertise you are trying to promote in your project management business.

On the other hand, if you have a lot of training business, you can hire independent contractors as needed to conduct on-going programs while you focus on developing additional programs for new clients.

The Future for Training Programs

There is always a market for training programs, especially during periods of dramatic economic and technological change. Corporations need to train their workforce to master the new technologies and address the ever increasing competition. Governments need to train displaced workers in order to minimize social upheaval and produce citizens who are productive and can pay taxes. In this environment, companies that develop and deliver innovative training programs to address corporate and government needs will capitalize on the opportunities that change brings.

Summary

Training should always be a business unit in your company. When you provide training, you generate revenue and you open the door for other business opportunities. Your training programs can include:

- Customized Client Programs—Training programs that you develop for a specific client to enhance the capabilities of their corporate and project staff
- Train-the-Trainer Programs—Programs that you develop for a client to give them the capability to do their own training
- Product Training Programs—Specific training on the capabilities and application of some specialized product you are selling
- Professional Seminars—Training offered to and conducted at a conference or seminar sponsored by some professional organization

- Public Training—Training programs that you provide to the general public that you can conduct at resort areas, convention centers, cruise ships, country clubs, universities, or churches

- Contracted Training—Training that you provide as a contractor to a university or private or professional organization

- First-rate training programs emphasize maximum participant involvement, learn by doing and provide value-added benefits

Chapter 13

How to Conduct Study Projects

Why Clients Need to Study Their Projects

Clients almost never retain consultants to study their projects or their project management capabilities when things appear to be going well. Typically it is only after a major disaster or continued poor performance that a company decides they need outside help to figure out what is wrong and how to fix it. The only good news in all of this is that project failure—and we define project failure as not meeting cost, schedule, or technical/performance objectives or stakeholder expectations—is very high across all businesses, corporations, and government agencies. Hence, there are plenty of consulting opportunities for your project management company.

Study projects generally fall into three categories: studies of the client's project management capabilities, studies of on-going projects, and studies of completed projects.

Clients commission studies of their project management capabilities when they see poor performance across most of their projects, or they have experienced some embarrassing blunder. These study projects tend to be extensive assignments involving analysis of project process, procedures, tools, techniques, organizational structures, and staff capabilities. The client will want to know where they stand against the competition, and what they have to do to improve. Often these studies lead to assignments to implement the recommendations that come out of the study.

Astute clients will retain project management consultants to evaluate on-going projects when they sense things are headed in the wrong direction. When cost exceeds budget and schedules slip, it is time to have an outsider make an objective evaluation of the current state of the project and make recommendations as to what has to be done to get the project back on track. The study of on-going projects may generate opportunities to provide training, team building, and on-site support or redesign of the client's project planning and control methodology.

Studies of major project failures or blunders seek to determine the root causes of the problem and provide recommendations and safeguards to ensure that the situation never happens again. Unfortunately, far too often these types of studies are undertaken for blame fixing and punishment of the guilty.

Regardless of the type of study you undertake, the basic methodology will be much the same; that is: organize the study team, collect information, make an analysis, develop recommendations, and provide deliverables such as briefings, reports, and presentations. The duration, effort, and the level of detail involved in the study will depend on the study objectives and complexities involved in the assignment. Studies of a client's project management organization and capabilities—especially those studies that require benchmarking of other organizations' processes, procedures and organizational approaches—may span several months. On the other hand, a study of an on-going or failed project may be accomplished in a few weeks.

In my project management business, I employ a five-phase methodology which can be used on virtually any study assignment simply by adjusting the level of detail and number of tasks in each phase. The study methodology is given in Exhibit 13-1. Thus, let us review some of the important elements in each phase of this study methodology.

Study Methodology

Phase 1 Mobilization	Phase 2 Information Collection	Phase 3 Analysis	Phase 4 Recommendations	Phase 5 Deliverables
Mobilize study team. Meet project sponsor. Define objectives. Define study areas. Identify participants. Establish schedule. Announce study. Publish schedule. Hold kick-off meeting.	Conduct interviews to determine: *Client capabilities to plan, schedule, estimate, budget, report and direct their projects. Effectiveness of client project tools, process, procedures, systems. Level of staff skills. Effectiveness of training programs. Commitment to invest in desired changes.*	Synthesize interview data, define findings. Establish critical success factors for project tools, process, procedures, systems. Establish reference benchmark data for world-class project management. Perform gap analysis. Perform expert assessment — client vs. equivalent client organization.	Identify strengths and weaknesses. Define quick-hits for early improvements. Identify high pay-off areas for significant improvements. Define strategy for implementation. Quantify the cost of improvements. Outline plan and schedule for program implementation.	Present study report covering: *Project strategy, objectives, scope, plans, estimates, budgets, risk, and schedules. Project processes, procedures, tools and systems. Project reporting, corrective action, and lessons-learned processes. Personnel training programs.*

Exhibit 13-1

195

Phase 1—Mobilize and Focus

In Phase 1 we meet with the project sponsor, organize our study team, and prepare the client's organization to participate in the study. There are some critical issues you need to address in Phase 1.

First, be clear about the project sponsor's motivations and expectations for the study. I have found that quite often these can be considerably different from what may be spelled out in your contract scope-of-work. I have had project sponsors who tried to use the study to make themselves look good or to knock-off a rival manager in another department. If there is a hidden agenda, get it out where you can deal with it as soon as possible.

Second, if you are conducting a major study which requires expertise beyond your background, be sure to hire independent contractors (ICs) who are well recognized and have the credentials to substantiate their analysis and recommendations. Clients can be very defensive about what they did and how they did it, so for any criticism to be accepted, it must come from an undisputed authority.

Finally, the study sponsor must set the stage to ensure that the study is not seen as a threat and the participants do not take a defensive posture. Announcements, information, and communication, especially from senior management, are extremely important and will do much to reduce the anxiety that studies tend to generate.

Phase 2—Information Collection

Study information comes from two basic sources: interviews with appropriate personnel and a review of physical materials, which may include but not be limited to documents, data files, drawings, photos, videos, equipment, labs, testing facilities, offices, and construction sites. There are a number of diagnostic study instruments that you can procure from PMI, ASTD, and other professional organizations to aid in collecting the necessary information. However, I recommend that you develop an interview questionnaire and data collection checklist for your client based on the nature of the industry or business you are dealing with, the objectives of the study, and the specific issues and problems that you compiled from discussions with the project sponsor and others. If you are conducting a major study and employing outside experts, be sure they use a questionnaire for their interviews. In my company, we used an instrument that was developed and refined over the years in collaboration with my ICs and based on the experience we gained while working with clients in a wide range of businesses, industries, and government agencies

In most project management studies, you should collect information from the majority of the client's organization as well as from vendors, suppliers, customers, and major stakeholders. Quite often you can gain insight into the effectiveness or shortcomings of the client's project management capabilities by interviewing people outside the client's organization.

It has been my experience that in most cases, the people at the working level know the problems and how to fix them. However, as a study interviewer, your challenge is to ask the right questions, remove or reduce the fear element, filter out hidden agendas or pet projects of the individual, and get the participants to contribute in an honest and willing manner. The key to getting useful interview information is a well-developed script or questionnaire that you use consistently throughout all the interviews. This script must be appropriate for the business, industry, or organization you work with.

The willingness of participants to contribute effectively and honestly to your interviews will depend on your communication style, sociability, and demeanor as well as the nature of the client's culture and environment.

It is a joy to work with a client organization that has an open, can-do, let's make it happen culture. People contribute, make suggestions, and are honest about where they need improvement. In client organizations that tend to be static, paternalistic, or protective, you will get the party line and "everything is great" response. In draconian organizations, you will get guarded responses or ranting and venting from embittered people. You can do a number of things to filter and cross-reference the information you collect; however, discussion of these techniques is outside the scope of this book.

Finally, the review and evaluation of physical materials is usually straightforward. Either the client has the physical assets to do the job, or they don't, and you can validate this based on your experience, your IC experts, or from benchmark studies.

All the information collected from interviews and from reviews of physical materials must be compiled, organized, and made easily accessible to the study team. You must have a disciplined process for filing information and updating the study database on a daily basis, otherwise the volume of information can quickly get out of control and important details of the study can be lost or not get appropriate attention. Good information-housekeeping is essential to ensuring a well-run study.

Phase 3—Analysis

The analysis phase of the study should overlap the information collection phase of the project. I have found that it is very important to have a team meeting at the end of every day of information collection. Even though everyone may be tired, it is important to get an overview of the information collected that day, and to discuss and assess the feelings and impressions that were generated by the interactions and discussions with client personnel. More often than not, these inputs reveal more about what is going on in the client's organization than anything actually said in the interview.

In the analysis phase you attempt to answer some basic questions about the client's project management capabilities. Generally, these are: what are we doing right, what are we doing wrong, how do we stack up against the competition, and what corrective action is required?

The analysis process (see Exhibit 13-2) first examines the *present state* of the client's organization to define how the client is currently operating. This information is evaluated against some standard, usually recognized best practices for the industry or bench mark studies. This gives an overview of what the client is doing right and what they are doing wrong in each performance area. However, to assess actual performance, you should do a gap analysis to determine the difference between the client's current performance and best practice. The gap analysis is a powerful tool that identifies the areas most in need of corrective action (see Exhibit 13-3).

Analysis Process

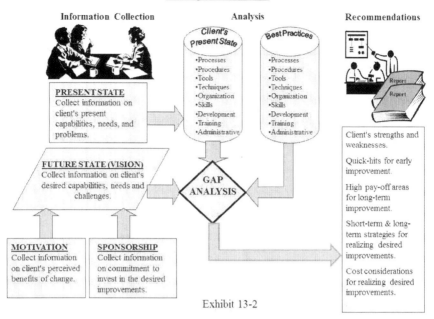

Exhibit 13-2

The gap analysis will also identify the areas that require action to help the client build the project management capability they desire. We define this as the *future state*; it reflects the client's vision of how they want to operate to meet the challenges of a changing world. The future state may envision a new business approach, such as operating as a lean organization, utilizing information technology more, or collaborating more with other project providers. Whatever the case, the future state must also be part of the gap analysis to establish the areas that require work and investment.

Gap analysis can be accomplished using objective and subjective measures. Subjective measures are usually based on the experience and judgments of experts. This is why I stress that in addition to your expertise and experience, you retain ICs who are recognized in their field to address issues that are not easily quantified. For example, we had a heated discussion with one client when we identified their deficiency in project planning and control. The client's project people insisted that what they were doing was new and involved a lot of creativity; therefore, they could not possibly do any serious planning and control. After listening politely to these arguments, my IC, who was an internationally recognized project management authority, gave a brief overview of what others in the industry were doing to plan and control projects, and explained that this was one of the reasons that the competition was rolling out their projects ahead of the client. Far too often, people are so busy and preoccupied with the environment they work in they think there is nothing else like it in the world.

The gap analysis not only highlights the disparity between client performances and best practice, but it also sets the stage for formulating the recommendations and action plans that you want to propose to the client.

Gap Analysis Identifies the Real Problems

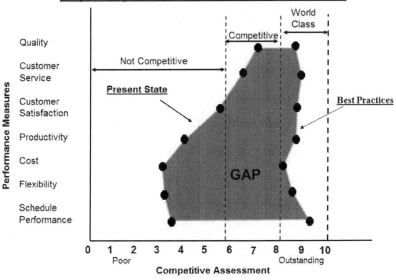

Exhibit 13-3

Recommendations

Recommendations must address the strengths as well as the weaknesses identified in the study. Identifying client strengths highlights the client's positive accomplishments and provides the foundation for building and improving in other areas of the organization. It is also a way of showing client personnel that in spite of whatever problems they may face, they have the ability to improve and prevail. This sets the stage to address client weaknesses in a more proactive and constructive manner.

I like to present recommendations in terms of quick-hits for early improvements and high pay-off areas for long-term improvements. Quick-hits are things that the client can do relatively quickly and at minimum cost to make improvements. These may include streamlining processes and procedures, eliminating redundant or ineffective functions, combining operations, and outsourcing low-value functions or operations. Long term improvements generally require major management commitments and investments. These usually encompass organizational redesign, process improvements, implementation and application of new technologies, and training. Often, making major improvements requires change management programs that, among other things, alter the culture of the organization.

In formulating recommendations, you must always be mindful of the client's ability to implement the desired improvements. Does the client have the courage to address the pain that change will require, do they have the skills and the time to implement the improvements, and can they afford the cost involved? Thus, your recommendations should include realistic strategies that the client can employ to move from their present state to the desired future state.

Study Deliverables

At the end of the study, you present your findings and recommendations in a comprehensive report with supporting backup data and information. Your report should include an executive summary followed by a comprehensive discussion of the study methodology, findings, recommendations, implementation strategy, plans, schedules, and cost estimates. In addition, most companies expect you to make a power point presentation on the study. One of my clients asked me to put together a road-show presentation for all the divisions and departments involved in the study. This turned out to be a smart move, because it helped to reduce the fear factor and facilitate the implementation of many of the process changes.

Implementation Issues

Study projects can be very rewarding, especially if you get follow-on work. Sometimes this work can lead to a long-term relationship with a client where you have the opportunity to be part of a major transformation of the corporation. There is a lot of professional satisfaction in taking part in an effort that enables an organization to change its processes, procedures, and culture and to grow and prosper in the face of a harsh business environment. On the other hand, you might complete an exciting study project with the high expectations that you are about to change the world—but then nothing happens.

I have had successful study projects where the client was generous with their praise, concurred with the result, and was enthusiastic about the implementation plan; however, the implementation program never got off the ground. There are several reasons why major improvement programs never take place despite the obvious need. Some of the reasons include cost, resistance, and deception. There are things you can do to help the client address the cost and resistance issues; however, there is nothing practical you can do about deception. Let me explain.

In most cases, the motivation for a study project is to improve the organization; however, there are times when the study is really a smoke screen to mask something else. A senior manager or executive is not performing well, his operation is in turmoil, and he can't explain why—what to do? Well, one answer is to conduct a study. Commissioning a study provides an opportunity to take the heat off the executive and give him or her time to do something else. Perhaps the executive finds another job, or as sometimes happens, the executive uses the study to show that things are really not so bad. It is not unusual to have an executive interpret study findings to their advantage. The net result is that if the study sponsor is not truly interested in changing, there is little you can do; however, if cost is an issue, there are strategies you can suggest that may help.

Budget constraints, such as a hiring freeze, often prevent implementation programs from moving forward. Yet there are some simple strategies you can propose that may help the client. For example, to get around a hiring freeze, suggest augmenting the client staff temporarily with your staff. Or, if budgets are a problem, try to break up the program into smaller segments and spread the effort out over a longer period of time. Or, better yet, try for some quick-hits to show improvements. There is nothing more effective for opening the corporate purse strings than to show cost savings and better performance. Helping your client to work around budget constraints will be invaluable towards establishing a long-term relationship and a continued stream of assignments. On the other hand, if the implementation program is stalled because of internal resistance, you and your client are facing a much more difficult problem.

Resistance to change, especially change that impacts the values, beliefs, and culture of the organization, is well recognized and is one of the major reasons why Reengineering, as postulated by Michael Hammer and James Champy in their best-selling book, "Reengineering the Corporation," fell out of favor after a brief period of euphoric application. If the client is facing resistance to change, be it overt or covert, it may be necessary to address this problem by way of a formal change-management program which I will discuss in the next chapter.

Summary

Some of the key points of this chapter are:

- Clients generally commission study projects when they have problems with their projects. These studies tend to focus on project procedures, tools, techniques, planning, scheduling, and budgeting methodologies

- Study projects can also include organizational structures, and staff capabilities

- Study projects involve setting up a study team, collecting information, making an analysis, and developing recommendations and strategies for implementation

- The end product of a study—the deliverable—is a report and management presentations

- Study projects can lead to implementation assignments if the client is ready, willing, and able to undertake the programs given in the study recommendations

Chapter 14

How to Manage Change Projects

Change is Great for Business

As I said in Chapter 10, one of the lessons that I learned over the course of my career is that there are minimal opportunities for business growth in a static environment. Dramatic change, both good and bad, provides the best opportunity to generate new business and make money. Probably one of the worst things that can happen to you in your business is to be very successful and very comfortable in one specialized niche. If this happens, I guarantee that one day you will wake up and find that you are obsolete, irrelevant, and no longer in demand. To avoid this trap, you must be in tune with a changing environment and offer products and services that help businesses, industries and governments deal with the trauma that change generates.

In this chapter I will review some of the change projects that I worked on and discuss the techniques employed in managing these projects. It is hard to predict the type of change projects that you may be involved with in the future, but I am certain that you will find them challenging, educational, and profitable.

Types of Change Projects

Basically there are two types of change projects: improvement projects and transformation projects. Improvement projects tend to focus on making incremental enhancements to existing processes, procedures, tools, and techniques in order to solve a specific problem, eliminate a bottleneck, or enhance the organization's efficiency and effectiveness. These projects usually have minimum impact on the overall organization and can be accomplished by using the organization's available resources, skills, and personnel.

On the other hand, transformation projects strive to completely redesign the processes, procedures, tools, techniques, and structures of the organization. Transformation projects are complex and expensive, involve considerable risk, and can have a significant impact on the people in the organization.

Improvement Projects

Improvement projects may come out of recommendations from a study, or as a result of suggestions that you make in your work on a client's project, or because of problems and issues that the client has identified. In most cases, improvement projects focus on revamping existing process and procedures or implementing new tools, techniques, or technologies. Generally, these projects are straightforward, involve minimal impact on the organization, and usually build on the experience of the project participants.

The tasks involved in these projects include: study the problem or requirement; identify what needs to be changed; design the new process or procedure; review the designs with the project team; implement the change; test and verify that the change is effective; monitor results to ensure that the benefits have been achieved; and finally, make adjustments as needed to fine-tune the change.

Sometimes the implementation of a seemingly minor improvement can have unintended consequences. For example, on one project we worked to speed up the client's maintenance process; however, to improve the maintenance process, we found that we had to revamp the purchasing department's procedures to enable the sole-source procurement of critical parts and materials. In turn, we found that we had to revise project budgeting and scheduling procedures to deal with the additional cost involved in expediting.

I have found that it is worthwhile, even when dealing with seemingly routine changes, to develop a flowchart showing the interaction between all the organizational elements involved or potentially involved in the improvement project. Simple input-output diagrams can be very helpful in avoiding the unintended consequences of a seemingly minor improvement.

Improvement projects can also come out of a project's lessons-learned reviews. In most cases, lessons learned are performed at the end of a project; however, I believe that this is a mistake. Too often, much of the learning that takes place in a project is forgotten or deemphasized. Thus, when lessons learned are performed at the end of a project, people usually remember everything that went wrong, especially the glaring mistakes made by others. Many of the positive accomplishments will be forgotten or quickly skimmed over. Therefore, I recommend that lessons learned be an ongoing activity over the life of the project.

On my projects, I make lessons learned an agenda item in weekly review meetings. While events are fresh in everyone's mind, we identify what we did right, what we did wrong, and how we can apply what we learned. In this way, we can make improvements quickly and benefit from our lessons learned over the life of the project; also, we can identify any major changes that need to be made by the organization before it undertakes the next project.

Improvement projects generate only incremental enhancements; however, this may be all that is needed for an organization to accomplish its projects in a cost-effective manner. When incremental improvements fail to solve critical problems or the needs of the organization, then it is time to consider a major transformation project.

Transformation Projects

As I noted in a previous chapter, I became interested in change management as a result of my involvement with a corporation that launched a major transformation project. Since most of my experience was in aerospace and construction, I was intrigued by the change management philosophy, and I eventually became a certified change management consultant. As a result, change management became an important part of my project management business, and I had change management engagements with corporations as well as foreign governments.

A transformation project is a major undertaking with the goal of making significant improvements in the way an organization accomplishes its mission. These projects focus on changing every aspect of the organization; the objective is to tear down or dismantle the existing processes, procedures, structures, and values of the organization. In the 1980s and 90s, Reengineering, as promoted by Michael Hammer and James Champy, was the driving philosophy for transforming organizations to a new way of doing business. This philosophy and the legions of Organizational Development (OD) consultants who were hired to implement this philosophy had a major impact on corporate America—most of it bad.

My views of OD consultants were shaped in part because of their participation in some of my client project meetings. For example, several engineers would be involved in a heated discussion trying to resolve some technical problem, when the OD consultant would interrupt the conversation and say something like, "Chuck, it sounds like you are really upset by the way things are going; please tell the group how you feel about this." Then, the meeting would grind to a halt while Chuck vented his frustrations about not having his technical expertise accepted by the group. The OD consultants tried to change the behavior of the project team members through this type of intervention and through the use of games and other activities to show how the existing culture prevented the organization from moving in a new direction.

The OD initiatives were well intended; however, engineers are poor candidates for the touchy-feely approach, and in a short time, "How do you feel about that," became a standing joke. Often, when there was a difference of opinion on some issue or problem, one of the engineers would stop and say, "tell me how you feel about that," and the other engineer would respond and say, "I am glad you shared that with me," and then they both would laugh. As far as I was concerned, these OD initiatives provided a lot of entertainment but did little to enhance the capabilities of the organization.

Much of the change management methodology that was applied by the OD consultants came out of Clinical Psychology studies of human behavior. Behavior is an important part of any major change program; however, people's behavior, especially engineers, must be influenced in a way that enables them to understand, value, and internalize the change. Furthermore, major change projects require much more than behavior modification. At a minimum, everyone impacted by a change project must understand why it is necessary to change, the goals of the change, the strategy for changing, their role in making the change, and how the change will impact them.

After I completed my change management certification program, I was convinced that what change management needed was a disciplined management approach, not an OD approach; hence, I developed a project management methodology that I used on different transformation projects.

Why Change

The basic reason for any organizational change is either a significant danger or an opportunity. Participants in a change program must believe there is a valid reason for the change; otherwise, they will not support the effort and may even work hard to defeat the program. When people have a clear understanding of the compelling need to change, they will participate in the process even though they may not like it. I saw plenty of examples of this when I worked on transformation projects in the United States, Eastern Europe, and the former Soviet Union. In almost every case, people hated the transformations taking place, yet they knew that things had to change and were going to change regardless of how they felt.

How to Change

Major change projects are complex, expensive, and prone to failure. Experts estimate that project failure may be as high as 50 to 70 percent. However, we have learned a lot about managing major change projects over the past twenty-some years, so we can be more optimistic about our chances for success. One of the major things we have learned is that there are prerequisites that must be met before an organization undertakes a major change project. These are:

1. Information—The organization must have accurate and timely information that clearly identifies the dangers or opportunities they face.
2. Motivation—There has to be an overpowering reason to launch a change project. In many cases, the very existence of the organization may be at stake.
3. Action—Decisions must be made and strategies developed to launch the change project in a decisive manner.
4. Leadership—There must be a central point of power and direction to initiate and sustain the change project.

5. Structure—There must be specific plans, processes, systems, and sufficient resources dedicated to the change project.

Experience clearly shows that if all the prerequisites are not fully met, the change project will fail.

The objective for all major change projects is to significantly transform an organization from its present way of functioning to a new way of operating, by a certain date, and within a specified budget. Major change projects have been undertaken by corporations as well as governments around the world. In many cases, the organizations involved may not have called their initiatives a change project; however, the improvements they sought to make required a major transformation in everything they did as an organization.

I will give you two examples of transformation projects I experienced, one with an American electric utility company, and the other with the Russian government.

Transforming an American Electric Utility Company

The American electric utility company that I worked with had a number of aging fossil fuel power plants. When deregulation hit the electrical utility industry, many of my client's fossil fuel plants could not generate power at a competitive price. Management had two choices: tear down the plants and ship them to China, or find a way to make these plants competitive in a deregulated marketplace.

A transformation project was initiated to see if the corporation could find a way to operate their plants more competitively. This was a do or die situation for everyone involved; if the plants were shut down, most of the personnel would be out of a job. The reason and the motivation for a transformation project was clear and virtually everyone bought into the program even though they did not like it.

To get started, management organized a transformation project team made up of personnel from various disciplines from several of the power plants. A senior corporate executive was put in charge, and he laid down a time table for the total effort. He also retained outside expertise to support the transformation project team. My involvement was to provide project management expertise and support as explained below.

Project Management for Transformation Projects

Over the years of working on major transformation projects, I evolved a structured project management approach to managing this type of undertaking. A model of my approach is given in Exhibit 14-1. I will use this model and my experience with the power plant transformation project to show how to manage these projects. The first step in managing a transformation project is to assess the present state of the organization and conceptualize what the future state should look like.

Organizational Transformation

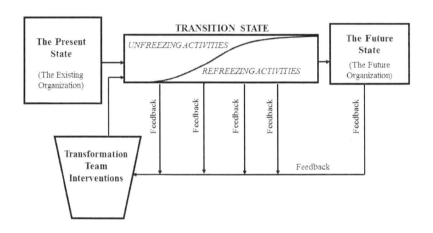

Exhibit 14-1

THE PRESENT STATE

This is the organization before the transformation. In the case of the power plant change project, the client had a traditional, hierarchical organization based on subdivision of work and specialization. Everyone in the plant knew their job, most had been there for many years, and everyone considered it a great place to work. The pay and benefits were good, they had job security, and there was a lot of camaraderie. The plant staff often tried to get family members jobs at the plant, and it was not unusual to find sons and daughters working at the same facility with their fathers or mothers.

The work at the plant tended to be predictable; occasionally, there would be a crisis, a breakdown, or an outage and the organization would respond with great energy and dedication. However, there would be long periods of routine or limited activity, and employees would occupy themselves by reading or inventing games. For example, the maintenance shop invented floor shuffle board where they would slide large, open-end wrenches twenty yards across the shop floor to see who came closest to the finish line without crossing it

Most of the employees at the plant realized that they were not operating as efficiently as they could, but they were comfortable and they were loath to change; however, when management announced the change program, everyone agreed they had to do something. Otherwise, they would be out of a job.

However, because things are going to change does not mean that everything in the present organization needs to be thrown out. It is important in any transformation project to take a hard look at the present organization and identify the processes, procedures, tools, techniques, experience, skills, and values that should be carried forward into the future state. The prevailing reengineering idea that everything has to be thrown out is wrong and counterproductive. Certain elements of the existing organization are valuable and should be incorporated into the future organization. The challenge, of course, is to ensure that you are not saving elements of the existing organization solely to preserve someone's job. It is important to ensure that anything from the present organization that is incorporated into the future organization accomplishes the objectives of the transformation project.

THE FUTURE STATE

The future state represents the ultimate goal of the transformation project. This state required the participants to function using new behavior patterns, expectations, and modes of operation. Much that the organization valued in the past will change, especially the organization's culture.

Initially, you need to develop a concept of what the transformed organization should look like. It is important to develop a conceptual model of the future state that fulfills the vision for the new organization. This model will serve as a reference to evaluate the processes, procedures, and systems that are developed as the organization works to transform itself. Throughout the transition effort, you need to ensure that you make the right process changes and develop and implement the procedures, tools, and technologies that will enable the transformed organization to fulfill its vision.

On my project, the transformation team envisioned a multi-disciplined team-based organization that could operate and maintain the plant with a greatly reduced staff. And they envisioned using information technology to streamline and automate many of the administrative and management functions of the plant. However, the specific design and details of the future state would be developed and tested during the transition state.

TRANSITION STATE

The transition state is where the actual work of transforming an organization takes place. During transition, unfreezing activities are initiated to breakdown the status quo and establish the pattern of expectations for the new organization. Training, coaching, and mentoring programs are implemented. In addition, the transformation project team conducts studies of other organizations to evaluate different approaches for their new organization; they also conceptualize new processes and procedures and engage in brainstorming to evaluate different management approaches.

During this phase, management plays a critical role by demonstrating their commitment and support to the transformation project. Management must convince everyone that they are dedicated to ensuring the success of the total effort.

Management shows their support and commitment by providing ample resources and outside expertise to aid the transformation team. They also encourage the team to explore new and different approaches to accomplish the transformation objectives.

In the power plant transformation project, management demonstrated their support by sending members of the team to visit and study other organizations in the United States and overseas. This had a powerful effect on team members. As one individual told me, "I worked at this plant for twenty years, and I never even went to corporate headquarters to attend a meeting, but now I am traveling the world like a consultant; clearly, management is serious about this project."

Every project initiative undertaken during the unfreezing and refreezing phase of the transition state is evaluated against the vision for the future organization. Project management's role in this effort is to critique transition results, make recommendations, and initiate programs and interventions to move the team forward.

Various test programs and pilot programs are undertaken to validate the processes, procedures, tools, and techniques being considered for the new organization. Discussion of these test programs is outside the scope of this book; however, for more information refer to the "Field Guide to Project Management, by David I. Cleland, Chapter 30, Managing Reengineering Teams."

The concepts, processes, procedures, and systems that are validated in the test programs are integrated into a cohesive organizational structure during the refreezing phase of the transition. It is also during this period that the transformation team works to establish the values, behaviors, and norms for the new organization. It is very important that the culture for the new organization be quantified and made known early and often; otherwise, there is a strong possibility that people will slip back into the old way of working.

In addition to designing a new way of doing business, the transformation team had to decide who would be brought into the new organization. The critical requirements in selecting personnel for the new organization were: skills, adaptability, the flexibility to work on a multi-disciplined team, and the capability to embrace the new culture. Individuals who were not selected or did not want to participate in the new organization were retired or given a buy-out package.

A multi-disciplined team was put in place to install the new processes, procedures, and systems and to operate the plants to demonstrate that they could be competitive in a deregulated environment. As it turned out, some plants were very successful; others were only marginally successful and required additional work to become competitive. Some plants had to be shutdown. This project demonstrated that organizations can change if management invests the time, money, and leadership to take its people through all the painful steps needed to transform their way of doing business. We Americans are very fortunate to live in a society where anyone can challenge the status quo and invent new concepts and philosophies to implement change. This was not the case in the former Soviet Union.

Transforming a Management Philosophy

I had the opportunity to travel through Eastern Europe before the fall of the Berlin Wall and through the Soviet Union sometime later. In all cases, traveling through the socialist paradise was like traveling to a different planet. People stood in long lines with their plastic shopping bags hoping to buy something at the state-owned stores, highways were devoid of traffic, and individuals would bump into you on the street and whisper, "sell dollars." What a bleak picture of the lives of average citizens.

Certainly, the citizens had job security, they could count on a modest pension if they followed the rules, and they might even get a decent place to live if they got recognition for some achievement. However, in these powerful, centralized governments in which every aspect of life was regulated, I found that productivity and initiative were almost nonexistent. In one city I was visiting, I was given a tour of a cultural center the Russians had under construction. I was shocked to learn that they had been working on the project for almost ten years. When I asked my host why the project was taking so long he replied, "Well, you know the government pretends to pay us, and we pretend to work." I found out later that this was a standing joke in the Soviet Union.

Some years later, as their economy started to crumble and the Soviet Union began to break up, I obtained an engagement from the World Bank to participate in a Russian training program. In an effort to better relations between East and West, the World Bank initiated a program to bring Russians from various industries and government agencies to the United States to learn American management techniques. There were a number of American consultants and experts from various fields involved in this program. I was responsible for project management.

Looking back, it is hard to appreciate the magnitude of the changes that we and the Russians were dealing with. In the first meeting at the World Bank, we sat at a long table, some dozen Russians on one side and an equal number of Americans on the other side, with the lead World Bank executive at one end of the table and an interpreter at the other. As I looked at the Russians across the table, I whispered to a World Bank staffer next to me, "I can't believe this is happening and I am here; I spent most of my early career working on projects to destroy these people." The bank staffer said, "Don't be shocked, see that fellow over there, he used to head up the Russian ICBM projects, working hard to destroy us; now he is looking for a job." After the initial meeting where we designed the total program, the Russians sent a team of some sixty men and women from academia, industry, and government to the World Bank's headquarters in Washington, DC.

The program we developed for the Russians consisted of a series of lectures, workshops, and visits to American businesses, factories, and on-going projects. The goal was to explain American management techniques and show how these techniques were applied by various corporations. Another, but more subtle goal, was to show the Russians that the American management philosophy and techniques produced abundance for most everyone; this was not discussed in our training sessions but was shockingly evident to the Russians when they traveled around the DC area.

Even though the Russian delegation was made up of the elite of their country—engineers, scientists, managers, and executives—none had ever experienced a supermarket or a beltway traffic jam; initially they were in awe of the material abundance of America—they took pictures of supermarkets, restaurants, and parking lots to show people back home. Things we Americans took for granted, like major appliances, were new to the delegation; this became evident when we discovered that our Russian visitors were not familiar with the automatic washing machine and dryer. For example, one member of the Russian delegation had washed his shirts in the kitchen sink and hung them on chairs in front of the oven to dry; then he went out to dinner. Unfortunately, when he came back from dinner, he found his apartment on fire.

I found it amazing that the nation that beat us into space could be lacking in so many areas. It was particularly surprising to me that the Russians did not have or use project management. There was not one Russian project management book in the whole of Russia. All undertakings were organized and managed by a bureaucratic, hierarchical management structure. Subdivision of work and specialization were the management philosophy, and everyone looked to someone above them to tell them what to do, when to do it, and in most cases, how to do it. It was clear to me that this monolithic approach to everything was responsible to a large degree for the lethargy and inefficiency that permeated the Russian economy.

I had a tough time getting the Russians to accept project management. They found it difficult to believe a team could have the power to plan and manage the work of a major undertaking without being directed by a higher authority. In addition to explaining project management concepts, I had the Russians meet and talk with project managers from different businesses and industries. The Russians began to understand project management; unfortunately, in the early stages of our program, I don't think the Russians fully believed they were going to apply much of anything we were showing them. I think most of them were hoping that all this change would go away and they could return to the security of the world they knew well. It was only after the breakup of the Soviet Union and the government shift to a more democratic structure that many of the participants in our program begin to change in a substantial way.

When the Russians returned home, many of them took advantage of the changes taking place in their country. Some of them bought their apartments, others started their own businesses, and still others emigrated to the West to find jobs in major corporations. Also, the first Russian book on project management was written and published by several of my program participants; in addition, project management courses were offered at the universities, and several Russians became project management consultants.

Changes in Russia and Eastern Europe were dramatic and swift. For the first time, the average citizen was free to travel outside their country. In the old days when I traveled overseas, I would see legions of tourists from the United States, England, France, Germany, and Japan; then, almost overnight there were hordes of tourists from Russia and Eastern Europe. The contrast between the early days of my travel and the changed world still rather amazes me; frankly, I never expected to see all these changes in my lifetime. Yet the changes continued, and after the success of the Russian program, I participated in similar World Bank programs for the Ukrainians and the Chinese.

The lesson in all of this is that major change will not be accepted and supported by any organization unless there is a compelling reason to change, a danger or an opportunity, and the participants can see the benefits of the change. However, in order for the participants to change, they must go through some type of unfreezing process that tears down the status quo and a refreezing process that helps them deal with the new environment they will work and live in. Sometimes this transition process can be managed through a formal transformation program, like my power plant project; at other times, the transition process is a series of historical events that impact peoples' lives and force them to deal with change—the breakup of the Soviet Union is a stark example of this.

The world has been transformed dramatically since I started my professional career in 1960; however, I believe that advances in science and technology, and evolving cultural, economic and political philosophies will generate even more profound changes. These changes will spawn limitless business opportunities, provided you can see, think, and react positively to the trauma these changes will produce. In the next chapter, I will discuss the most challenging aspect of running a successful project management business; that is, the challenge of managing yourself.

Summary

Change, good or bad, creates opportunities for your project management business. Some of these opportunities include:

- Work on improvement projects to make incremental improvements in process, procedures, tools, and techniques

- Manage transformation projects to completely re-cast the organization to a new way of operating

- Conduct training, workshops, and management interventions to help personnel move from the present state to the desired future state for their organization

- Assist change teams to study, evaluate, and design new processes, procedures, tools, and techniques for their transformed organization

- Conduct test and pilot programs to validate the concepts, processes, procedures, and systems for the new organization

Chapter 15

How to Manage Yourself

You are the Architect of Your Success and Happiness

As I look back at all the people I knew and worked with over the years, I often wonder why some were very successful and others were not. There were those who had many advantages, yet wound up living disastrous lives, while others were very successful despite their modest resources. Certainly there are degrees of success where some individuals amass a fortune while others live an enjoyable middle-of-the road life. But as we all know, success is more than money. Successful people are happy with what they have accomplished in their personal and professional lives, they know that they did well with what they had to work with, and they have few or no regrets. Unsuccessful people are discontented or disappointed and harbor regrets about their professional or personal lives, or both.

There are many things in life that influence your success and happiness, some of which you can control, some you can manipulate, and some you can't do anything about. However, to a large degree, your success and happiness in life will be determined by how well you manage yourself.

Self-Management and the Seven Phases of Life

Self-management means that *you* direct your thinking and actions on every aspect in your life. In most management literature, self-management is discussed primarily in terms of how to be successful in the corporate world. Peter Drucker wrote about Managing Oneself in his book, "Management Challenges for the

21st Century (HarperCollins, 1999);" and Daniel Goleman addresses many of the same issues in, "Emotional Intelligence (Bantam, 1995)." From my point of view, much of this writing falls short of the needs of the entrepreneur. As soon as you start your project management business, your self-management demands will be more in line with a marathon runner then a member of the corporate team.

Success and happiness is governed by how well you manage yourself in every phase of your life, starting when you are very young. I can identify seven, distinct phases of life (see Exhibit 15-1) that present specific self-management opportunities and challenges and which set the stage for success or failure in future life stages. These seven phases include Youth, College, Early Career, Mid-career, Late Career, Early Retirement, and Late Retirement.

A word of caution to the reader who is in the early phases of his or her career; if you think the other phases have no bearing on your life beware—you need to examine the youth phase of your life to understand how your self-management skills developed and shaped your present life; furthermore, you need to evaluate your present self-management skills to prepare for the future phases of your life. Regardless of what phase of life you are in, it is never too late to enhance your self-management skills.

Let us look at the seven phases of life to see how self-management impacts your success and happiness.

YOUTH

From the time you are born until you leave home to go to college, your frame of reference, the mental model of your world, is shaped by the environment you live in and the people around you (see Exhibit 15-2). Your parents, relatives, and friends inculcate you with their views and standards of religion, morals, values, ethics, politics, work, goals, and everything else. During this phase of your life, you are influenced and shaped by others. But, it is also a time of self-discovery. You begin to find what interests you, what you can do well, what you are not good at, what excites you, and what bores you. You may even begin to develop goals for yourself. When people ask you what you want to be when you grow up, you may be able to answer them with conviction.

John Tuman, Jr.

Seven Phases in the Life of a Working Professional

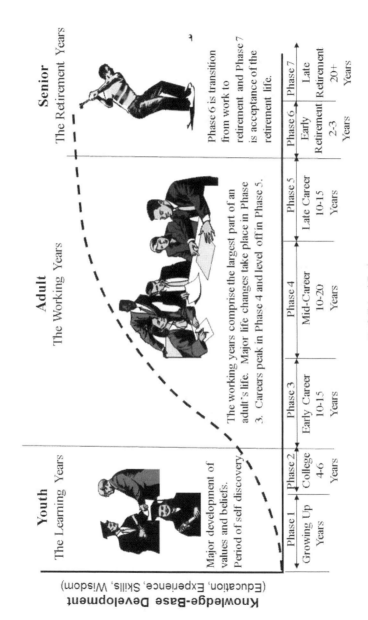

Exhibit 15-1

221

Mental Model (Frame-of-Reference) Development

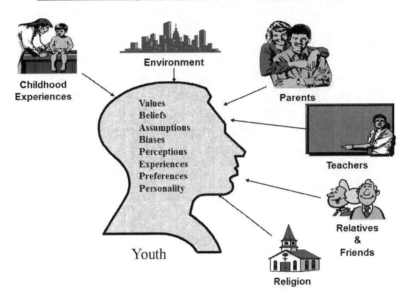

Exhibit 15-2

I have noticed that young people who develop goals early tend to do well in their future lives. An example of this is Taylor Swift, who at one time lived not too far from my home in Pennsylvania. Taylor won a national poetry contest when she was in the fourth grade; by the time she was ten years old, she was writing songs and singing them at festivals and fairs; by age seventeen, Taylor was well on her way to fame and stardom as a singer-songwriter and actress.

I do not know if there are studies that bear out my belief that there is a strong correlation between early formulations of life-goals and success and happiness.

Those who are driven to succeed tend to come from goal-oriented families that emphasize education, hard work, and practice a lifestyle that reinforces this philosophy. But there are exceptions; I know individuals from dysfunctional families or disadvantaged backgrounds, yet they set goals, work hard, and improve their lives. I would like to know the source of this drive and how to instill it in others who are destined to fail because they do not know how to set goals and manage themselves.

The youth-phase of your life, especially the several years before college, is probably responsible for 70 to 80 percent of the values and beliefs you will use throughout most of your life. It is very rare that anyone can transmute themselves from the mental model that was wrought in their youth to something completely different.

Furthermore, youth is the phase of your life when you begin to form and solidify your interests, goals, and self-management skills. It is my observation that the people most successful throughout their lives are those who developed good self-management skills early. I am certain you have seen or know a high-school student who seems to be outstanding in academics, sports, arts, and everything else. These students know how to set goals and priorities and manage their time and work efforts to achieve maximum results. Students who have not developed these self-management skills usually have a very difficult time when they go to college.

COLLEGE

In my experience teaching at the undergraduate and graduate level I noted that students who failed or had a hard time keeping up with their courses lacked more self-management skills than mental ability. I'll give you an example of a typical conversation that I have had with students who struggled with their courses.

> Professor, I work very, very hard, but I just can't get it. I don't know how these other guys can just breeze through this course; the material is hard and the work load is impossible. Oh, I say, "Sorry to hear that you find it so difficult; let me ask you some questions; do you watch TV in the evening? "Yes," my student replies, "But only one hour when I take a break." Then I ask, "Did you go upstate to attend the big game this weekend?" "Yes," my student replies, "But I did try to get in some study on the way up and back." "Do you go out with your girlfriend during the week?" I ask. My student replies, "Yes, I do; I need some recreation in my life, and besides what's the use of going to college if you can't have a little fun." "Well," I tell my student, "the top performers in this class do not watch TV, they rarely go out, and they work hard all the time." My student replies, "Who wants to live that kind of life; if all there is work, it's not worth it."

The reality is that this student, and most others who do poorly, do so for one basic reason—they have not developed the self-management skills that enable them to maintain the right balance between work and everything else in life. They are motivated by the pursuit of pleasure and the avoidance of discomfort (work). Frankly, my teaching experience has led me to believe that the most dangerous word in the English language is, "Fun."

The college years are critical for most students because it is the first time they will not be under the daily influence of their parents and other family members; thus, they have to develop and apply self-management skills on their own. In college, self-management is especially important with regard to setting priorities and managing the workload. For example, I never expected to go to college, my parents could not afford it, and I never even considered it. I left home, took a job in another state, and worked for several years until I decided that I wanted to go to college. As a result, I had the barest of qualifications to get into college, and I did not know how to study. Hence, my first year of college was brutal.

But I had a goal; I did not want to be another blue-collar worker waiting on the street corner with his lunch bucket for the bus to take him to the mill or the mines. I did not want to spend forty years doing the same thing day after day while trying to support myself and my family through strikes, layoffs, deindustrialization, and every other economic trauma that I saw my parents and relatives live through.

I am certain that I was more motivated to pass my courses than my fellow freshmen. I had only one chance; if I failed, it was back to the mill and forty years of toil. During my freshman year of college I had to work day and night just to keep up; however, I was determined to get an education, become an engineer, and change my life. I accomplished my goal and improved my life in ways that I could not have imagined. This was possible because I learned two of the most important elements of self-management, namely, *goal setting* and *motivation*. You have to know what you want, it has to be important to you, and you must have a burning desire to accomplish your goal.

In addition to becoming your own person, college is the time to prepare yourself for your chosen career. Unfortunate is the student who does not know what they want to do in the working phase of their life. From what I have seen, too many students take courses that do little to help them earn a living.

Worse yet is the student who is in a course of study he or she does not want. When I was in my senior year of college, a bunch of us engineers were sitting around musing the fact that we had made it, and we were about to graduate and start our careers in engineering. We were startled when one in our group said, "I hate engineering; I never wanted to study engineering." Someone asked, "Why in the world did you spend four years suffering through engineering—what the hell did you really want to do?" "My parents made me take engineering because they figured that was how I would get a good job; I really wanted to be a coach," was the reply. To this day I am still shocked when I think about that incident. I know that the individual in question spent his working career bouncing from one job to another; and, as far as I know he never became a coach in any sport—a good example of dreams unrealized.

An important part of self-management is finding what you are good at, being realistic about your strengths and weaknesses, and taking charge of your life to move toward your goals no matter what someone else wants. This is especially critical when you transition from college into the early phase of your career.

EARLY CAREER

A typical working career will span some forty-five years. I define the early-career phase of your life as the first ten to fifteen years after leaving college, your mid-career phase will run about fifteen to twenty years, and finally your late-career phase will be at least another ten to fifteen years depending on when you decide to retire.

The early-career phase is probably the most dramatic period in a person's life. It is during this period that most people start working at the profession they will pursue for most of their lives. In this phase, most get married, start a family, and make major investments in cars, furniture, homes and everything else. It is also during this period that no small majority will change jobs, get divorced, remarry, and basically start over again. From my observations, by the end of the early career phase, most people are locked into a type of life that will change little until they die.

Those who have created a foundation of effective self-management skills in their youth and college years will tend to build on this foundation as they grow and mature through their early career years. A small majority who did not have a basis for effective self-management will address their weaknesses and begin to construct the necessary self-management capabilities in order to prevail in their professional and personal lives.

Regardless if you are a corporate soldier or an entrepreneur, you must know yourself, know what you like, what you are good at, and where to direct your efforts for maximum results. Individuals who rise up the corporate ranks quickly and entrepreneurs who grow their enterprises successfully, do so because they produce results—they make things happen. The average performer or poor performer will do what is proscribed and obvious but little more. The top performers know how to get the most out of the time available and the resources (mental and physical) they have to work with; they know how to manage themselves through the volatility of the world they live and work in.

Unfortunately, people who have not developed effective self-management capabilities will never change or improve. The difference between those who are effective self-managers and those who are not becomes dramatically evident by the time an individual reaches the mid-career phase of his or her life.

MID-CAREER

Most people will reach the peak of their career in about fifteen to twenty years. Some of these individuals will become high-level managers, others successful entrepreneurs, some will be stuck in dead-end jobs, and some will bounce from one undertaking to another or drop out completely. With few exceptions, most will continue to do the same thing for the remainder of their working life. Mid-career is also that point in time when many men and some women will experience a mid-life crisis.

From what I have seen, individuals experiencing mid-life crisis tend to be disappointed and unhappy about where they are and what they have accomplished in their lives. "Is this all there is?" is the question they ask themselves. I think many of these people subconsciously feel that they should have done better or accomplished greater things.

I will not describe some of the foolish things that I have seen victims of a mid-life crises get into; however; it seems clear to me that many of these individuals never formulated meaningful life goals or developed the self-management skills necessary to realize their true potential.

On the other hand, I do know a few individuals who, during mid-life crisis, took stock of themselves, reshaped their lives, and moved into a new and more fulfilling career. In particular, one person I had mentored from time to time left a mid-level management job, started his own business, and spent the remainder of his professional life as a very happy, creative, and financially successful entrepreneur. This transformation was a direct result of an in-depth self-analysis, a striking change in thinking, and a realignment of self-management skills. This transformation did not happen overnight, but as my friend said, "My mid-life crisis scared the hell out of me and motivated me to do something to change my life."

Mid-career is an important phase in your life, especially if you are unhappy or dissatisfied with what you are doing. If you are not satisfied with your life in mid-career, you need to change; otherwise, you will be dissatisfied and unhappy the rest of your life. However, in order to change you need to know what to change, when to change, how to change, and the motivation and self-discipline to actually make the change.

It is sad that many people will not even make the attempt to change. They continue in their well-worn-grooves until retirement, where they continue to be dissatisfied and unhappy. Worse yet is that some of these individuals will be blasted out of their groove by downsizing, layoffs, or forced early retirement. Sometimes these traumatic shocks are enough to motivate people to change; however, there are those who just give up and drop out.

When you move into the late-career phase of your life, you will face another set of challenges that will determine how well you will live in the retirement years of your life.

LATE CAREER

The last ten to fifteen years of your working life can be happy and rewarding or stressful and disappointing, depending on how well you manage yourself. In late career, many individuals in the corporate environment will have reached their peak position and earnings level and will spend their remaining years hoping they can make it to retirement. Still for others, late career is an opportunity to capitalize on the skills developed over the years to beat out the competition and get that big promotion. The difference between those who are just hanging on and those who still have the potential to advance has to do, in large measure, with their level of motivation, intellectual development, and self-management capabilities.

For the entrepreneur, late career is the opportunity to expand your business to the level commensurate with your interests and lifestyle. It is also the opportunity to enhance and cultivate your non-business interests and to optimize your wealth in preparation for retirement. You must start preparing for retirement ten to fifteen years before you actually retire. There is a whole range of issues that you need to deal with to get ready for retirement, and we will discuss these in Chapter 19.

Late career is the time to start thinking and planning for where you will live in retirement, what you will do when you retire, and how you will live without the purpose, energy and discipline that you derive from your work. This is not as simple as it sounds because, to have a rewarding and enjoyable retirement, you need to re-frame your mental model and create one that is appropriate to a lifestyle that is completely different from the one you have experienced for the past forty to fifty years.

EARLY RETIREMENT

I define early retirement as the first two to three years after you stop working. The early-retirement phase is a stressful period of adjustment and adaptation. Making the transition from forty to fifty years of work is difficult; it is especially difficult for those who, for one reason or another, were forced into early retirement. Many of these individuals can still be productive; however, most will never have any meaningful work for the rest of their lives. Some of the people I know in this situation have become bitter, resorted to drink or worse, and have experienced serious emotional and health problems. On the other hand, I know others who took their forced retirement as an opportunity to do what they always wanted; some started a business, others became teachers and mentors, still others became volunteers in their communities.

As I see it, transitioning successfully from working life into early retirement has a lot to do with physical, mental, emotional, and ethical resources. These four resources are also critical to ensuring success and happiness in the late-retirement phase of your life.

LATE RETIREMENT

Late retirement is the final phase of your life which may run another twenty years or more. The key to enjoyable and successful living in this phase is your health. If you employed prudent self-management during all the phases of your life, you will more than likely be in good physical health. And if you are in good physical health, you will more likely be happy and enjoy sound mental health. Late retirement is the period in your life when you can realize your life-long dream outside of your work. But you have to be careful; your retirement dream may not be as great as you expect.

I have friends who dreamed of retiring and playing golf every day for the rest of their lives. Some got bored after a few years and actually went back to work; others had conflicts with their wives who did not want to be golf widows.

In another case, there was a guy and his wife who dreamed about sailing around the world in their boat. Upon retirement they immediately set out to pursue their dream; they made detailed preparations and set sail from San Diego to Hawaii; however, by the time they reached Hawaii they decided they hated each other, sold the boat, and got divorced.

I have noted that just as there is a mid-life crisis, there is also a late-retirement crisis. I have seen retired people squander their money on gambling, drinking, fast cars, extra-marital affairs, and eventually, divorce. It is tragic that people who have worked hard, raised their families, and positioned themselves to live a comfortable retirement should wreck their lives at the very end. This is not the way to manage a life.

Effective Self-Management

Effective self-management means that you manage and direct your physical, mental, emotional, and ethical resources (see Exhibit 15-3) in a way that enables you to realize your maximum human potential. These four resources are interrelated, and they determine to a large degree the level of happiness and success you will achieve in your personal and professional life. Let us take a look at each of these important components.

PHYSICAL

How well you manage your physical resources will determine if you remain healthy, strong, energetic, and vital throughout your life.

People who effectively manage their physical health eat sensibly, avoid health killers (tobacco, alcohol, drugs), and exercise regularly. I cannot emphasize strongly enough the importance of maintaining good physical health consistently over your lifetime. This is especially true for the entrepreneur just starting out. When you work on your own, everything depends on your being able to work. It's unfortunate, but I have seen too many entrepreneurs cut down in their prime by heart attacks or strokes brought on by their high blood pressure or their being overweight. Many of these problems are a matter of simple neglect. In addition to effectively managing your physical health, you must also manage your mental well-being.

Effective Self-management

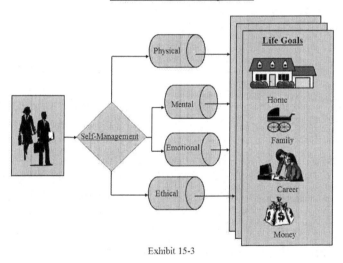

Exhibit 15-3

MENTAL

A sound mind in a sound body is the classical criteria for a happy and successful life. To grow and prosper you must manage your intellectual development to continually expand your knowledge and understanding of yourself and the world you live in. Continuous learning should be a way of life; I know too many people who, once they left college, never read a book or explored anything outside of their work or business environment. Truly successful people enhance their understanding, creativity, and problem solving abilities by expanding their knowledge-base in many different areas.

Those who practice life-long learning are more self-confident, resilient, and open to new ideas, concepts, and change. Enhancing your mental resources will also improve your emotional strength.

EMOTIONAL

To be successful in your project management business as well as your personal life you must be able to deal with ambiguity, change, conflict, and stress. Individuals with a sound emotional foundation will be able to thrive in chaos, establish order, and solve problems effectively. Typically these people are confident, fearless, optimistic, and happy. A sound emotional platform is the result of physical well-being, mental stimulation through learning, and ethical and spiritual development.

ETHICAL AND SPIRITUAL

At the core of self-management is a set of values. You are what you believe, you manage what you consider important, and you conduct your affairs based on what you think is right. The starting point for effective self-management is to look deep inside yourself and determine what you truly value. What is most important in your life? Is it your family, career, money, fame, reputation, religion, salvation, or something else?

Those who do not have a strong set of ethical and spiritual values will adjust their views, goals, and priorities to suit the situation and their desires at that moment with little regard for the impact on others. Those who lie, cheat, or steal can always justify their actions despite the harm and pain it may cause their associates, friends, or loved ones. Without a solid ethical and spiritual foundation it is easy to rationalize everything you do even when you know it's wrong.

How to Develop the Essential Self-Management Skills

When you are on your own, everything is on your shoulders. Like the lonely long distance runner, your speed, endurance, and resolve determines your success, and this, to a large degree, is based on the self-management you use to prepare yourself for the big race and to sustain yourself during the race. Some people seem to have natural, inbred, self-management skills while others have to work hard to develop and master these skills. For most of us, it is a matter of recognizing our weaknesses and mastering the needed skills in order to become better at managing ourselves.

Self-management effectiveness depends on the environment in which you live, the influence of family, friends, and associates, and your natural preferences based on your personality and genetics. However, there are fundamental skills everyone can master that are indispensable to success and happiness. You can learn and master these skills through a process of self-analysis, development, and application.

SELF ANALYSIS

You cannot manage yourself effectively unless you know yourself well. Most people believe they know themselves, but at best they have only a vague feeling of their strengths, weaknesses, and desires. Self-analysis requires an in-depth, objective probing of oneself with appraisal and feedback from others.

A good friend of mine was convinced he had a great sense of humor; he even admitted to me that he secretly wanted to be a stand-up comedian. However, after two failed marriages he decided to get some professional help. What he discovered was shocking; he was not funny, he did not have a good sense of humor, and he was using humor to mask his fears and insecurity. After considerable in-depth analysis my friend came to grips with who he really was and became a better man because of it. As a result he did not become a comedian to make people laugh; instead he became a minister who was very successful helping people with serious addictions.

The average person will probably not have these deep-seated self-understanding problems; therefore, the following appraisals will be enough to set the stage for understanding your self-management capabilities and needs.

Define your preferences—Identify your interests, what you do well, and what you most like to do. Also try to identify why you enjoy doing these things; are they easy to do, do they give you personal satisfaction, do they make you look good, or do they set you apart from others?

Define your temperament—Are you basically a field marshal, analyst, politician, or care giver? Are you an introvert or extravert? It is extremely important to understand your temperament (See Chapter

7) because this is at the core of your self-management skills and is the one area that you cannot change in any meaningful way.

Define your values—What is important in your life? Is it your religion, family, career, money, lifestyle? How solid are your values? In other words, are they deep-rooted or are they influenced by what others think? Understanding your personal values is critical because they will subconsciously drive your thinking, decisions, and actions.

Evaluate your self-management capabilities—Qualities that form the foundation for effective self-management are goals, plans and schedules, motivation and self-discipline, self-reliance and resilience, and tolerance of ambiguity and change. You must determine how effective you are in each of these areas and develop programs to improve your self-management skills.

DEVELOPMENT AND APPLICATION

To develop or sharpen your self-management skills, ensure that you take the time to do a self-analysis to determine your preferences, temperament and values. These are to a large degree interrelated and are the foundation for almost everything you do in life. If you are certain that you know yourself, begin by working on goal-setting skills.

Goals—Goals are the targets you set for yourself. Well-defined goals give you a purpose and a sense of direction. When you have no goals or poorly defined goals, you wander around in the fog and confusion of life's conflicting demands and priorities.

Well-defined goals are specific, realistic, measurable, and are congruent with your preferences, temperament, and values. You must write out your goals; if you can't write them out, you do not have well-defined goals. Get in the habit of developing and documenting long-term goals (five, ten, twenty-year goals) and short-term goals (monthly and yearly). Post your goals where you can see them daily. Also keep a log book of your goals to check and record progress at regular intervals.

Goals must be realistic; in addition to being congruent with your preferences, temperament, and values you must also have the skills to accomplish your goals. If you don't have the prerequisite skills, then develop a plan to obtain these skills. In order to inculcate your goals, practice visualization and self-talk about your goals. Reinforce your visualization and self-talk with plans and schedules for accomplishing your goals.

Plans and Schedules—Goals by themselves will never come to fruition without a specific plan of action. Develop a written plan and a schedule for the resources (mental and physical) and tasks (work) required to accomplish your goals. Make it a habit to review and evaluate your progress against your plan at regular intervals. Revise and expand your plan as needed to reflect real world conditions and changes in your life.

In addition to laying out a realistic path to accomplish your goals, plans and schedules are also tools that aid motivation and self-discipline to ensure that you work your plans as scheduled.

Motivation and Self-Discipline—The passion and desire to accomplish a specific goal and the self-discipline to keep working toward that goal are reinforced and amplified every time you review your plans and schedules. When you develop and document the specific steps toward your goals, you establish a contract with yourself that mentally obligates and disciplines you to achieve your goals.

Motivation and self-discipline are interrelated. Motivation provides the psychological energy to keep you working on your goal and helps to reinforce your self-discipline by mentally shielding you from other diversions. However, self-discipline is a learned skill and can be improved through practice. In the same way that the long-distance runner builds strength and endurance by adding extra miles to his or her training schedule, the individual improves self-discipline every time he or she foregoes a pleasure or some diversion to keep working on their goals.

Self-Reliance and Resilience—Your psychological makeup determines the degree of your self-reliance and resilience; however, everyone tends to improve their self-reliance and resilience as they deal with changes in their lives. The student who leaves home for college or the stay-at-home housewife who suddenly loses a husband and has to go to work and take care of her family on her own, all build up their self-reliance and resilience. You can improve your self-reliance and resilience by moving out of your comfort zone. You need to undertake new and different challenges, travel to different places, and associate with people outside your family, friends, and profession.

Constantly testing yourself with new and different situations will condition you to stand on your own and deal with the unexpected.

Tolerance of Ambiguity and Change—If you are fortunate to live in a stable and secure environment, you more than likely will not be comfortable in a situation where you must face ambiguity and change. If you are suddenly thrust into such an environment, you either learn to adapt or you become dysfunctional. Learning to adapt is to a large extent a matter of attitude. If you believe that ambiguity and change are a normal part of life and business, then you will make the necessary adjustments to function in this environment. However, if you believe ambiguity and change are out of the ordinary and should be avoided, you will never develop the necessary coping skills. You can only develop the appropriate coping skills by working in areas that present high levels of ambiguity and change. The longer you work in these areas, the more you will build up your tolerance and coping skills.

It is important for the entrepreneur in a project management business to be especially adroit at dealing with ambiguity and change. This ability is vital in showing clients that you have the leadership, confidence, and skills to prevail regardless how chaotic and difficult their project may be.

Developing and improving self-management skills is a lifelong process. You need to retune and reinforce your self-management skills as you transition through the various phases of your life. Regardless of the phase of life you are in now, you can always improve your self-management skills to enhance your success and happiness.

Summary

Everything you are and everything you hope to be depends on the effective self-management of your physical, mental, emotional, ethical, and spiritual resources.

To become an effective self-manager you need to know yourself, your preferences, temperament, and values; furthermore, you must evaluate your self-management capabilities.

To develop or sharpen your self-management skills you should:

- Establish long term and short term goals

- Practice visualization and self-talk to inculcate your goals
- Design plans and schedules to accomplish your goals
- Use motivation and self-discipline to implement your plans and schedules to work toward your goals
- Enhance your self-reliance and resilience to deal with obstacles you encounter in working toward your goal
- Learn to tolerate ambiguity and change across all the phases of your life

It is never too late to develop and improve your self-management skills.

Chapter 16

How to Manage Risk

Avoid Getting Hurt

The potential for business failure scares the hell out of most individuals and is one reason why many do not go into business. People do not want to take the risk of working hard only to lose their savings and perhaps go into debt for the rest of their lives. Risk of failure is certainly an ever-present possibility in any entrepreneurial undertaking. However, in today's global economy, the possibility of losing your job to outsourcing or downsizing is also a very real risk. As I see it, when you have your own business you have a significant advantage because you are in a position to manage your risk. As an employee, there is little you can do to deal with the possibility of losing your job. In this chapter we want to take a pragmatic look at risk and what we can do to control risk in a project management business.

Project Risk Fundamentals

To be a successful provider of project management services you must understand the subject of risk, both the risks inherent in client projects as well as the risk issues that are unique to a project management business.

By definition, risk is the exposure to the *chance* of injury or loss. In business as well as in life, we want to manage risk to prevent the possibility of getting hurt or losing money. Equally important, we want to manage risk to create the best odds for success. Therefore, we may take risks to realize a gain or reward. Unfortunately, the prevailing philosophy seems to be that you have to take high risk to make big gains. I suspect this philosophy comes out of Wall Street and the financial world of speculative investments. However, I don't buy this philosophy; as far as I am concerned, you want to be smart and make big gains with little or no risk. This has been my over-arching philosophy for my project management business.

Many books have been written on the subject of risk and risk management, and virtually every college and university around the world offers courses on these topics. In addition, numerous computer programs have been developed to analyze and evaluate risk. Managing risk is an especially important topic in project management because project success or failure can literally determine the financial viability or even the survival of a corporation. Project risk is characterized by three risk factors:

- The Risk Event
- The Risk Probability
- The Impact of the Event or the Amount at Stake

The Risk Event is a specific, unwanted occurrence; in other words, what can go wrong that will harm the project's cost, schedule, or performance objectives.

The Risk Probability is the likelihood that the event will actually happen. We are particularly concerned with events that have a high probability of coming to fruition; we focus on those events to determine how much harm may result, which brings us to the impact of the event.

The Impact of the Event is what we might lose if the risk actually happens. The question of how much harm the risk event will cause is important because a risk event may have only minor consequences so we don't have to worry too much about it. On the other hand, we must be concerned about those risk events that can seriously hurt a project. Typically a risk management program will concentrate on the high probability, high impact events and develop specific plans to mitigate the risk. A comprehensive risk management process is shown in Exhibit 16-1.

Risk Management Process

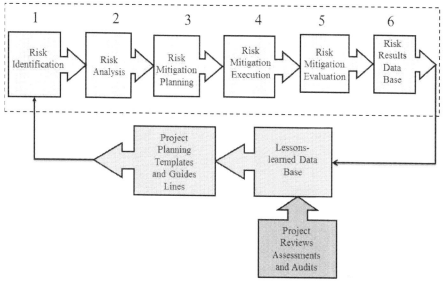

Exhibit 16-1

In most projects risk generally boils down to:

- **Cost Risk**—It will cost more than planned. There may be a potential for a significant cost overrun, so much so, that the project will be terminated. This is not an uncommon occurrence on military projects, software projects, or R&D projects. Therefore, managing those events or activities that can lead to cost escalation is a major risk-management task.

- **Schedule Risk**—It will take longer than planned. Schedule delays can mean that new products do not get to market ahead of the competition, or facilities are not made operational when needed, or deliverables are not turned over to the client as promised. In today's highly competitive global marketplace, most projects are intensely schedule driven. Also, virtually all schedule delays can be translated into cost overruns.

- **Technical Risk**—The product or service is not working as specified. Technical risks are all too common in the world of project management; for example, computer programs that don't work or are released minus all the promised functionality; operational systems and/or structures that perform poorly or fail completely. We need only to look at the Three Mile Island project to appreciate the impact that technical issues have on a corporation. In addition to customer or consumer dissatisfaction, technical issues almost always contribute to cost and schedule overruns.

- **Other Risk Issues**—In today's complex society there are numerous stakeholder, political, social, environmental, and legal issues that projects deal with. These risk issues must be identified early and managed before they become insurmountable problems. In addition, Acts-of-God risk issues such as floods, earthquakes, lighting strikes, and severe weather situations must also be taken into consideration. Finally, the specter of terror attacks, criminal acts, and cybercrime are all risk issues that cannot be ignored by prudent project managers.

Risk management is an integral part of project planning. All project plans must identify and evaluate the risk involved in the project and develop strategies to mitigate the risk. As a rule, the level of detailed planning and control required for a project must be commensurate with the risk involved. It is commonsense that high-risk undertakings should be planned in-depth and firmly controlled to ensure success. On the other hand, routine projects, especially those where we have a lot of experience, will not require extensive project plans or sophisticated project control systems. Most of the literature on risk management tends to make it a complex subject; however, risk management consists of five basic steps (see Exhibit 16-2).

Risk Management - Five Step Process

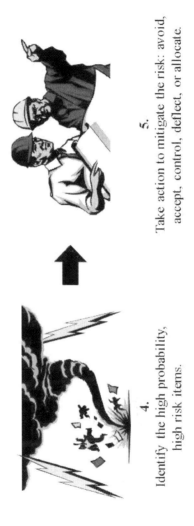

1. Identify the project risk. What can go wrong?

2. Determine the chances (probability) of the risk actually happening.

3. What is the impact if the risk actually happens?

4. Identify the high probability, high risk items.

5. Take action to mitigate the risk: avoid, accept, control, deflect, or allocate.

Exhibit 16-2

241

1. Identify the project risk; ask, "What can go wrong?" There are a number of ways to determine this. Use historical data from past projects, lessons learned, weather reports, and private and public databases. Confer with experts, experienced personnel, consultants, universities, government agencies, and research firms. Review each phase of the project plan and conduct what-if reviews to explore worst-case scenarios.

2. Determine the chances of the risk actually happening. As a start, you can classify risk events as high, medium, or low. Later, a more analytical evaluation of the probability of the risk can be made. There is an extensive portfolio of software tools available to help assess the probability of things going wrong. In addition, past experience can aid in determining the probability of risk in certain types of project undertakings.

3. Ascertain the impact on the project if the risk actually happens. How much harm can a particular risk issue create? Many risk issues have only a moderate impact on a project and these can be dealt with easily. It is important that the impact analysis identify the risks that can have a significant bearing on project success.

Keep in mind that the risk analysis should also examine the potential for reward or gain. It may be appropriate to take prudent risk in order to realize a substantial gain. It may be possible to take short cuts in some processes and procedures to reduce cost or improve the schedule without compromising quality or technical performance.

4. Identify all of the project's high probability, high impact risk items. These are the risks that must be mitigated in order to give the project the best chance for success.

5. Finally, take specific action to mitigate the high probability, high impact risk items. There are four basic ways of dealing with the risk items: avoidance, acceptance, control, and allocation or deflection.

Avoidance—If the impact of the risk is severe, we may choose not to engage in the effort. In other words, we avoid the risk by not doing a task or by doing something differently. Risk can also be avoided by eliminating unknowns, conducting tests, getting additional information, and so on.

Acceptance—On the other hand, if we can live with the consequences of the risk, or if we decide that the potential reward or gain justifies the risk, then we may accept the risk.

Control—Develop plans to eliminate the risk or reduce it to acceptable limits. Strategies may include: subdividing tasks into smaller, more easily managed work packages; allocating more cost, schedule, or human resources to the task; and improving processes, procedures, and work practices.

Allocation or Deflection—This strategy moves risk to the party who is in the best position to handle the risk. Typically this party has the right experience, skills, expertise, and resources to deal with the risk.

When you are working on a client project, it is important to understand the conditions and situations that create project risk. This knowledge will enable you to provide meaningful products and services that contribute to project success. When you provide services or products that reduce or eliminate risk to a client's project, you will build a relationship that gives you significant competitive advantage.

Understanding the risk inherent in client projects is only one facet of ensuring your business success. The other aspect is to understand the risk issues unique to your project management business.

Risk Issues in a Project Management Business

Risk issues over the life of a typical client engagement (see Exhibit 16-3) must be assessed for each phase of activity. Failure to address the risk in one phase of a project will generally set the stage for additional problems in succeeding phases. Some of the risk issues we will address are unique to a project management business; others are common to all businesses.

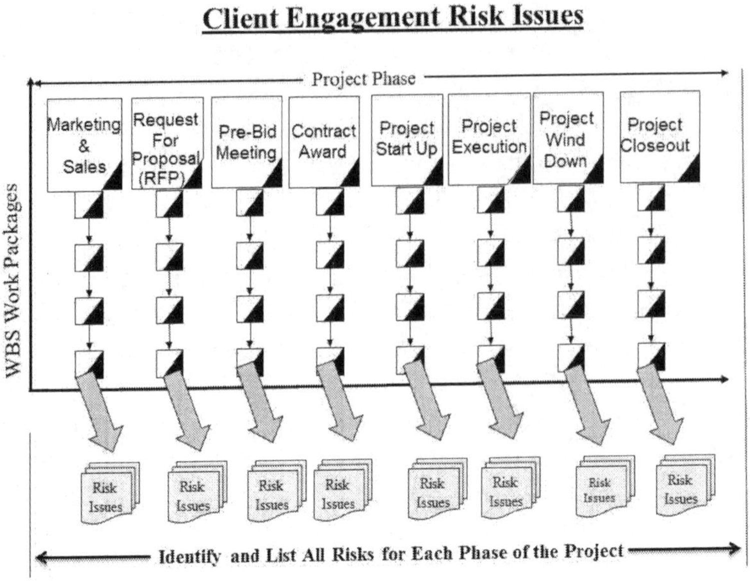

Client Engagement Risk Issues

Exhibit 16-3

Marketing & Sales Phase—The risk in this phase is that you may spend too much time and money promoting services that are not in demand or are widely offered by other firms.

This is a common risk, especially if you are just starting out. You can spend a lot of money on advertising that will not generate any business. You may be tempted to advertise in professional journals or to mail promotional materials; in most cases this is a waste of money. Some professionals I have talked with believe you need just one big hit and the advertising will have paid for itself. I know enough people who have gone broke using this approach. The shotgun method does not work for a knowledge-based business like project management. As far as I am concerned, the only effective marketing involves eye ball to eye ball contact with a potential client or powerful referrals from credible sources, i.e., other clients, or through professional venues such as conferences, seminars, or technical publications.

Furthermore, you can spend a lot of time making cold calls to clients to promote services that many others are offering. Before you go into business, you must know exactly what products and/or services you will offer to your target clients. These offerings must set you apart from the competition. To the maximum extent possible, you should offer products and/or services that are unique or customized specifically for that client. This is how you obtain significant competitive advantage.

Proposal Phase—Probably the greatest risk for all new project management businesses is spending time and money on proposals that you have a low probability of winning. You can actually put yourself out of business by proposing job after job and never generating any revenue.

Early in my business I responded to a Request for Proposal (RFP) from a major aerospace corporation. The project involved development and implementation of an extensive project management training and support program. Since I had considerable experience in this area, I felt that I had a good shot at getting this project even though I had never provided services to this client before. More than a dozen firms were bidding on this job. My associates and I traveled to the client's headquarters, several states away, to attend the bidder's conference. We prepared a very extensive proposal and competitively priced our services.

I was delighted when we made the short list. However, we had to undergo another round of proposal refinements, price re-bidding, and responding to questions. Of course, while doing this work we were not generating any revenue. The whole process consumed about three months before the client made their decision. Up to the very end, the client gave us clear indications that we were one of the top contenders. Therefore, I was stunned when we were informed that we did not get the job. I requested a debriefing to find out where we went wrong.

In reviewing the client's selection criteria, item by item, we found that we rated high on every point. Furthermore, we found that we actually scored higher than the winner in several key areas. The contract manager admitted they had a real problem in not selecting us for the project. When I asked why we were not selected he said, "Well frankly, we did not know you; however we know the other firm because they worked for us before." I was upset to hear this and I said, "What you are telling me is that there was no way I could win this job." The contract manager said, "Look, contact the winning firm; perhaps they will subcontract some of the project work to your organization, and we would be happy to support this."

Just to satisfy my curiosity I did contact the winning company. They were a small consulting firm located on the Washington DC beltway. I met the principals and discovered that they were retired military officers. They knew the contracting manager and project managers at the aerospace company who were also retired military personnel. The picture was clear; everyone who bid on this job was up against the old boys' club, the double-dippers, retired military personnel who now had a second career in industry. The professional bonds among them were very strong. Despite all the regulations to make the government contract bidding process as fair and equitable as possible, the old boys' network prevailed.

I figured I would have to generate at least several months of revenue to pay for this ill-fated proposal effort. Clearly, small organizations cannot afford to undertake major proposal efforts without assurance that they have a better than average chance of being successful. I was happy that this costly learning experience happened early in my business career. From that point on I made it a policy not to take the lead on any major proposal efforts. Furthermore, I avoided going after jobs where another firm had been working for the client for a long time, except when I discovered that the competition had screwed up and was on the outs with the client.

Whenever possible I avoid writing proposals; often, when I do submit a proposal package, the bulk of the material is boilerplate. In other words, I make extensive use of templates; hence, my investment in proposal preparation time is minimal. As we got smarter about proposals, we even got clients to write the proposal for us. Also, over the years we built up a strong rapport with several clients, and we often received sole-source contracts.

Contract Award Phase—A major risk in the contract award phase is accepting onerous contract terms and conditions or poorly defined contract deliverables primarily because you need the work.

It is imperative that you take on only work that you are capable of doing under conditions that enable you to be successful. As a matter of policy, corporations lay out terms and conditions that are most favorable to them, and they strive to move as much risk to the contractor as possible. In many cases the client's contract requirements are standard boilerplate and may not be applicable to your particular assignment. I have found that most clients are reasonable, and they will modify the contract if you explain why you cannot accept the contract as written. If you cannot get some relief from the client, it may be wise to walk away from a particularly risky or demanding contract.

Project Start-up Phase—Initiating a project assignment with little or no planning will generate considerable risk. It is a great feeling to beat out the competition and win a challenging and hopefully profitable contract. There is a tremendous urge to jump right in and start doing the work. The project tasks may be obvious, and you may have scoped the project thoroughly; however, if you do not step back, review the contract in detail, and develop an appropriately detailed project plan, you will live to regret it. One of the classic reasons for project failure is poor or inadequate project planning.

Project plans discipline the work effort and provide a beacon to guide all the project participants. To ensure a well-managed and profitable project engagement, you must put in place an appropriately detailed plan and you must manage to that plan. Otherwise, you will get caught up in daily firefighting and problem solving and slip into cost and schedule overruns.

Project Execution Phase—In this phase of the project there is a risk of getting caught up in the client's internal conflicts and political struggles. In today's downsizing, outsourcing, corporate-world conflict, competition, and turf wars are commonplace. You have to work hard not to get caught up in the organization's internal politics because no matter who wins, you lose. The only way to avoid this is to remain totally professional and to focus on the goals of the project, your contract commitments, and working your project plan.

Project Wind Down Phase—A major risk in any project is that key personnel will begin to leave the project before the final phase is completed. Since all projects are life limited, project personnel know that they will be out of a job when the project is over. Hence, project participants move to position themselves with a new assignment before the end of the project. This issue must be addressed in the project plan and appropriate incentives and transition routines put into place to deal with this problem.

Project Close Out Phase—There is always a risk that excessive project cleanup work will adversely impact the project cost, schedule, and performance objectives. The adage that the last 10 percent of the project contributes to 90 percent of cost and schedule overruns has a lot of truth to it. This problem is almost always due to poor or incomplete project planning.

If you step back and look at the risk inherent in a project management business, you can see that in most cases the risk is easily identified and can be managed. Common sense, good planning, and disciplined management of work against the project plan will address 99 percent of most risk issues that you will face in your project management business. Nevertheless, there is always that remaining 1 percent of unexpected risk for which you must prepare.

Personal Risk

In my experience, unexpected risks tend to involve the low probability, high impact risk that you may encounter over the life of your project management business. These risks include health, accidents, Acts of God, fraud, crime, and terror attacks. You may not think these are significant risk issues; however, these risks are real, and unless you implement appropriate safe guards, you could suffer devastating losses. Consider the following situations.

Health Risk—As an individual entrepreneur, maintaining good health is absolutely vital. If you become seriously ill and cannot work, your business will fail. If you do not keep physically fit you will not be able to perform with vitality and energy. The net result is that the stress and demands of everyday work and life will take its toll, and you will become overweight, suffer high blood pressure, and a host of other modern ills.

Managing health risk is simple and well known: exercise regularly, maintain a healthy diet, and avoid tobacco, alcohol, and drugs. Maintain a life balanced between work, family, and other activities to foster good mental health. If you want to be successful over the long run and glide into retirement fit, happy, and rich, you must have a systematic program for sound mental and physical health.

Accidents—Accidents can and do happen, usually at the worst possible time. Travel is necessary in a project management business. Driving provides the greatest risk of all accidents. To minimize this risk, don't drink and drive, avoid long drives when you're tired, and don't drive in severe weather.

A number of years ago I was returning from a business trip when I got caught in a nasty ice and snowstorm on the Pennsylvania Turnpike. I should have gotten off the highway and headed for the nearest motel; however, I had been away from home for some time, I was really beat, and I just wanted to get home and go to bed. As conditions worsened, I had to drive slower and slower; however, I felt I had things under control and was confident about making it. Nevertheless, I did not count on the other driver who shot past me, hit a patch of ice, spun out, bounced off the divider, and forced me into a ditch. Luckily I was unhurt; however, while I sat in the ditch, several cars whizzed by me and smashed into the first car. Many people were hurt; it took hours to clean up the mess. Right then and there I resolved to never again drive in really bad weather.

As you grow your business you will probably have to do a lot of air travel. In my case I did a lot of international travel. Based on advice from a friend who is an aviation expert, I avoid flying third-world airlines. My friend warned me that the maintenance practices of third-world airlines were poor at best.

In the 60s and 70s I also avoided flying Eastern Block airlines. On one of my business trips I flew Aeroflot from Moscow to Tbilisi. When I got to my seat near the back of the plane, I noted that every seat was taken, but people were still boarding the plane and jamming the aisle. I thought certainly they are not going to fly with people standing in the aisle. The doors closed, the engines fired up, the plane began to move; and then the plane stopped abruptly. The cockpit door flew open and the pilot came out and started yelling at the passengers standing in the aisle. The pilot opened the plane's door and literarily threw a number of the standing passengers off the plane. The pilot, who had a pistol strapped to his waist, did not clear all the people out of the aisle. About a half a dozen big guys were still standing in the aisle, talking to each other, laughing, and hanging on to the luggage rack when the plane took off. Apparently, during those days, standing room only was not uncommon on domestic Russian flights.

A fellow passenger, an Armenian rug merchant from New York City, noted my apprehension and tried to assure me that this was a very safe plane and the pilot was very experienced. I believe the pilot was a former MIG pilot. The plane was being flown like a fighter plane; abrupt climbs, hard banks, and steep descents. The landing in

Tbilisi was something to talk about; we hit the runway so hard that a section of the ceiling light fell out. Not to worry; the Russian air stewards came down the aisle, picked up the light fixture, and slammed it back into place. The Russian guys standing in the aisle paid no attention to the whole affair and just continued talking and laughing. My first task when I got off the plane was to find the bar and get a stiff drink.

Over the years that I traveled around the world I had a strict policy to fly only major American or European carriers.

Acts of God—Acts of God are those unexpected events of nature that you really can't plan for. For example, the first month I set up my home-based office, we experienced a terrific summer thunderstorm. At the height of the storm our house was hit by lightning. We lost our brand new computer, printer, fax machine, and telephones. In a flash we were out of business. Fortunately, I had business insurance and home-owners insurance, and I had backed up all of our critical files. Nevertheless, it took weeks to collect on the insurance, buy new equipment, and get our office back up to speed. Fortunately, I had associates who let me use their office until we recovered enough to get back to our place. Clearly, there is little to do to prevent the risk of Acts-of-God incidents, but you can reduce the impact somewhat with insurance, backup plans, and support from others.

Fraud and Crime—No law or contract will prevent an individual from resorting to fraud or committing a crime if they are unethical and want to profit at your expense. An entrepreneur friend I know, who traveled a lot, hired the wife of one of his consultants as an office manager to take care of bills, invoices, payroll, insurance, and all the other administrative requirements of his business. She was efficient, dedicated, and freed my friend from all the paperwork that he hated; unfortunately, she was also a clever thief who defrauded my friend of tens of thousands of dollars.

When she was discovered, her defense was that she was suffering from emotional problems and she resented the fact that my friend was making so much money. She promised to repay everything she took, so my friend did not prosecute; however, she left and took a job with another company and did the same thing. When the other firm found out what she was doing, they had her arrested and prosecuted and she was sent to jail. My friend was never able to recover his losses.

The risk of fraud and crime is real, and you must protect yourself; be vigilant, deal only with ethical people with a proven track record of trust, and avoid putting people into situations where they may be tempted to stray to the dark side. Giving people easy access to large sums of money, not exercising prudent oversight, and failing to implement checks and balances in your business is asking for trouble.

Terror—The world has changed much, and America is no longer the island of security that we enjoyed through much of our history. Like most people, I took for granted the safety of our country.

Over the years I established a client base in New York City. I really enjoyed working in the city and having the opportunity to take in a show or two, go to my favorite restaurant, or just absorb the energy of the city. I had several clients in the World Trade Center. For more than fifteen years I was in and out of the World Trade Center working on a variety of projects. I should have been working on a client project in the South Tower of the World Trade Center on September 11, 2001. However, I had to change my schedule to be present at a civil trial in Pennsylvania. Part way through the trial, the judge stopped the proceedings to take a message from the court clerk; you can imagine our shock when the judge announced that he was halting the trial because the country was under attack.

To this day I cannot forget the scenes of aircraft crashing into the twin towers, people jumping from the flaming building, and the horrific collapse of the towers. I had a number of friends and associates who did not survive the attack. I could have been there, but for the hand of fate.

There are many risk issues that you can manage with foresight and planning; however, there are others that are in the hands of a higher power.

Risk Management Rules of Thumb

Here are a few rules of thumb that I have used over the years and that have served me well in running my project management business:

- Don't believe that you have to take high risks to make big gains
- If there is any doubt about the risk, rewards, or probability of success, don't take the risk
- Don't count on good luck to save a bad situation; you never have good luck when you need it most
- If the potential reward is great and you can absorb the impact of the risk if things don't work out, then take the risk

There are stories about famous entrepreneurs who have taken high risk, made and lost great fortunes, only to come back and do it all over. I know gamblers who win big and lose big many times. However, what I have noticed is that over the years these individuals never really get ahead. They seem to love the challenge and excitement of the gamble and are willing to live the traumatic up and down lifestyle when they win and lose. However, I am interested in positive incremental growth and progress, and my guiding principle is, "never lose money."

Summary

To be successful in your project management business you must understand and manage risk.

Risk is characterized by three factors:

- The Risk Event—something that could harm the project
- The Risk Probability—the likelihood of the risk actually happening
- The Impact of the Event or the Amount at Stake—the harm if the risk actually happens

Project risks typically encompass the cost, schedule, and technical parameters of the project; however, they may also include political, social, environmental, legal, and stakeholder issues. In addition, you must consider risk associated with your health, accidents, Acts of God, fraud, crime, and terror.

Risk management is a key element in project planning and must be addressed in every phase of any project that you undertake in your project management business.

Chapter 17

How to Maximize Profits

Getting Rich While Enjoying Life

Far too many management books imply that you have to constantly work hard, take risks, and totally devote yourself to your business, sacrificing everything else in the process in order to get rich. As far as I am concerned, this is stupid and certainly no way to enjoy life. In our project management business the goal is to make more than enough money to support our lifestyle, run our business without killing ourselves, and enjoy life. The key to making this possible is to maximize profit; that is, put into your pocket more of every dollar you can squeeze out of your business. You do not have to be an accountant or a financial expert to know how to do this. You only need to know the most powerful business equation ever invented, that is:

PROFIT = INCOME - EXPENSES

Many years ago I had a course in Engineering Economics, and on the first day our instructor, who was a successful business consultant, put the above equation on the blackboard. He then said: "There are only two ways to generate wealth: spend less and make more." Frankly, this is about the only thing I remember from that course; however, this equation has been a powerful influence on my business life. Therefore, in this chapter we will discuss how to spend less and make more in your project management business.

Spend Less

There are a number of ways you can increase your profits by spending less; these include: control expenses, reduce taxes, leverage discounts and rewards, and optimize your time. Let us consider each one of these.

CONTROL EXPENSES

One of the keys to ensuring a profitable business is to control expenses. Expenses are the cost of doing business. This is money that comes right out of your pocket even if you are not generating revenue. The bad news is that you will have expenses to go into business, you will incur expenses to generate business, and you will have more expenses to operate and grow your business; hence, expenses cannot be totally eliminated. The good news, however, is that for a knowledge-based business like project management there are a number of simple and practical ways to keep these expenses low.

Start-up Expense—It costs money to start a business. You need a place to work, you need tools and equipment, and you need to market and sell your products and services. But, before you start, remember my first rule (see Chapter 4): never borrow money to start your business. If you do, you will have the expense of paying off your loan even when you are not making money. What's more, the cost of starting a project management business is very modest so you should not have to borrow money to go into business.

As I discussed in Chapter 5, don't rent an office when you start your business; instead, set up your business where you live. You don't need a lot of space, but it should be quiet and free from the normal household noises, TV, kids and the dog. Associates I know have set up their offices in bedrooms, basements, garages, and even their RVs. When you have a home office, you can pay yourself rent, save commuting costs, and have more time for billable work; also, if you have extra space you can share it or rent it to fellow entrepreneurs. I know one person who was pressed for space and who operated out of a shopping mall, library, or coffee shop for the first six months he was in business until he teamed up with another individual in his home office.

As far as tools and equipment are concerned, the most important rule is, and this rule applies over the life of your business, buy only what you need. If you are a typical knowledge-worker you probably already have a computer, printer and a cell phone. If not, buy the basic no frills devices; buy what is on sale, or buy used equipment. Shop around to get the best deal for everything you buy for your business;

insurance, supplies and equipment will take a big bite out of your savings, so shop wisely.

When I started my company, money was tight, so I had no choice but to take the time to look for the best buys. I was amazed to find very large price variations on many items I needed for my business. I also found that I could make significant savings by buying used and surplus items. All of my original office furniture came from a company that was modernizing their offices and installing the latest color coordinated cubicles. I was able to purchase solid oak desks and conference tables for $5.00 each. The ironic thing was that when I closed my office, I found that solid oak desks were selling for several hundred dollars.

Don't hesitate to buy used equipment or last year's models. When we set up our office, we bought our copier, fax machine, computers, and answering machine for pennies on the dollar from a consulting firm that went belly up. Sorry to say that another's problems can be an opportunity for you.

Keep in mind that you can avoid spending a lot of money on software by using open source and freeware. Also, consider buying last year's computers from a techie who upgrades with every new release. Get to know these techies by joining a computer club. You can save money on hardware and in many cases get help with your software and hardware problems. Computer clubs are also a good source for independent contractors you may want to employ on future projects.

I strongly recommend incorporating your business; you can do this yourself, you do not need a lawyer. Go on line, download the forms from your state, and setup a Limited Liability Corporation (LLC). The protection of the corporate shield is well worth the minimal cost involved in setting up your LLC.

To get started you have to market your business; however, do not spend money on advertising; instead, use the social networks, teach at local community colleges or universities, speak at Chamber of Commerce meetings, professional association meetings, and any place else where you may have the opportunity to talk about your expertise and services. Another strategy you may want to consider is to start your business part time; that is, moonlight in some specialized area to make contacts and gain recognition.

You may have other startup expenses to deal with, but some or all of these costs may be tax deductible. Keep in mind that taxes are an expense, and the more you can do to reduce your taxes, the more you will increase your profit. I will discuss how tax deductions can be used legally to enhance profits in the next section.

A final note about start-up expenses—keep them to the absolute minimum, and defer the majority of your purchases until you are actually running your business. There is a tax advantage to deducting your expenses as operating costs instead of as start-up expenses.

Operating Expense—It is imperative to reduce expenses not only to save money but also to develop good, expense management habits for the life of your business. From what I have seen over the last thirty years, entrepreneurs who are disciplined expense managers have a better than average chance of running a successful and highly profitable venture than those who do not watch their pennies.

Typical operating costs for a project management business include:

- Rent
- Equipment (computers, printers, etc.)
- Software
- Internet
- Utilities (telephone, electricity, etc.)
- Insurance
- Supplies
- Subscriptions
- Licenses
- Professional Dues
- Marketing, Sales, Advertising
- Travel
- Auto Expenses
- Entertainment
- Out of Pocket
- Contributions
- Payroll

Virtually all of the above items are tax deductible business expenses, provided that they are incurred specifically for your business and not your personal use. Therefore, it is important to keep good records.

You can keep your operating costs low by shopping for the best deals. For example, I found that the rates for business insurance varied considerably, so be sure to get quotes from a number of different insurance agents; also, you can get package deals on telephone and internet service. Keep business auto expense low by buying a reliable, non-luxury car that gets good mileage, or use your own car. If you use your car instead of a company car, keep good records of your mileage for tax purposes; also, find a small local garage to service your car—they are typically less expensive than a dealer.

I recommend that you buy all your office supplies from a bulk supplier. I shop primarily at Costco; their prices and quality are good, and they have an excellent rewards program.

LEVERAGE DISCOUNTS AND REWARDS

For my business I make it a policy to pay for virtually everything by credit card. Credit cards are useful for tracking your expenditures, and many credit cards will give you rewards for purchasing office supplies, gasoline, utilities, and many other things. I find it useful to use credit cards; however, I have a strict policy to never carry a balance or pay interest or late charges. Therefore, I never put anything on a credit card that I cannot pay off at the end of the month. I am fanatical about this and in the past thirty years or more I have had only one or two late payments due to family emergencies that totally consumed me. Credit cards can be a useful business tool; however, credit cards can also be dangerous. They are like a pistol for home defense; they can help you in an emergency, but if you're not careful, you can shoot yourself in the foot.

In addition to rewards and the twenty some days of free credit, your business credit card will give you monthly and annual reports of all your transactions. This is invaluable information for you to review your spending habits as well as backup information for tax audits.

In addition, I make it a habit to document all business expenditures on my smart phone and save all receipts. It is especially important to keep details on travel and entertainment expenditures.

Keep brief notes on who, what, why, where, when, and how much for every meeting, lunch, dinner, party, gifts, or anything else where you pick up the tab. Socializing and entertaining is an important part of generating business and building rapport, so be prepared to deal with this expense in a responsible manner and keep good records.

One final note—keeping good expense records does not have to be a chore if you make it a habit to record the expenses as soon as they occur. After a business lunch, I sit in my car for a few minutes and enter my expenses into my smart phone. I do the same thing while on a plane or train returning from a business trip. When I get back to the office, I hot sync my business meeting and trip expenses into my accounting program. I also make it a habit to review all expenditures weekly to ensure that I am not letting things get out of control. At the end of the month, I pay all the bills, tally up accounts receivable, and quickly assess profitability.

It is especially important when you are first starting out to be fanatical about controlling expenses. In the beginning you will probably be in a negative cash flow situation; hence, every dollar you spend comes out of your pocket. I have seen too many businesses never get off the ground because the founders spent all their money, and perhaps their creditor's money, before they ever generated a profit. In addition to positioning yourself for the highest probability of financial success, fanatical expense management at the start of your business will help to develop an ingrained practice that will pay handsome dividends over the life of your business.

Make Maximum Use of Tax Deductions

A tax deduction is the amount of money you subtract from your gross income to arrive at your taxable income. Obviously you want to keep your taxable income as low as possible so you can retain more of your profits. There is a whole range of tax deductions that the business man or woman can legally take advantage of; therefore, I strongly recommend that before you start your business, you learn all you can about business tax deductions. If you use your business tax deductions effectively, you will be able to generate more wealth than the average employee who has virtually no opportunity to shield his or her earnings.

To understand just how important tax deductions are, take a look at the income tax savings for each dollar in deductions as shown in Exhibit 17-1. For example, if you are in the 28 percent tax bracket for married filing jointly, you can save 28 cents for every dollar deducted as a business expense. Include the effective self-employment taxes which come out to about 12 percent, then you have a 40 percent savings. If you have to pay state income tax (the average is about 6 percent) you may be able to also deduct your business expense to give you a savings of 46 percent. So if you buy a piece of equipment for your business for $1,000 you can save $460 in taxes.

Married Filing Jointly

Tax Bracket %	Tax Bracket Rate ($)	Savings for Each Dollar in Deductions
10	0 – 16,750	$0.10
15	16,750 – 68,000	$0.15
25	68,000 – 137,300	$0.25
28	137,300 – 209,250	$0.28
33	209,250 – 373,350	$0.33
35	373,650 - Above	$0.35

Exhibit 17-1

Since Congress is constantly changing the tax laws, and I am not a tax expert, I will not attempt to discuss the tax codes. What I will do is show you how tax deductions can be used to maximize your profits; however, you must research the latest IRS regulations to get the detailed information needed for your specific situation. Let's start by considering tax deductions for the start-up phase of your business.

Start-Up Expenses—Remember I said to spend only a minimum amount to start your business. The reason for this is that you have to spread start-up-expense deductions over the first sixty months that you are in business. However, once you are running your business, the expenses you incur are deductible in the tax year you incur them.

Operating Expenses—The Government understands that you have to spend money to operate your business, so it allows you to deduct these expenses from your gross income to compute your taxable income. Obviously, the more deductions you can take legitimately, the lower will be your tax bill and the greater will be your profit. Operating expenses are those that directly relate to running your business, are reasonable, necessary, and current.

Operating expenses for your project management business are fairly straightforward and virtually everything you spend to run your business is tax deductible. Nevertheless, when it comes to taxes, always check the latest tax codes to ensure that you have a legal deduction. If you are using an accountant or a tax preparer, be certain that they understand your business. I had to try three different accountants/tax preparers before I found one who understood my business and could effectively optimize my tax deductions. All the others were what I would call, "spreadsheet mechanics."

Long-Term Assets—As you grow your business, you will need to purchase things to remain viable and competitive. These things may include buildings, equipment, furniture, vehicles, computers, software, and books; most of these purchases will be classified as a capital expense. Capital expenses are those that have a useful life of more than one year. Some capital items will be deducted by using depreciation; others can take advantage of Section 179 of the IRS codes, wherein you can deduct the full price of items purchased each year. Since depreciation is a complex topic I recommend that you defer to the tax experts when you have to deal with this topic. However, for your project management business, Section 179 will probably be the primary vehicle for reducing your taxable income. The IRS defines Section 179 deduction as follows (see www.IRS.gov, Depreciation and Section 179 Expenses):

> "A qualifying taxpayer can choose to treat the cost of certain property as an expense and deduct it in the year the property is placed in service instead of depreciating it over several years. This property is frequently referred to as section 179 property.
>
> The Hiring Incentives to Restore Employment (HIRE) Act of 2010 extends the dates of the IRC Section 179 temporary

increase in limitations on expensing of depreciable business assets.

Under HIRE, qualifying businesses can continue to expense up to $250,000 of section 179 property for the 2010 tax year. Without HIRE, the 2010 expensing limit for section 179 property would have been $125,000.

The $250,000 amount provided under the new law is reduced, but not below zero, if the cost of all section 179 property placed in service by the taxpayer during the tax year exceeds $800,000."

Obviously Section 179 deductions are very important for your business, but again I must emphasize buy only what you need, and make certain you get the best deal on whatever you buy.

There are numerous other deductions that the IRS makes available; however, for your project management business, the most important deductions are: your home office, travel, meals and entertainment, medical, retirement, and payroll cost.

Home Office—Independent contractors and consultants have reservations about taking the home office deduction. It seems to be a widespread belief that taking the home office deduction will raise a red flag with the IRS and trigger an audit. It is true that the IRS has cracked down on those who misuse the home office deduction; in most cases, people deducting expenses for their hobbies were the prime offenders. If you have a real business, and especially if you have set up a corporation, you should not worry; what is more, the IRS can audit you at any time for any reason; it's all part of being an entrepreneur.

It does not make any difference where you set up your home office; it can be in your basement, garage, family room or part of a room in your apartment or condo. Regardless of where you locate your home office, it has to be used exclusively for your business. My first home office was in my family room; actually I walled off a part of the family room, installed a door, and mounted my company sign on the door—I also put a lock on the door to keep the kids out. Later when we moved to a larger house, I used the whole second floor as my office.

The easiest way to determine your home office deduction is to calculate the percentage of your home that you use for your business; thus, if your home is 2,000 square feet and you use 500 square feet for you home office, 25 percent of the total area is used for your business. This means that you can deduct 25 percent of the cost of your home expenses—what you actually deduct will depend on how you file your income taxes. Consult the IRS Web site WWW.IRS.gov, Home Office Deduction, for specific information.

Travel Expenses—Travel will probably be a major expense for your project management business; fortunately, you can deduct virtually all travel expenses so long as they are for business purposes; furthermore, you may be able to take advantage of business travel to work in some vacation time. Whenever I travel to a client site and work there for some period, I make it a point to take some personal time to sample the local food and take in the historical, cultural, and archeological sites of interest. As a result of my extensive business travel, I have visited places that many people could only dream about.

The expenses relating to your personal days are not deductible; otherwise, you can deduct everything else related to your business travel. Keep in mind that excessive travel expenses can trigger an IRS audit, so keep detailed records and receipts related to all business travel.

Meals and Entertainment—Marketing, building client rapport, and maintaining client relationships can usually be accomplished more effectively in congenial, off-site get-togethers; dining out and entertainment are an important part of your business expense. Unfortunately, as things stand now, you can deduct only 50 percent of the total you spend on meals and entertainment.

Because this tax deduction has been widely abused over the years, the IRS has imposed strict limits on what you can deduct; therefore, review the regulations carefully and keep detailed records of all your business meals and entertainment expenses.

A word of advice; some clients have strict policies for their employees on the gifts and entertainment they can accept. To avoid any embarrassing situations, get to know your client's guidelines on this matter. One time I was escorting several clients around New York City when I suggested that we stop at a popular night spot; one individual refused to go in because it might violate his company's ethical guidelines. It was somewhat embarrassing for me and the individual involved; in most cases, if you are not sure about your client's limitations or restrictions, keep your entertainment on the conservative side.

Medical—It's in your best interest, and the government's, to remain healthy so you can work, earn money, and pay taxes; hence, you can deduct medical expenses and the cost of various health insurance premiums. I recommend that you review Topic 502— Medical and Dental Expenses given in the IRS Web site (www.IRS.gov) to learn the basics; however, keep in mind that the provisions of the government's new health program are still being worked out as to how the new laws will impact small business. Nevertheless, medical deductions are important, so be certain to claim all the deductions that you are entitled to.

Retirement—As a business owner you have significant advantage over an employee when it comes to saving for retirement. You can establish retirement accounts that provide major tax benefits and enable you to maximize the amount you can save for your retirement years.

There is a wide range of retirement accounts or programs including IRAs, Roth IRAs, SEP-IRAs, and Keogh Plans to choose from. You need to study these programs and select one or more that best fits your needs. The only recommendation I would make is that you setup your retirement program as soon as you start your business. You need the tax deduction, and you want as much time as possible until retirement to build up your retirement accounts.

Payroll Cost—The amount you pay independent contractors (IC) is deducted from your business income for the year. You do not have to withhold or pay any state or federal payroll taxes for your ICs; however, you must file an IRS Form 1099-MISC to report how much you paid the IC. In addition to state, federal, and local taxes, payroll costs include salaries paid to yourself as well as any employees including family members on your payroll. You are responsible for issuing W-2 forms to all those receiving salaries as well as making timely deposits of any federal, state, and local taxes that you withhold and submitting quarterly tax reports.

Other Deductions—There are a significant number of business related expenses that you can use as tax deductions; these include but are not limited to: advertising, dues and subscriptions, education, insurance, interest on loans, legal and professional services, and licenses. As with everything else, when it comes to tax deductions, do your homework, get professional advice when you need it, and keep good records—tax deductions play an important role in enhancing the profitability of your business. In addition, your profitability depends greatly on how you use your time.

Manage Your Time Effectively

Time is a limited resource. In order to maximize profits and minimize expenses, you must study how you spend your time. All of your available time can be put into two boxes: non-billable time and billable time. When you are working you are billing clients and making money. Obviously, during your non-billable time you are not making money; more than likely, you are spending money. Let's take a hard look at non-billable time.

Non-Billable Time—The four main blocks of non-billable time are administrative time, development time, management time, and free time. Let us examine each of these blocks of non-billable time to see how you can optimize your time, save money, and position yourself to make more money and enjoy life.

Administrative Time—This includes all the activities and expenses related to the administration of your business. Administrative activities encompass all those boring tasks like paying bills, paying contractors, buying supplies, getting insurance, responding to e-mail, correspondence, telephone calls, voice mail, and everything else not directly related to actually performing billable work. But, make no mistake; well executed administrative routines are critical to business success. Your contractors must be paid on time—no excuses. Taxes and credit card bills must be paid on time to avoid penalties which eat your profit. Far too often, it is the little things left unattended that grow into big problems. I had a friend who did not get around to paying his business insurance. His insurers dropped him, his client was advised of the dropped coverage, and his contract was terminated. It took a lot of time and effort to get things back on track. Stay on top of the small stuff to keep your administrative demands from becoming big problems that eat into your profit.

The key to dealing with administrative tasks is to establish well-defined, simple routines which you use consistently. Also, automate every administrative task possible. Today you can set up on-line automatic bill payments for utilities, phones, Internet, and many other things. You should keep check writing to an absolute minimum.

Consider outsourcing your administrative tasks to family members—your spouse and even your children can handle some responsibilities. It is smart to have family members as backup for your business, especially if you have to be on the road for any length of time. In addition, when you put family members on the payroll, you keep part of your profit in the family.

In summary, in order to minimize administrative time, establish routines and automate everything possible. Furthermore, stay on top of your administrative tasks, and do things when they need to be done. Doing it right, at the right time, takes less time and is less stressful than having to fix the compound problems that develop when administrative tasks are neglected.

Development Time—This is the time you spend on creating new products and services for your business, enhancing existing products and services, or designing processes and procedures to operate your business more effectively or more efficiently. It is also the time you spend to keep yourself up to date on the latest management, business, and technological trends. You must constantly engage in some development work to ensure that your business is viable for the long run. Knowledge-based businesses that do not constantly upgrade their capabilities and portfolio of products and services fade quickly in today's global marketplace.

Keep in mind that all business is cyclical. You will have periods of intense work, followed by lulls; use slow periods to develop new products and services. Even when you are working on a hot project, be on the look-out for new ideas, emerging client problems, or comments and suggestions from clients and associates alike. I make it a point to file ideas, suggestions, and observations in a simple database that I maintain specifically for future development work. When things are slow or I have a few spare minutes, I query my data base for ideas and inspiration to energize my business. Your development time is an investment in the future of your business, so be certain to make regular deposits to development activities.

Management Time—You must spend a certain amount of non-billable time interfacing with your clients and your consultants to ensure that your projects are moving forward successfully. If problems develop, you will expend as much time as necessary to get things back on track. Over the years I have found that, on large projects where I am employing consultants or independent contractors, I have to spend most of my management time on the front end of the project. If I focus on the front end of a project, I find that I will have to spend less management time over the life of the project. Therefore, I make it a point to be heavily involved in the first 10-20 percent of the project. If I feel confident that an effective project plan has been implemented and tasks are being accomplished as planned, I transition into an administrative mode and spend less time in direct management.

If you follow my business model and employ independent contractors as I describe in Chapter 11, you should not need to spend a lot of time managing or supervising your staff or dealing with interpersonal problems.

Free Time—I define free time as non-business related time. This is the time you should set aside to enjoy family, friends, and everything you deem important to having a fulfilling, rewarding, and enjoyable life. The amount of time you expend on free time of course depends on you, your values, and your lifestyle; however, make no mistake about it, free time is important to keep you mentally and physically fit and positively engaged in life. If you truly enjoy your work, it is very easy to fall into the trap of allowing yourself to be totally consumed by your work. Keep in mind that a child's birthday party missed or an anniversary forgotten can never be replaced. I believe it is imperative that you discipline yourself to carve out plenty of free time from your business to ensure a fruitful and meaningful life.

No matter how hard you work to make more money, you will never have a truly profitable business unless you minimize expenses and control the time you spend on non-revenue producing activities. This is not rocket science; however, failure to control expenses and non-productive time will kill your business with the same certainty as death and taxes.

Make More

As discussed in Chapter 10, "How to Grow Your Business," if you run your project management business as a one-person shop, your capability to make money is typically limited to your billing rate and the number of hours you can bill. Also, your work load will vary; you will spend part of your time on billable assignments, and the rest of your time marketing to get new assignments. In order to make the maximum amount possible every year, you need to have a steady flow, or backlog, of assignments; however, in most cases this is difficult for a one-person operation.

On the other hand, you can make more money by expanding the products and services you offer clients. As discussed in Chapter 10, you can add new business units, such as training, consulting, and client support. By providing diverse services you may be able to generate a steady flow of revenue, but as a one-person operation, your income is still limited to the number of hours you can devote to providing these diverse services.

In order to substantially increase your revenue, you must hire staff; as we discussed in Chapter 11, the best way to do this for your project management business is to utilize independent contractors (ICs). Since the focus of our project management business is to provide services to a wide range of clients on a project-to-project basis, it is imperative to have a highly flexible and mobile staff of expertise. Thus, the independent contractor is ideal for our type of business. In addition to providing the flexibility needed for a project management business, the IC will enable you to generate more revenue by reducing costs associated with overhead, benefits, and taxes.

I have found that you will make more money if you grow your project management business in building-block fashion; that is, start with your area of expertise, obtain spin-off assignments, and then hire staff to work those assignments as you move into other areas. It may take several years to establish a foundation for your business, but once you start to grow you will find that every successful engagement generates opportunities for additional business in other areas. If you pursue this strategy, you will spend more time overseeing client engagements then actually working on them. By leveraging your business units and utilizing ICs, you can significantly increase your income.

Before you pursue different strategies to make more money you should ask yourself, "How much money do I truly need to enjoy life and live well?" The answer to this question will obviously depend on your interests, values, and lifestyle. Nevertheless, everyone has an optimum point where working harder and making more to live well will jeopardize enjoying life; consequently, you have to find your optimum point.

In this chapter we examined various ways to enhance the profitability of our project management business. Our goal is to make more money, work hard without killing ourselves, enjoy what we are doing, and realize a sense of happiness in our accomplishments. However, one issue we need to discuss is: what do you do with all the money you make? Will your financial success position you and your family for a better life or set the stage for failure in the future? We will discuss this and more in Chapter 18.

Summary

To maximize profits you must spend less and make more.
To spend less:

- Keep expenses to a minimum
- Leverage discounts and rewards
- Make maximum use of tax deductions
- Effectively manage your non-billable time to increase billable-time

To make more:

- Offer more products and services
- Hire staff to expand the services you can provide
- Increase the size and scope of your business units

Chapter 18

How to Build Wealth

The Structure of Wealth

When you think of wealth, I am certain you invariably think of money; however, your wealth is more than money. Your wealth consists of two components; your tangible assets and your human capital. You know about tangible assets; these are your possessions of value, your house, car, stocks, bonds, and money. Your human capital consists of your mental and physical assets. In general, the vast majority of people are born with about the same amount of human capital. Some individuals may excel in one area more than another; for example, athletes may have more physical capabilities, such as strength, speed, and endurance, than the average person; others may excel in mental abilities and may be able to extrapolate, correlate, and calculate more effectively than the average person. All of us have more than sufficient human capital to become rich. And by rich I mean you have enough money so you do not have to work, and you can live well because your money is working for you.

How to get Rich

The process for getting rich is deceptively simple—all you have to do is make money, save money, invest to make more money, and not waste money; however, simple does not necessarily imply easy. Getting rich is not easy because you must effectively use your human capital to get rich. The problem is that most people do not understand the importance or the significance of their human capital, and therefore ignore or even waste this important natural resource. Let us look at human capital to understand how to utilize this resource to get rich.

PHYSICAL ASSETS

The ability to get rich is more closely related to sound physical capabilities than most people realize. It takes physical endurance, strength, and energy to work effectively, long, and hard. The desire to accomplish demanding tasks in your job or business is sustained by the body's capacity to carry it through the stress and fatigue involved in the undertaking. Far too often, people give up on demanding tasks because they become tired, worn out, or ill. They lack the physical endurance and strength to stand up to the demands of the undertaking, the long hours, the problems, and the endless conflict. To beat out the competition in any undertaking you must be strong, healthy, and physically fit; hence, you must enhance, protect, and utilize your physical capital wisely throughout your life.

Failure to enhance and protect your physical capital can have catastrophic implications. For example, Stan, an associate I knew well, was a very successful business man. Stan lived the conspicuous lifestyle. Every dollar of profit was spent on a beautiful home, a vacation retreat, exotic travel, and lavish entertainment. Stan constantly kidded me about my conservative philosophy; he always said, "What's the sense of working hard and making money if you can't enjoy yourself." Stan's joy came from buying stuff and living the good life.

Unfortunately, Stan's overweight condition and the high blood pressure he had ignored for years finally caught up with him—he suffered a massive stroke. The enormous medical bills, extensive rehabilitation treatment, and loss of income proved disastrous. Since Stan had little or no savings, he was forced to liquidate virtually everything he owned. His wife had to give up her country-club lifestyle and get a job; his kids had to drop out of college and go to work. For some families, this type of traumatic experience would be an opportunity to bond, to work together, and to meet the setbacks head on. Unfortunately for Stan, his family had been so ingrained with their materialistic lifestyle that they could not deal with the setbacks they faced. Stan's wife blamed him for not taking care of himself, Stan blamed his wife for her superficial values, and the children blamed their parents for all their unhappiness. In relatively short order the family disintegrated, and Stan was left by himself.

I lost track of Stan after he sold his house and moved out of state; however, some twenty years later I ran into Stan quite by accident. I was in New York City showing some of my European associates around the city when we stopped at a street vendor to buy some souvenirs. To my shock it was Stan; I did not recognize him at first, he had not aged well, and he was bent over on one side due to his stroke. This meeting was more painful than I can describe. We spoke briefly, Stan said that he was doing OK, and he was happy because he had no pressures or problems to deal with. We promised to keep in touch, but we never did.

It's unfortunate, but when you are young, you never think about your physical assets. The human body seems indestructible up to about your mid-thirties; you can eat, drink, smoke, and do just about anything without ill effect; however, by the time you roll into your late thirties and early forties, you begin to notice the effects of your lifestyle. Your weight goes up, your endurance wanes, you get one cold on top of another, and it takes longer to recover from any illness. If you don't do anything to change your lifestyle, by the time you get into your fifties you will have serious health issues, and by then it may be too late. There is ample research that shows serious, life-debilitating illnesses like heart attacks, strokes, and even some cancers, can be prevented by adopting a sensible lifestyle.

Therefore, to enhance and protect your physical assets, you should adopt a smart lifestyle; implement a vigorous exercise program, eat sensibly, get enough sleep, and avoid the health killers: smoking, alcohol, drugs, and anything else that will destroy your physical capital.

One final note about physical assets—it is well known that if you are healthy and in good physical condition you will enrich your mental assets.

MENTAL ASSETS

To succeed in your business and get rich, you have to think clearly, make sound decisions, and live intelligently. You need a mental ability that enables you to deal with complex, vague, or ill-defined problems or situations. Good problem solvers and decision makers have a well-developed portfolio of mental capabilities. This means that you must constantly enhance your mental capital by adopting life-long learning as an integral part of your lifestyle. Today's world is a dynamic caldron of new ideas, concepts, processes, procedures, information, technologies, laws, and regulations. Those who do not maintain a rich knowledge-base will soon be obsolete and lose out to those who are intellectually more adroit.

In addition to a rich knowledge-base, your mental assets must include energy, toughness, and humor. Without sufficient mental energy and toughness, even highly motivated, smart people cannot hold up under the rigors of a complex business environment. Humor is the glue or the catalyst that binds and augments mental energy and toughness. Humor helps people under stress keep a proper prospective. Humor helps to provide the mental checks and balances between reality and perception, values and costs, deadlines and timeliness.

Expand and invest in your mental assets by engaging in life-long learning, interacting with a wide range of people from different backgrounds and cultures, and exploring new environments outside your comfortable niche.

Anyone can enhance his or her human capital; however, in most cases, significant human capital is developed and cultivated in families that have a particular advantage —intangible wealth.

Intangible Wealth

Some years ago the World Bank made a study to determine why some nations became wealthier than others despite having limited natural resources. What they found was that there were certain intangible factors, such as an efficient judicial system, effective government, established institutions, trust among people in society, and other intangibles that enhance a nation's wealth-generating capabilities. In similar fashion you can find intangible factors in families that enable them to generate wealth while others cannot.

I am certain that you know families that seem to prevail regardless of their socio-economic backgrounds or limitations. These families work hard and prosper; their children do well in school, go to college, become professional or business people, build wealth, and move up the economic ladder. What are the intangible factors that set these families apart from those who do not advance?

Successful families have a well-defined ethical foundation. They raise their children to be honest, trustworthy, mannerly, and respect authority. These families are goal orientated, have a solid work ethic, and tend to have conservative, practical values. Roles and responsibilities are well-defined, and the family emphasizes self-reliance and individual responsibility. Also, the family has a primary source of authority and discipline on all important matters. The nature of families has changed over generations; however, the intangible factors that enable families to succeed remain the same.

For example, when I was growing up fathers were the undisputed head of the family and the sole bread winner. Mothers stayed home, kept house, prepared meals, cared for the children, and educated them on the standards, values, and expectations of the family. Fathers brought home the pay and mothers managed the money. All the children had chores to do at home; when they got older and went out to work, they gave their pay to mother who allocated an appropriate allowance for spending money. Parents preached and practiced honesty, hard work, and thrift. The children were expected to do the same. Parents did not hesitate to use consequence-management when necessary to align children with the standards set down for the family.

Parents prepared their children for their future roles as adults. Mothers taught their daughters how to cook, sew, and keep house. Fathers taught their sons how to use tools, repair equipment, and how to get a job. Children were made ready for the labor-intense, manual skills-based economy of my generation.

Families that functioned in this manner provided a secure and solid foundation for their children regardless of what happened in the world; hence, it was a safe environment to grow up in, there were no ambiguities or gray areas about right and wrong, and there were no excuses for non-performance—low self-esteem did not exist as a malady.

The traditional family of my generation may be gone, but the intangible factors that gave it the ability to generate wealth still exist in today's family. I know families of my grandchildren's generation where both parents work, yet they have a solid, ethical foundation, and raise their children to be honest, trustworthy, mannerly, and respect authority. They also have a solid, work ethic, they set high goals for themselves and their children, and they emphasize self-discipline and self-reliance. Despite the fact that these families live in a much more fluid environment than my generation—there certainly seem to be more distractions and temptations—these families communicate more with each other and actively reinforce and support each other in dealing with the stresses of modern life. The difference that I see is that the modern family tends to function more like a team than the hierarchical family structure I grew up in. Nevertheless, in the team-based modern family there is a leader (which may alternate between the father and mother), and there is structure, standards, goals, roles and responsibilities; furthermore, great emphasis is given to communication, education, and the skills needed for the information intense, knowledge-based, economy that they live in.

Families that possess intangible wealth will be successful regardless of the economic turmoil they may face.

The more you can do to foster intangible wealth, the better prepared you will be to address the actual mechanics of making money and getting rich.

Making Money and Getting Rich

The more money you make the easier it is to get rich. For example, if you reach the highest levels of the corporation where you earn an enormous salary, you can get rich; or, if you are really lucky and get equity shares in a successful start-up, like a Microsoft or a Google, you can get rich. But if you are a typical employee, you will never be able to take home enough money to pay all your bills and have enough left over to save and invest to get rich. Federal, state, and local taxes will take a big chunk out of your paycheck, and there is little you can do to shield your earnings from these taxes

The only way for the average man or woman to get rich on their own is to have a successful business—which is what this book is all about. However, making a lot of money is only part of the story; to get rich you have to manage your money to produce a surplus that you put to work to make more money. This means you must save consistently and invest wisely. Many people do not know how to save consistently, and there are quite a few who do not know how to invest wisely; these are the two main reasons why so few people actually become rich.

John Tuman, Jr.

Save Money Consistently

To save money, you have to take part of your income and put it into a secure savings instrument. The key to getting rich is to save consistently—week after week, month after month, year after year, until it becomes an ingrained habit. You can mentally program yourself to save consistently by making it a routine like going to bed, waking up, and eating meals at a certain time. Start by making small deposits until you make savings a deep-rooted part of your life; then slowly adjust your lifestyle to increase the amount you want to save.

This is where most people fail; they do not have the savings habit, and they lack the discipline to develop the habit; hence, they will never get rich. If you save consistently, time will enable your money to grow through the power of compounding; in other words, the interest you earn on your money will grow to make more money. Individuals who are thirty to forty years away from retirement have the potential to generate in excess of a million dollars simply by saving consistently.

I am amazed at the number of people I know who claim they cannot save anything. I know a number of two-income families, well-educated, well-paid professionals who have little or no savings.

Once, I was invited to a party given by a young couple who were celebrating the wife's recent promotion. This couple lived in New York City, they had a well-furnished apartment in a high rent neighborhood; they had the latest in electronic gadgets, I-pods, high fidelity sound systems, high-resolution wide screen TV, all resting neatly on expensive furniture. After a tour of their apartment and a few cocktails, the conversation, turned to politics, taxes, the cost of living, and why it is impossible to save money. I know better than to try to offer advice, so I just politely listened to the conversation; however, mentally I was screaming, "Just stop buying stuff and you will have money to save." Unfortunately for this couple when the bottom fell out of the economy they both lost their jobs. The last I heard about them is that they were selling their belongings for pennies on the dollar.

I wish I could say that this couple was the exception, but from my travels and observations I have concluded that far too many people have fallen into the trap of believing that they must buy things to be happy. For many Americans, shopping is entertainment; however, we know from research and experience, buying new things does not make you happy, it offers only short-term pleasure. Thus, like the addict, the shopper has to quickly get another fix to feel good. The result is that savings are replaced by massive credit card debt. God have pity on those people, because the credit card companies will not.

Invest Money Wisely

In addition to putting money into savings to create a cushion for tough times and to build a foundation for your retirement, you should also put some of your money into investments. I am not about to advise you on how to invest your money, there is a world of information out there on how to do that. What I will do is give you two rules that have served me well over the years. These are: Rule 1—Manage your own money, and Rule 2—Don't lose money.

RULE 1—MANAGE YOUR OWN MONEY

There are legions of experts available who will help you manage your money for a handsome fee. However, I believe that if you are smart enough to make money, you are smart enough to manage your investments. The experts will tell you that you don't have time to manage your money. Nonsense! Managing your money is just an extension of managing your business. You must allocate time to managing your money, just as you allocate time to managing your business.

Also, the experts will imply they have access to information that you don't have. Don't believe it; in today's information intense, Internet-based world, you have access to all the information you need to make informed and sound investments. Take time to do the research, make decisions, and then invest your money wisely to make more money. But when you invest, keep in mind Rule 2—Don't Lose Money.

RULE 2—DON'T LOSE MONEY

When you hire an expert to manage your money, you believe you will make more money and your money will be safe. Wrong! There are people like Lou Pearlman and Bernard Madoff who turn out to be good con artists that defraud thousands of very smart people. This is not unusual—there are dozens of fraud cases uncovered every year, yet the con artist does not have a shortage of suckers. All a con artist has to do is promise great returns on an investment, and the gullible will trip over each other in the rush to give his or her hard earned money to the con artist.

Even ethical money managers can lose your money; if you don't believe it, talk to your friends who have taken a beating in the last market crash. Each and every major downturn in the stock market reveals the fallacy of putting your trust in others to manage your money. Now I am not against investing in the stock market; quite the contrary—I have realized some very nice returns from the stock market. But all my investments are based on my research and focus on businesses and industries I know something about. I never invest in anything I don't understand. Furthermore, all my investments reflect my risk tolerance. What is your risk tolerance? A better way of posing this question is to ask, "How much money can you afford to lose?" If you are like most people, your answer is none!

Far too many people are programmed to believe that if you invest in the stock market for the long term, your investments will be safe and you will increase your wealth. Financial advisors point out that the stock market over any twenty-year period in history, in any market, has outperformed everything else; thus, many investors are convinced that if you hold stocks long enough, you don't have to worry. This is just plain nonsense.

There are several things you must take into consideration when making any investment: first, you do not have an infinite amount of time; life is limited and in the long run we are all going to die. The reality of time is that you have at best only forty to fifty working years to make money, save, invest, and build your fortune. Second, over any forty to fifty year period the market can have significant downturns—it can even crash.

What happens to you when, right before you are ready to retire, the market drops and wipes out 50 percent or more of your wealth? I have seen it happen to several of my friends and associates, and I can tell you the impact on their physical and emotional well-being has been devastating. Many of these individuals will never recover what they lost—they do not have the time.

As we have seen in the recent economic collapse no one, not even the experts, can predict what the stock market will do or how the economy will react; clearly, it is impossible for an individual to control the economic turmoil that impacts his or her life. However, an individual can control the goals, plans, actions, and decisions in every phase of their life. It takes time to build wealth; the sooner you start the more wealth you can create, provided you have a goal and a plan for getting rich.

The Twenty-Five Year Plan

In Chapter Two I laid out a twenty-five year plan for building your project management business. This plan is based on experience and a pragmatic approach to starting your own business, making money, and creating wealth. Experience shows that it takes about the first five years to establish the foundation for a successful project management business. By the end of the fifth year, you should have a solid client base and a steady stream of revenue.

Nevertheless, if you want to get rich, you must, in your first year, set up a savings and investment program. This program may be very modest in the beginning, you may be able to save and invest only a very small amount; however, the most important thing in the first five years is to get into the habit of saving and investing on a regular basis. You must develop an ingrained saving and investing routine like eating and sleeping—you want to develop this habit to the point where you feel really bad if you miss making a deposit to your savings and investment program. Once you develop this habit, you are well on your way to getting rich.

As your income increases, you need to allocate more to your saving and investment program. By the time you reach your fifteenth year in business, your savings and investments should be generating substantial returns on their own because of compounding interest and dividends. Nevertheless, you must continue to save and invest the maximum amount possible in line with your desired lifestyle. To create substantial wealth you need to structure a lifestyle that enables you to have money left over after all your expenditures.

There are two basic lifestyles: conspicuous and minimalist. The conspicuous lifestyle focuses on the acquisition and consumption of material objects for the sake of comfort and happiness, while the minimalist lifestyle acquires only what is needed to live a healthy and rewarding life. The minimalist lifestyle will generally produce funds for saving and investing, whereas the conspicuous lifestyle will generally produce debt.

Lifestyle Cost

You will probably spend the largest part of the profits from your project management business to support your lifestyle. Lifestyle cost includes living expenses (food, clothing, shelter, etc.), education, entertainment, political, social, and everything else you spend money on to live well and enjoy your life. You may live a conspicuous lifestyle, a minimalist lifestyle, or a lifestyle somewhere in between. Regardless of your lifestyle preference, your business profits must be able to support your lifestyle needs and wants and, if you want to get rich, you must ensure that there is money left over for savings and investments.

The curse of a successful business is that it can create the illusion that things are always going to be this way. We all know from experience that there are ups and downs in every business and every life. To deal with these cycles, you must construct a lifestyle that can be sustained through good and bad times, and you must make prudent decisions about critical issues in your life to ensure that you don't waste your money.

How Not to Waste Money

All the money magazines and money advisors on the Internet offer pithy advice on how to save money by giving up things like lattes, dinners out, luxury cars, and so on; however, even though trading down will save you money, this is not where people squander the money that keeps them from becoming rich. The wealth destroyers are the big, crippling, life decisions people make that consume their income for years. I have compiled a list of the top ten things you should not do if you want to get rich:

1. **Don't marry the wrong person**—Never marry a person whose values are vastly different from yours, especially when it comes to money. Disagreements on how to make money, how to spend money, and how to save money are one of the major sources of stress and conflict in a marriage.

2. **Don't divorce**—In addition to the stress and pain that divorce creates, it is also expensive—multi-divorces are very expensive; I know individuals who are supporting three families around the country.

3. **Don't go into debt**—When you go into debt, you in effect dig yourself a financial hole. When the hole gets deep enough, you can never get out; this is especially true of credit card debt where interest rates are in the 20 percent range.

4. **Don't commit a crime**—Breach a contract, steal from your own company, defraud others, or commit any violation of the law that causes financial or physical harm to anyone, and you will have destroyed your reputation, your livelihood, and your wealth-generating potential.

5. **Don't develop an addiction**—People who are addicted to drugs, alcohol, gambling, or anything else all have one thing in common: they cause pain and suffering to their loved ones and they all die poor.

6. **Don't get sick**—Overweight issues, high blood pressure, heart attacks, strokes, and many other maladies destroy an individual's productivity, consume their wealth, and shorten their life.

7. **Don't get hurt**—Avoid taking chances and doing stupid things that will incapacitate you so you can't work. After a major snow storm, a friend went to clear snow from the roof of his house; he fell off the roof, broke two legs, his hip, and fractured several ribs—he was unable to work for over two years.

8. **Don't jeopardize your life**—A brilliant, young engineer I knew drank too much at a Christmas party, drove off the road, hit a tree, and was killed. He left a wife and two small children who struggled for years.

9. **Don't stagnate**—I know smart, well educated people who, once they left college and got a job, were content to do little else for the rest of their lives. By the time they reached middle age, they were obsolete, out of work, and unemployable.

10. **Don't retire too early**—Don't retire before you have made more than enough money to support yourself in comfort for the rest of your life. Also, do not retire if you truly enjoy your work, are actively engaged, and physically fit.

If you manage your business successfully, live sensibly, save and invest wisely, by the time you are ready to get on the glide path to retirement, you should be physically fit, mentally sharp, and rich.

Summary

To build wealth you must:

- Develop, cultivate, and enhance your human capital—the physical and mental assets that you possess

- Be healthy, physically fit, strong, and energetic to stand up to the stresses and demands of modern life

- Be mentally sharp, intellectually curious, and open to new ideas, concepts, and different ways of dealing with the challenges you face

- Lead a healthy lifestyle based on moderation, sensible diet, and exercise. Avoid addictions that cripple a healthy body

- Embrace life-long learning as a way of life

- Create a family environment that fosters intangible wealth

- Save consistently, invest wisely, and don't destroy your wealth by making any of the big, life-crippling decisions

- Not retire too early

- Have more than enough money in the bank to support yourself for the rest of your life

Chapter 19

How to Get on the Glide Path To Retirement

Why Retire

When I was an employee in the corporate world, I lived for weekends, holidays, and my vacation. I counted the years, months, weeks, and days to retirement. My job was so arduous that I could not wait to get out. After I started my project management business, all of that changed. From that point, on I so enjoyed the work I was doing I did not give much thought to retirement. Not long ago I visited associates of mine that I left behind in the corporate world. It was heart wrenching to hear about the stress and anxiety they were enduring. They had to work longer hours because of their downsized organization. They lived with the fear that their job would be outsourced or eliminated. Worse yet, they worried that their pension might be reduced or abolished before they retired. As one friend of mine put it, "I am hanging on by my finger nails until the day I retire and get out of here." Is this what retirement is all about, escape from Devil's Island?

Rationale for Retirement

For many of today's corporate workers, retirement is about escape. Certainly, when I was an employee that was how I looked at retirement; however, after I started my project management business I really did not plan to retire. Sure, I might slow down a bit, but why give it up completely? As far as I am concerned, as an employee you work to earn a living; as a retiree you work at what gives you satisfaction. When you are doing work you love, you are living the ideal retirement—you are working, happy, and enjoying yourself. You can see examples of this when you look at people like financier Warren Buffet, media tycoon Rupert Murdoch, Penn State coach Joe Paterno, and many others.

So why retire? Well, everyone mellows at some point in their lives. You have seen it all; many projects and problems look similar, and there are few, new challenges. The only difference is the next generation working their way up the ranks. When you reach this stage, you are ready to move on and find what will vitalize and enrich the final phase of your life; thus, it's time to get on the glide path to retirement.

On the Glide Path to Retirement

After pursuing an active professional and business life for more than forty years, I began to think about retirement because many of my friends and associates had already retired. However, I noticed a disturbing turn of events for a number of those who retired well before me. More than just a few died within a relatively short time after retiring. I wondered if this was fate or did it have something to do with the stress associated with the life-altering transition to retirement. I decided that moving to retirement was a significant change and required careful preparation. Thus, I laid out a four phase program (see Exhibit 19-1) to deal with what I considered the most important pre-retirement planning issues. Let us briefly review some of the critical issues you should consider when you start thinking about retirement.

ASSESSMENT PHASE

Start thinking seriously about retirement at least five to seven years ahead of your actual retirement date; give yourself plenty of time, and above all, avoid snap decisions—mistakes in this phase of your life can be very expensive. It is important from a financial and tax point of view to start as early as possible. Also, starting well in advance will minimize the physical and emotional stress on you and your loved ones. Moving from an active, professional life to retirement requires significant changes in many dimensions of your life; therefore, it will be less painful if these changes are done in small increments.

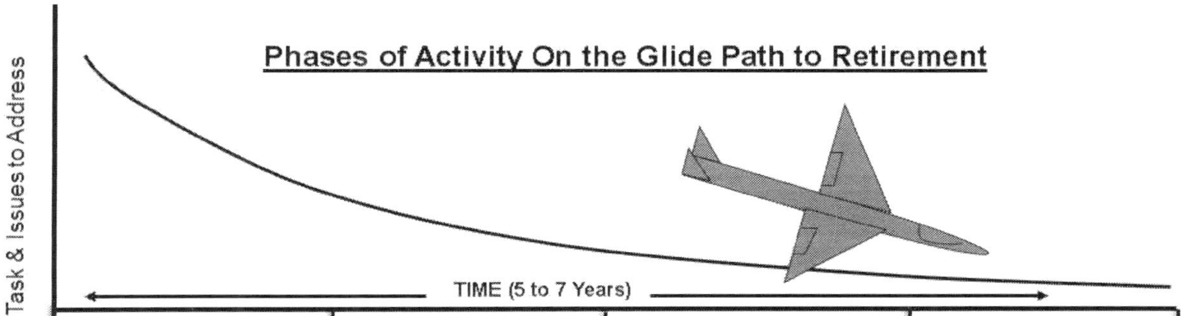

Phases of Activity On the Glide Path to Retirement

TIME (5 to 7 Years)

Task & Issues to Address

Assessment Phase	Study Phase	Action Phase	Transition Phase
What has changed in your life?	Determine where you want to live.	Realign your portfolio and finances – reduce risk.	Consolidate all personal finances – zero risk.
How much work do you want to give up?	Do research.	Reduce/eliminate debt.	Address family legal requirements: wills, trusts, and related.
When do you want to retire?	Visit potential retirement sites.	Address health issues.	Close home office.
How will your retirement impact family, friends, and associates?	Test locations: visit retired friends and relatives; query residents, take mini-vacations, rent. or lease for short periods.	Address care-giver issues.	Downsize client base.
		Develop plan, schedule, and budget to transition out of business.	Dispose of business equipment, furnishings
What will keep you happy in retirement?	Decide where and when to retire.	Develop plan, schedule, and budget to transition into retirement.	Purchase retirement home.
Do you have enough money to retire?		Implement plans.	Prep house for sale - sell house. **Move.**

Exhibit 19-1

285

Some of the more important issues to think about in the assessment phase are: do you have enough money to retire in comfort; what will keep you and your spouse vital and happy in retirement; and when should you actually retire? Narrow your retirement date down to within a year or two.

My friend and professional associate Jack started seriously planning for retirement some ten years in advance. He and his wife fell in love with the Southwest and decided that was where they wanted to retire. They bought a small ranch and spent their holidays and vacations renovating the house and making improvements to the property. They got to know the area and made friends in their community. They made it a point to check out all necessary service providers, doctors, dentists, auto repairs, shopping, and entertainment venues. By the time Jack was ready to retire, he had everything in place for a painless and pleasant transition.

The key to making the glide path to retirement as stress free as possible is to decide as early as possible *when* to retire and *where* to retire. These two decisions have a profound impact on the financial and physical effort it takes to get to retirement.

As you get within a few years of your target date, move into the study phase of your retirement program.

STUDY PHASE

Deciding where you want to live when you retire basically boils down to retiring in place or moving to a new location. If you retire in place, you don't have to worry about selling your house, finding new doctors or other health-care providers, etc.; furthermore, your ties to friends and relatives remain secure. However, keep in mind that as your friends and associates retire, many of them may move away. Likewise, as your children grow up and pursue their careers they will most likely move to other locations. For the most part, the days when two or more generations lived in the same neighborhood are a thing of the past.

Retiring in place is the most cost effective and stress-free way of moving into retirement. However, there may be many reasons why you may want to move to a new location when you retire.

Years before I retired I had decided that I would not really retire. I might slow down, take it a bit easier, be more selective about client engagements, and spend more time on creative pursuits. My situation was ideal. I lived in a rural area of Pennsylvania and I could run, mountain bike and go hunting in one of the last major wooded areas in eastern Pennsylvania. Yet we lived close enough to a major network of highways to have easy access to New York City and Philadelphia for cultural interests, the shore for summer fun, and points north for skiing. The house was paid off, comfortable, and decorated to suit our lifestyle. I felt very fortunate to have everything in place for my retirement.

However, things can change in unexpected ways that significantly alter the best of plans. In my case, a skiing accident tore up my knee to the extent that my skiing and running days were over. In addition, developers discovered our rural paradise. Housing developments, industrial parks, and landfills transformed our bucolic area. Like it or not, I had to do some serious soul searching about my retirement plans. So keep in mind that the environment around you can change, and as you grow and mature, you will change also. In my case, the world around me had changed and I had changed. I could no longer do all the strenuous things I used to do; winters became depressingly long, cold, and gloomy; so, I decided I needed to move to a warm, sunny place.

Moving is expensive, stressful, and requires major life alterations. Therefore, it's important to take enough time to get it right the first time. This is why I recommend that you start your retirement planning several years in advance. Take time to identify what you and your life partner want to do in retirement. Focus on those interests that you always wanted to pursue but never had time for. Think about the retirement lifestyle you want to live, and how you will satisfy your value based goals; in other words, what will make you happy and keep you vitalized. Take time to research the many options available for retirement.

My wife and I spent the better part of three years investigating and evaluating retirement communities. We visited our retired friends and got their advice and recommendations. We used the Internet and retirement magazines to identify potential retirement sites. We developed a short list of promising locations and visited each one. Many retirement communities offer attractive packages for you to visit and evaluate their community. With careful planning, you can do your research and work in mini-vacations at the same time.

Since there are so many fine places to retire, it will be difficult to make a final decision. Nevertheless, you will know when you find the right place. In our case, it turned out to be a community *we both agreed* we liked. After seven years in our community, there is no doubt we made the right decision. Getting it right the first time is critical to your financial and mental health; however, picking the right retirement location is not the only critical decision you need to make—you have to pick your retirement date, and you have to move into the action phase of your program with determination and speed.

ACTION PHASE

There are a lot of practical issues to deal with when you get ready to retire; however, the first order of business is to ensure that you have enough money to retire in comfort—that is, if you don't keep working. If you have saved and invested wisely, you should have more than enough money; however, you have to be careful to ensure that your investment portfolio does not crash and burn just before you retire. I have seen that happen to a number of my friends and associates.

I took a risk averse approach several years before I retired (see Exhibit 19-2) contrary to the advice I received from a number of so called financial experts who insisted that I had to have an ample supply of equities in my retirement portfolio. I liquidated my portfolio of stocks and bonds over a period of years well before I retired and moved all my money into minimum risk accounts.

For anyone nearing retirement, I recommend moving your money into insured Certificates of Deposits (CD), Treasuries, and Treasury Money Market Funds. Start laddering CDs and Bonds (see www.bankrate.com, for advice and recommendations). You will not make a lot of money with these investments, but you will not lose money.

Consolidating Your Investments On the Glide Path to Retirement

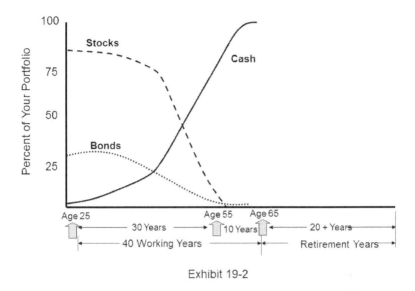

Exhibit 19-2

Contrary to all the advice from the money magazines and financial advisers, I do not believe you should have any of your money tied up in the stock market—not if you want to sleep well during retirement. As I write this, the United States and the rest of the industrial world is going through the worst financial crisis since the great depression. I shudder to think how I would feel if I still had investments in the stock market.

You should also start clearing up all debt; you do not want to move into retirement with mortgage payments, car payments, or large credit card balances hanging over your head.

Your financial health is important, but so is your physical health. Be sure to take care of all health issues for yourself and your loved ones well before you retire. Use your business medical insurance to address all potential health needs before you wind down your company. Have a complete physical, get your eyes checked, and take care of any dental problems. If you move to another location you will discover that it is a real pain to find new doctors, dentists, and other health-care professionals you may need. You do not want to start retirement spending time visiting doctors or dentists.

Also, if you are a caregiver for elderly parents or others, you need time to make appropriate arrangements for them, so start addressing these requirements well in advance. It takes time to properly deal with all the important issues in your life, so don't wait until the last minute, and don't make snap decisions.

I have a friend who, at the drop of a hat, decided he had had enough, closed shop, and moved to a retirement community. He has spent the better part of two years unscrambling business and personal financial issues as well as a myriad of family problems. It's been my experience that anything important that is not planned will go wrong.

Exhibit 19-3 gives a summary of many of the tasks you should address on the glide path to retirement. Note that the stress associated with this effort can be reduced by spreading out the effort over a long period. It takes time to make an orderly adjustment to move from your professional life to your retirement life. So work consistently and deliberately to get your financial, personal, and family affairs in order, then move into the transition phase of your retirement program with deliberate speed.

TRANSITION PHASE

In the transition phase, you get serious about winding down your professional life and moving to your retirement life. The transition phase is a period of high stress, so I recommend that as much as possible you spread out the tasks you need to do. For example, close your home office (stop taking the home office deduction) two years before you sell your home. This will avoid capital gains tax if you plan to sell your home; however, if you plan to stay in your home, the transition to retirement will be an order of magnitude simpler. Nevertheless, you have to decide what to do about your business.

You may just want to downsize the business and keep yourself busy in retirement with a few select clients, or you may want to transition the business to your children. Of course, you can sell the business or just close-up shop.

Tasks & Issues On the Glide Path to Retirement

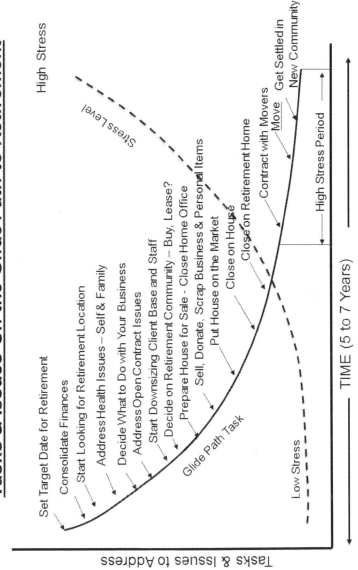

Exhibit 19-3

What about your clients; do you want to maintain some type of business relation in the future, or just make a complete break? Many of these decisions will depend on your personal interests and your vision for retirement. As far as I am concerned, the deciding factor should be what will keep you vital and challenged during your retirement years. I have more than a few friends who, after a brief period in retirement, decided to go back to work. Again, if you love what you are doing, it's not really work.

Another important issue is what to do with your house—keep it and be a snowbird, just going to Florida or some other warm location for the winter—sell it or rent it?

Once you decide that you want to retire, don't procrastinate; there is too much to do. If you have done your homework and laid out your plans, start implementing your plans immediately; events can change quickly and impact the best laid plans. When we decided to sell our home, it was a sellers' market. Housing prices were at a record; in addition, when we contracted to build our retirement house, prices were just starting to accelerate at a record pace. Within a year after we closed, our retirement property cost tens of thousands more. Two years after that the housing bubble burst, and many retirees we knew could not sell their homes. As I write this, the housing market is the worst it's been in many years. As I look back, I realize how fortunate I was to implement my plans as aggressively as I did; truly, timing is everything.

Moving also brings up a host of other issues. For instance, what do you do with all the personal possessions you have accumulated over the years—sell, donate, or trash? What about the friends and relatives you are leaving behind—how will they react and what relationships will you maintain in the future? After being comfortably ensconced in one area for a long time, it is hard to tear down everything and start out afresh.

Moving can be an expensive proposition as well as a difficult emotional adjustment. I will not bore you with all the tribulations we had while on the glide path to retirement; however, I will call your attention again to Exhibit 19-4 where I tried to identify the major issues on the glide path to retirement.

Major Issues on the Glide Path to Retirement

Personal Issues	Business Issues	Move Issues
Health – Evaluate your health. Get complete physical. Address dental and eye requirements. Take care of all health issues for you and loved ones before you retire and move. **Financial** – Make detailed review of your savings and investments. Start shifting investments to minimum risk accounts. **Legal** – Update wills, trusts, and contracts as needed. **Personal Items** – Inventory all personal possessions. Identify items to keep, sell, give away, or junk.	**Clients** – Decide how much client business to keep, turn over, or phase out. **Staff** – Determine when to downsize staff – reposition to other firms, etc. **Legal** – Assess all contract obligations – close out per retirement schedule. **Company** – Sell, turn over to family, downsize, go dormant, or phase out. **Assets** – Take action on company equipment, furniture, supplies. **Tax Issues** – Close home office two years before retirement. Address state and local tax issues.	**House** – Prep house for sale. Contract with realtor. Final inventory of all household items – keep, sell, give away, or junk. **Family** - Address care-giver and dependent children issues. **Retirement Home** – Take sufficient time to study and evaluate retirement locations. Decide where and when to retire. Contract for retirement home. **Move** – Contract with movers. As needed, put items into storage; move to retirement home.

Exhibit 19-4

Identify the issues that are most relevant to your situation, and focus on dealing with them as far in advance of retirement as possible. The amount of time you take on the glide path to retirement will determine the kind of transition you will experience. If you take enough time, your transition will be relatively smooth; if you procrastinate, you will have a rough landing; and if you make snap decisions, you will crash and burn.

Taking the time to plan carefully and to address all the important issues involved in moving from forty to fifty years of a professional life to a retired life will ensure that your retirement life is happy, secure, and rich.

Summary

Making the transition from your working life to your retired life is more complex and stressful than you might believe; therefore, to minimize the stress and do it right the first time you should:

- Decide *when* you want to retire
- Decide *where* you want to retire
- Ensure you have enough money to retire and live in comfort the rest of your life
- Consolidate and secure your investments well in advance of retirement
- Address your major personal issues well before retirement
- Realign your business to suit your retirement life
- Address all your move issues in small increments to minimize stress

Chapter 20

How to Retire Rich

More than Money

To have a truly rich retirement you need three things: good health, a smart lifestyle, and money.

Good Health

After living in an active-adult retirement community for several years, I have observed that the people who really enjoy retired life are those who are physically fit, mentally sharp, and in good health. Sadly, I found that there is a segment of the retired population that does not fall into this category. There are many retired people who are overweight, have high blood pressure, and are battling a host of medical maladies. Many but not all of these problems are the result of sheer neglect. Here we have well educated, successful professionals from all walks of life who have accumulated enough wealth to retire comfortably. Unfortunately, during their working years they concentrated on their professions or businesses and paid little attention to their health or physical well-being. They now find themselves spending an inordinate amount of time visiting doctors, filling prescriptions, and commiserating about their aches and pains.

Retirees who live a much more enjoyable life are the men and women I see working out regularly at the fitness center, swimming laps in the pool, running or walking on the track, playing tennis, baseball, or some other active sport. These people made physical fitness and good health maintenance a routine part of their lifestyle; as a result, they have an active, positive outlook, unlike those who wish things were different.

My advice to the reader who is years away from retirement is to make certain you manage your physical condition and health just as aggressively as you manage your money. This effort will pay handsome dividends in later years. Be advised that if you wait until you retire to get in shape, it may be a lost cause.

Smart Lifestyle

Retirement can be heaven or hell depending on where and how you live your life. First and foremost, you need a secure and comfortable place to live. If you retire to a high-rise apartment in a crime-ridden city, you will always be subjected to stress and anxiety. Everyone needs a measure of security for tranquility and peace of mind.

You also need an environment that provides for healthy living, pleasant surroundings, and sufficient diversity of activities to stimulate and feed your social and creative desires. People who find this type of environment will be positively engaged on a daily basis and you will hear many say, "I don't know how I ever had time to work at my job."

Most importantly, you need to live a smart lifestyle. By this I mean a lifestyle that promotes good habits that safeguard your mental and physical health. I have friends who love to play golf. Now that they are retired, they can play every day—something they always wanted to do. So they get up early, play eighteen holes, then visit the bar, and spend a good part of the day telling war stories and drinking. One acquaintance of mine admitted that he has gained twenty pounds since he retired. You don't get much exercise riding a golf cart; couple this with all the calories in alcohol, and you see the pitfalls of not living smart. I can give you other examples of how not to have a rich retirement, but I think you get the point. The message here is that retirement requires you to make major adjustments in your life. And these adjustments are not as easy as you may think. It requires planning, implementation, and discipline to create a smart retirement lifestyle.

Money

To enjoy retirement you must be worry free about money. You have to accumulate enough money during your working years to have your money work for you for the rest of your retirement years. How much money you need to live well during retirement is a subject of debate. Certainly it depends on your specific preferences and circumstances. Most people would say, "I could live comfortably if I had a million dollars." Well, a million dollars is not what it used to be; today, you need to have close to three million dollars to have the same purchasing power. This sounds like a lot; however, it is not out of reach if you follow my twenty-five year plan, systematically grow your business, and carefully manage your financial portfolio.

In retirement, your money should be working for you; in other words, you should have sound, safe investments which give a reasonable return on your money. How do you make this happen? Well, as I said before, I believe if you are smart enough to make the money, you are smart enough to manage your money, especially in retirement. The Internet gives you access to almost unlimited financial information you can use for research, analysis, and decision making; furthermore, when you are retired, you will have more than enough time to actively manage your money.

Nevertheless, if you are still concerned about how to manage your money in retirement, don't fret because there are plenty of people out there who want to help you. When you retire, especially if you move to an active-adult community, you will discover legions of organizations that are ready to help you manage your money—for a fee, of course.

In my community, hardly a week goes by without a seminar or workshop on some financial topic of concern to retirees. Typically you are enticed to attend these informational sessions by a free breakfast, lunch, dinner, or some kind of gift. I have attended many of these sessions and found most to be well organized and informative. It is a good way to keep up to date on tax laws, annuities, estate planning, investment strategies, and long-term health care. However, almost all of these workshops are designed to sell you something. Furthermore, I find that the fees involved for the services being offered are quite high. If you want to ensure that your retirement money does not run out before you do, do not pay someone two to three percent or more to do what you can do for yourself. In addition, I find that tax avoidance schemes that some of these financial advisers are proposing are questionable at best. The last thing you need in your retirement life is conflict with the IRS.

MONEY MANAGEMENT

If you saved consistently, invested wisely, and lived a sensible lifestyle, you should not have any money worries in retirement; however, if you start to entertain lavishly, travel frequently, and make regular trips to the casinos, you can burn up your retirement nest egg at an alarming rate. To make certain your spending is not out of control, review your finances every month, and adjust your lifestyle accordingly.

A critical issue in managing your money during your retirement years is risk. Most financial advisors and money magazines recommend that you invest part of your money in the stock market. The argument is that the stock market will protect your money against inflation. But as I said in the previous chapter, this may be true in the long run, but in retirement you don't have a long run. On average it takes seven to ten years to make up major stock market losses. If you have not moved all of your money to safe investments before you retire as I recommend in Chapter 19, you should do so now; you will sleep more peacefully when you don't have to worry about your money.

If you listened to your expensive, high-powered financial advisor and your portfolio has gone into the dumpster, you may have to make some radical adjustments to your retirement strategy and lifestyle. I know people who have had to go back to work just to make ends meet. In a few cases there have been individuals who have suffered staggering losses because of Bernie Madoff; as a result they had to move out of the community.

It is especially important in retirement that you do not do foolish things with your money. During the height of the housing boom in Florida, I know of retired people who bought a second and third home for the express purpose of flipping them to make a killing. When the bottom fell out of the housing market, these people suffered huge losses; most will never be able to recover their money.

Adjusting to Retirement Life

After working for many years, it is not easy to transition to a new lifestyle. Furthermore, it may be especially difficult for you and your spouse as you spend more time together. Nevertheless, the difficulties that people encounter in adjusting to retirement life are varied and many. I will discuss only those problems that seem to be most prevalent among the people I have met over the last several years.

LETTING GO OF WORK

Maybe you spent years dreaming about leaving your job or your business and pursuing your retirement dreams. When the day finally arrives, you may find that it is extremely difficult to forget your work life. For years you have been regimented to a schedule that defined when you slept, ate, traveled, worked, and played. Your work life had a calendar and a cycle almost as consistent as the motion of the planets. To a large extent, your success in moving to retirement depends a lot on how you make the transition and the adjustments to a new lifestyle. I find that those who dream, plan, and take deliberate steps to reposition themselves to retirement are usually successful and happy with their new life. On the other hand, those who just jump into or are forced into retirement have a tough time.

I had a friend who had a very good job at GE. Without much advance notice my friend was forced into early retirement. He received a beautiful retirement package—good income, medical benefits, and support services. When I heard what he was receiving I jokingly asked if I could take his place. My friend did not see the humor; he was lost and did not know what to do. As far as he was concerned, his life was over and he fell into a deep depression. I thought to myself how pathetic; here is a fellow, still young and healthy, who does not have to worry about money for the rest of his life. He could start a second career, write the great American novel, go into the community and make a difference, travel, take courses, broaden his intellectual life, help his children and grandchildren, get to know his wife, and so on.

Unfortunately, if the center of your life is work, life becomes dark when your work disappears. For those who are still years away from retirement, I recommend that you start thinking about a life without your work; identify the value-based pursuits that will enrich your life. Make it a point to lay out a retirement plan based on these pursuits. Revisit your plan at least once a year; make adjustments as you grow and mature and as the world around you changes.

MAKING ADJUSTMENTS

Adjusting to retirement life is not as easy as you think. If you have decided to retire in place, you will be comfortable in the environment you know well; however, your daily routine will be different. You will have a lot more time on your hands. Also, you will be spending a lot more time with your life partner. This combination can lead to stress and conflict. In the retirement community where I live, I hear people talk, especially women, about how difficult it is having their spouse or partner at home all day long. Think about it; we spent years living with another person according to a well-established routine of sleeping, eating, shopping, working, and socializing—suddenly, it all changes. Like it or not, we are all creatures of habit and sudden change can bring stress and discomfort.

If you move to a new community, there are a host of administrative things to take care of. You have to change addresses, get telephone, Internet, TV hook up, driver's license, auto registration, and insurance. You have to find new doctors, dentists, druggists, auto services, shopping, restaurants, places of worship, cleaners, and support services of every type. You can get suggestions and advice from friends and neighbors, but you still have to check things out for yourself. Based on my experience, it takes a good year to get settled and take care of the basic needs of modern living. Even then you may not be satisfied with what you find, especially if you move from an area where you have lived for a long time. I find many people complain, women in particular, that everything was better where they lived before; shopping was better, dining out was better, the hair dresser or barber was better, traffic was better, and the list goes on; for my part, the only complaint I have is that you can't get a really good Philly cheese steak sandwich in Florida.

It's tough not to keep looking back; however, the joy of retirement is that you now have the time and flexibility to explore, test, and learn new things.

MEETING NEW PEOPLE AND DEVELOPING FRIENDS

Most professional people live, work, and play within the boundaries of their professional lives. Typically the friendships we develop and the people we know are much like ourselves. My world tended to be made up of engineers, scientists, and technologists of all types. I rarely had the opportunity to associate with writers, artist or musicians. I certainly would have liked to meet people like this, but I just did not travel in that environment. In retirement, I now have the opportunity to explore other worlds. In our community we have a rich cross section of artists, writers, lawyers, doctors, engineers, educators, poets, entrepreneurs, and other well educated professionals. There are people from virtually every State in the union and from many countries around the world. I meet these people in clubs, meeting places, and social activities that are a regular part of retirement community life. If you are interested in breaking out of your shell, select a retirement community that offers a diverse population and many clubs and activities. You will enrich your life, enhance your vitality, and not look back with regret at the life you left behind.

AVOIDING LEISURE TRAPS

When you retire you might say to yourself, "I worked hard all my life, so now I can take it easy." So you sleep late, play a bit of golf, have a few drinks, take a nap, go out to dinner, stay up late watching TV, sleep late the next morning, and do it all over again. The result is you get bored; you start thinking about the good old days when you worked and your life had meaning, or you start thinking about all the things you could have done differently, or all the mistakes you made, and then you get depressed.

Leisure time is too valuable to waste in taking it easy. Leisure time is the reward you earned for all your years of hard work; hence, you can now use this precious resource to pursue the value-based activities that give meaning and purpose to the final phase of your life.

SPENDING MORE TIME WITH YOUR SPOUSE

Since my wife and I spent years working together in our project management business, I would never have thought that spending more time with a spouse or life partner in retirement would be a problem; however, it turns out that in some marriages, this can be an issue. As I see it, part of the problem is a lack of meaningful activities. If the husband does not know what to do with himself and is home all day with his wife, they are bound to get on each other's nerves. The solution is for both partners to get involved in outside activities that give them meaning and purpose. When you live in an active-adult community, this should not be a problem because there are so many clubs and activities to choose from—see the section below.

DEALING WITH END-OF-LIFE PLANNING

End-of-life issues are one topic that most people do not want to think about or talk about; nevertheless, it is an issue that everyone has to deal with at some point in time. Having to address final arrangements for a loved one is especially difficult and can be more expensive than necessary when left to the last minute. Prudent individuals will address end-of-life arrangements well in advance; however, if you have not taken care of this important task for yourself or your loved ones until now, it is critical for your peace of mind to get this difficult issue out of the way—it will help the grieving process and reduce the burden on family members.

All end-of-life arrangements should be recorded in writing, shared with family members, your attorney, and filed where readily accessible. If you or your spouse do not want to deal with this important issue, then it is up to one or the other to exercise leadership, do the necessary planning, and tell the other partner or another family member where to find the important documents.

Happiness and Satisfaction in Retirement

The key to a happy and enjoyable retirement is to find what gives you satisfaction and fulfillment. If you live in an active-adult community, you will have access to an almost unbelievable wealth of resources that can enrich your life. For example, in the community where I live, there are over one hundred clubs that cater to virtually every interest, from art to wildlife preservation. If you are interested in culture, sports, fitness, religion, politics, computers, photography, gardening, dining, dancing, theatre, travel, socializing, or just having fun, there is a club for you.

The community also offers health and fitness programs from aerobics to yoga; lectures and seminars delivered by doctors, specialists, lawyers, and financial advisors; movies, shows, and specialty acts by well-known entertainers; also, there are numerous parties and celebrations throughout the year. There is no shortage of activities to keep people entertained, happy, and full of life.

There are many in the community who remain viable and active by operating businesses that provide a variety of services to residents. Some of these services include shuttle transportation to airports, train stations and other places, painting, paving, pressure washing, plumbing, computer repairs, custom woodworking and carpentry, golf cart maintenance and repairs, house sitting, cleaning, shopping, and special help to handicapped or shut in residents, just to name a few.

In addition, many residents enrich their lives by contributing to the surrounding communities. There are groups that provide food, clothing, and school supplies to children of migrant workers; others regularly visit assisted living facilities, nursing homes, and hospitals to give aid, comfort, and support. Still others act as mentors and teachers to young people who may be struggling in school or living in dysfunctional homes. And there are many people who are active in their churches or synagogues and help at food banks, soup kitchens, or other charitable activities.

The idea that retirement is for old people who sit around and watch TV, play bingo, or shuffleboard is a thing of the past. Today, retirement is a time when people enter a new and exciting phase where they grow, contribute, and enrich not only their lives but also the lives of everyone around them.

Summary

To have a rich retirement you need good health, smart lifestyle, and money. However, to make the adjustment to retirement life you should:

- Plan to reposition yourself to retirement life
- Avoid leisure traps
- Manage your money carefully
- Meet and cultivate new people outside your former life and profession
- Deal with end-of-life planning requirement
- Find the interests and activities that give your life meaning and purpose

Appendix A

John Tuman, Jr., P.E., PMP
PUBLICATIONS

Technical Papers

"The Problems and Realities Involved in Developing an Effective Information and Control System," The Project Management Institute Seminar/Symposium, Chicago, Illinois, October 1977.

"Innovative Techniques in Training and Development of Project Management Personnel," The Project Management Institute Seminar/Symposium, Phoenix, Arizona, October 1980.

"Building Information Systems for Major Advanced Energy Projects," The Project Management Institute Seminar/Symposium, Boston, Massachusetts, September 1981.

"New Vistas for Project Management Planning and Control of International Projects," The 7th World Congress on Project Management, Copenhagen, Denmark, 1982.

"System Technology Developments and the Future Direction of Project Management," The Project Management Institute Seminar/Symposium, Toronto, Ontario, Canada, 1982.

"Improving Productivity in the Project Management Environment Using Advanced Technology and the Behavioral Sciences," The Project Management Institute Seminar/Symposium, Houston, Texas, October 1983.

"The Technological Revolution in International Project Management," The IABSE Journal, Zurich, Switzerland, February 1984.

"Project Management Modeling and Simulation For Planning, Organizing and Team Building," The Project Management Institute Seminar/Symposium, Philadelphia, Pennsylvania, October 1984.

"Modeling and Simulation Techniques For Project Planning, Organizing, Training and Team Building," The 8th World Congress on Project Management, Rotterdam, The Netherlands, May 1985.

"Success Modeling: A Technique For Building A Winning Project Team," The Project Management Institute Seminar/Symposium, Montreal, Canada. September 1986.

"Entrepreneurial Project Management: An Organizational Strategy For Innovation and Growth," the Project Management Institute Seminar/Symposium, Milwaukee, Wisconsin, October 1987.

"Transnational Project Management for the Global Marketplace," The 9th World Congress on Project Management, Glasgow, Scotland, September 1988.

"Project Management for Turbulent Times: Creating the Rapid Response Proactive Organization," The Project Management Institute Seminar/Symposium, San Francisco, California, September 1988.

"Information Technology Organizational Culture and Engineering Management for a Volatile World," The American Society for Engineering Management, Knoxville, Tennessee, October 1988.

"Project Management as Catalyst for Strategic Change: Restructuring the Corporate Environment for the 1990s," The Project Management Institute Seminar/Symposium, Atlanta, Georgia, October 1989.

"Project Management-Agent for Change: Building a New Culture for a Nuclear Engineering Organization," The Project Management Institute Seminar/Symposium, Atlanta, Georgia, October 1989.

"Projektmanagement als Katalysator fur Strategische Veranderung," Project Management Austria, April 1990, p. 42-48.

"Project Management in Different Organizational Cultures: A Tool for Creating Competitive Advantage," The 10th World Congress on Project Management, Vienna, Austria, June 1990.

"The Mission of Project Management in the '90s is to Enhance Competitive Advantage," The Project Management Institute Seminar/Symposium, Calgary, Alberta, Canada, October 1990.

"From Vision to Realization: Strategies for Implementation of Organizational Change with Project Management," The Project Management Institute Seminar/Symposium, Calgary, Alberta, Canada, October 1990.

"Quality, Culture and Personal Effectiveness: Strategies for Project Managers," The Project Management Institute Seminar/Symposium, Dallas, Texas, October 1991.

"Moving to Win-Win Contract Management," Contract Managers Owners Group, Summer Meeting, Atlantic City, New Jersey, August 1992

"Using Project Management to Create an Entrepreneurial Environment in Czechoslovakia," The Project Management Institute Seminar/Symposium, Pittsburgh, Pennsylvania, October 1992.

"Group Think, Blunders, and the Psychology of Choice in Project Management Decision-Making and Risk Management," The Project Management Institute Seminar/Symposium, San Diego, California, October 1993.

"Designing A Corporate Management Process," The Project Management Institute Seminar/Symposium, San Diego, California, October 1993.

"The Psychology of Choice in Project Execution Decision-Making and Risk Management," The 12th World Congress on Project Management, Oslo, Norway, June 1994.

"Project Management Decision-Making and Risk Management in a Changing Corporate Environment," The Project Management Institute Seminar/Symposium, Vancouver B.C., Canada, October 1994.

"The Triad for Reengineering Success: Communication Dynamics, Team Diversity and Project Management," The Project Management Institute Seminar/Symposium, New Orleans, Louisiana, October 1995.

"Project Management Strategies That Ensure Reengineering Success," The IPMA World Congress on Project Management, Paris, France, June 1996.

"Creating A Revolution In Project Management Thinking, Tools, and Techniques to Manage Reengineering Projects," The Project Management Institute Seminar/Symposium, Boston, Massachusetts, October 1996.

"Project Management for the Twenty-first Century: The Internet-Based Cybernetic Project Team," The Project Management Institute Seminar/Symposium, Chicago Illinois, October 1997.

"Shaping Corporate Strategy with Internet-Based Project Management," The IPMA 14th World Congress on Project Management, Ljubljana, Slovenia, June 1998.

"Making the Vision Work Using Reality-Based Project Management," The IPMA 18th World Congress on Project Management, Berlin, Germany, June 2002.

Project Management Books

"Development and Implementation of Effective Project Management Information and Control Systems," Chapter 25 of the Project Management Handbook, Van Nostrand Reinhold Company. New York, 1983.

"Development and Implementation of Project Management Systems," Chapter 27 of the Project Management Handbook, Van Nostrand Reinhold Company. New York, 1988.

"Project Management: A Tool for Creating a Corporate Culture as Competitive Advantage," Handbook of Management by Projects, MANZ. Vienna, 1990.

"Models for Achieving Project Success Through Team Building and Stakeholder Management," Chapter 15 of the AMA Handbook of Project Management Handbook, AMACOM. New York, 1993.

"Culture Strategies for Global Project Management," Chapter 11 of the Global Project Management Handbook, McGraw-Hill. New York, 1994.

"Managing Reengineering Teams," Chapter 30 of the Field Guide to Project Management, Van Nostrand Reinhold Company. New York, 1998.

"Energizing Project Teams," Chapter 34 of the Field Guide to Project Management, Second Addition, John Wiley & Sons, Inc. Hoboken, New Jersey, 2004

"Studies in Communications Management: Achieving Project Success Through Team Building and Stakeholder Management," Chapter 13A of the AMA Handbook of Project Management Handbook, Second Edition, AMACOM. New York, 2006.

Articles

"Training and Development of Project Management Personnel," Project Management Quarterly, September 1983, p. 78-86.

"Shaping Corporate Strategy with Information Technology," Project Management Journal, September 1988, p. 35-42.

"Using Project Management to Create A Customer-Focused Nuclear Engineering Organization," Project Management Journal, September 1990, p. 25-29.

"Developing Corporate Hustle.," Project Management Monthly, November 1991

"It's Time to Re-Engineer Project Management," PM NETwork, February 1993, p. 40-41.

"Using Project Management in the Czech and Slovak Republics," The PM NETwork, April 1993, p. 19-24.

Other Publications

"The Ubiquitous Management Action Network," The University of New Haven Graduate School, West Haven, Connecticut, 1973.

Index

Destiny, 1-2, 8, 13, 30-31, 35, 40, 52, 69, 159
Downsizing, 40, 46, 159, 162, 170, 227, 237, 247
Dream, 6, 19, 19, 21, 26, 39-40, 46-47, 52-53, 229, 262, 299
Dysfunctional, 103, 109, 112, 120, 126, 177, 181, 222, 235, 303

E
Early career, 215, 220, 225
Early retirement, 128,164, 220, 227-228, 299
Eastern Europe, 41, 148, 152, 156, 209, 215, 217
Education, 2-3, 6, 26-29, 34, 37, 49-50, 112, 159, 166, 222, 224, 263, 274, 279
Emotions, 55, 88, 96
Employees, 10, 13, 17, 24, 47, 63, 107, 1121, 116, 143, 160-163, 167, 171, 212, 262-263
Employer, 43-44, 46-50, 59, 65, 129, 170
Endorsements, 76, 79, 81, 101
Energy, 1, 12, 30, 32-33, 35, 40, 44, 48,75, 182, 211, 228, 234, 348, 251, 270, 272
Enjoy life, 1-2, 5-8, 18-19, 253, 264, 267
Enrich your life, 55, 79, 100, 209, 301-302
Entrepreneur, 7-9, 14-15, 23, 29-31, 36, 39, 41-42, 49-50, 52, 54, 61, 69-70, 84, 111, 129,152, 154, 220, 226-230, 235, 238, 250, 261
Equipment, 10, 57, 63, 108, 138,150, 161, 171, 181, 186, 196, 250, 254-256, 259-260, 273
Estimating, 15, 51, 79, 146, 184
Ethics, 30, 33, 36, 115-116, 220
Exercise, 33, 44, 153, 173, 176, 189, 230, 248, 271, 281, 296, 302
Expense, 67, 97, 111, 130, 132, 250, 254, 256-262
Experience, 1-2, 7-8, 13-15, 17, 21, 26, 28-29, 34, 37, 41, 44, 46, 48-50,

52, 54-55, 62, 69-70, 74,77-80, 84, 85, 87, 89, 99-104, 108, 109, 111-112, 115, 117, 119, 126, 129, 132, 138, 140, 144-145, 147-148, 150-154, 156, 159, 162-163, 166-167, 175-177, 179, 181, 186, 188-189, 197, 199, 206-207, 210-212, 223-224, 226, 240, 242-243, 245- 246, 248, 270, 275, 278-279, 290, 293, 300
Expert, 5, 34, 119, 138, 249, 253, 259

F
Facebook, 50, 64, 128, 131, 165
Facilities, 10, 51, 108, 171, 181, 186, 196, 239, 303
Failure, 1, 10, 54, 73, 141, 193, 209, 220, 237-238, 243, 247, 266-268, 270
Family members, 59, 65, 211, 224, 263, 265, 302
Fast track, 48, 85, 87, 97
Fear, 10, 53, 155-156, 197, 201, 283
Fees, 122, 124, 161, 166, 172, 177, 184, 297
Forming alliances, 138, 144, 148-149, 157
Free time, 2, 54, 70, 264, 266
Freeware, 63, 66, 68, 255,
Funding, 97, 112, 122, 127
Future state, 199, 201, 211-213

G
Gap analysis, 198-200
Generate revenue, 11, 17, 80, 138, 143, 151, 155, 180, 190
Glide path, 22, 281, 283-284, 286, 290, 292-293
Global economy/marketplace, 2, 6-7, 9-11, 151, 237, 239, 265
Goal, 1, 7-8, 22-23, 53-54, 90-91, 93, 100, 112, 143, 208, 220, 222-223, 225-226, 233-236, 247, 273-274, 278, 287
Good clients, 96, 107-108, 117, 120, 125
Google, 50-51, 64, 274

H
Happiness, 1, 8, 33, 51, 70, 219-220, 222, 228-229, 235, 268, 278, 302

Pension, 156, 215, 283
Personal life, 29, 32-33, 47, 55, 176, 231
Phase of your life, 220, 222-223, 225, 227-229, 284, 301
Physical assets, 197, 269-271
Physical condition, 33, 44, 271, 296
Place to work, 57, 60, 172, 211, 254
Planning, 14, 19, 42, 48, 50-52, 64, 146, 154, 181, 184-185, 189, 194, 199, 203, 228, 240, 247-248, 252, 284, 287-288, 296-297, 302-303
Pleasure, 1, 120, 224, 234, 275
PMP, 17, 29, 77, 167
Probability, 7, 25, 100, 238, 242, 245, 248, 252, 258
Professional credentials, 27-29, 37, 80
Profit, 9, 22, 50, 108, 111, 143, 148, 162, 250, 253, 256, 258, 260, 264-265, 270
Progress payments, 122, 130, 174
Project failure, 141, 193, 209, 247
Project Management Institute (PMI), 17, 29, 43, 68, 184-185, 187
Project manager, 18, 100, 103, 109, 124, 127-128, 175-176
Project plan, 14, 42, 85-86, 97, 242, 247-248, 266
Project success, 11, 14, 74, 141, 238, 242-243
Proposal, 77, 111-112, 144, 150-151, 184, 245-246
Psychological, 25, 32, 37, 234
Publications, 146, 244
Purchasing, 74, 76, 206, 257, 297

Q

Qualified, 18, 23, 76-77, 83, 103, 174
Quality, 18, 70-71, 78, 81, 94, 99, 172, 242, 257

R

Rapport, 54, 61, 79-81, 83-84, 87, 92, 95-101, 104-105, 109, 117, 126, 128, 136, 138, 151, 176-177, 246, 258, 262
Recognition, 21, 60, 70, 80-81, 100, 117, 138, 215, 255
Recruit, 159, 164-165, 174, 177
Reengineering, 16, 78, 155, 179, 186, 203, 208, 212, 214
Referrals, 78, 81, 118, 167, 244
Relations, 43, 83, 105, 215
Rent, 62, 181, 254, 256, 275, 292
Respect, 35, 104, 108, 162, 272, 273
Retire, 1, 5-8, 18-19, 23, 137, 225, 228, 277, 281, 283-284, 286-289, 294, 295-298, 300-301
Revenue, 79-80, 138-140, 143, 145-146, 151, 155, 180, 183, 185, 190, 245-246, 254, 266-267, 278
Risk, 4, 7, 13, 15, 35, 44, 54, 59, 65, 123, 137, 140-142, 146, 148, 151, 154, 173, 206, 237-240, 242-248, 250-252, 277, 288, 298
Role model, 52, 54
Russian, 210, 215-217, 249-250

S

Self-management, 167, 219-220, 223-229, 231-233, 235-236
Self-reliance, 35, 234, 273
Site support, 13, 17, 24, 143, 194
Skills and expertise, 78-79, 137, 161, 179
Slovak, 41, 156
Smart lifestyle, 271, 295-296, 303
Social networks, 64, 77, 131, 136, 255
Software tools, 57, 63, 68, 242
Sole source, 76, 118, 137, 171, 206, 246
Soviet Union, 209, 214-215, 217-218
Specialized products, 13-14, 24, 139,146-147
Spirit, 25-26, 30, 32-33, 35, 37, 46
Sponsor, 142, 196, 202
Staff, 9-19, 12, 17, 47, 50, 75, 85, 109-110, 112-113, 126-127, 138-140, 142-143, 145, 159, 162-165, 170, 174-175, 177, 188, 190, 193, 202-203, 211, 213, 266-268
Stagnation, 3-5, 8
Stakeholder, 112, 197

Strategies, 107, 111, 116-117, 153, 177, 201-203, 209, 240, 243, 267, 297

Stress, 96-97, 109, 118, 159, 187, 231, 248, 270, 279, 283-284, 286, 290, 294, 296, 300

Student, 50-51, 223-225, 234

Study team, 112, 194, 196, 198, 203

Success and happiness, 8, 33, 219-220, 222, 228, 232, 235

Successful business, 7, 22, 253, 270, 274, 279

Successful project management, 116, 218, 278

Support services, 57, 66, 111, 143-144, 299-300

T

Taxes, 3-5, 8, 58, 66, 71, 145, 160-162, 167, 171-172, 190, 253, 256,259-260, 262-264, 266-267, 274-275

Teaching, 77-78, 81, 118, 133, 156, 188-189, 223-224

Team building, 142, 161, 194

Teaming, 148-153, 157

Temperament, 7, 9, 13, 19, 25, 30-31, 33, 35, 37, 84, 87, 94, 105, 175, 232-233, 235

Templates, 14, 62, 142, 246

Tolerance, 102, 119, 233, 235, 277

Training, 13, 15-16, 24, 28, 43-44, 51, 53, 69, 75, 79, 108, 114, 138-140, 142, 146, 155-157, 159, 166-167, 179-191, 194, 201, 213, 215-216, 218, 245, 267

Transformation projects, 205-207, 209-211, 218

Twenty-five Year Plan, 7, 18-19, 23, 278, 297

U

Ugly clients, 111, 119, 120, 125, 129-139, 136

Unethical, 98, 105, 114, 154, 163, 166, 250

Unhappy, 112, 177, 226, 227

Universities, 50-51, 180-181, 187, 191, 217, 242, 255

V

Value-added, 9, 16, 18, 80, 180-182, 188

Value-based goals, 1, 7-8, 287

Values and beliefs, 101, 103-104, 151

W

Wage stagnation, 3-5, 8

Wealth, 3-8, 21-23, 69, 95, 138, 228, 253, 258, 269, 272-274, 277-281, 295, 302

Website, 64, 76-78, 126-127

Wisdom, 27, 29, 34, 54, 102

Work life, 299

Working relationship, 54, 68, 84, 89, 97, 102

World Bank, 215, 217, 272

48649537R00200

Made in the USA
Lexington, KY
08 January 2016